THIRTY THOUSAND BOTTLES OF WINE AND A PIG CALLED HELGA

A NOT-SO-PERFECT TREE CHANGE

Also by Todd Alexander

Tom Houghton
Pictures of Us

TODD ALEXANDER

THIRTY THOUSAND BOTTLES OF WINE AND A PIG CALLED HELGA

A NOT-SO-PERFECT TREE CHANGE

SIMON &
SCHUSTER

London · New York · Sydney · Toronto · New Delhi

A CBS COMPANY

THIRTY THOUSAND BOTTLES OF WINE AND A PIG CALLED HELGA:
A NOT-SO-PERFECT TREE CHANGE
First published in Australia in 2019 by
Simon & Schuster (Australia) Pty Limited
Suite 19A, Level 1, Building C, 450 Miller Street, Cammeray, NSW 2062

10 9 8 7 6 5 4 3 2 1

A CBS Company
Sydney New York London Toronto New Delhi
Visit our website at www.simonandschuster.com.au

A catalogue record for this
book is available from the
National Library of Australia

Cover design: Xou Creative
Cover image: Adobe Stock
Typeset by Midland Typesetters, Australia
Printed and bound in Australia by Griffin Press

The paper this book is printed on is certified
against the Forest Stewardship Council®
Standards. Griffin Press holds FSC chain
of custody certification SGS-COC-005088.
FSC promotes environmentally responsible,
socially beneficial and economically viable
management of the world's forests.

For Mel and Jesus
(no, not that *Jesus)*

'Never be afraid to laugh at yourself. After all, you could be missing out on the joke of the century.'
Dame Edna Everage

Contents

Prologue

Missing in Action: One Pig

April, 2018

As we trudged up to the vineyard, I wiped sweat out of my eyes. It had been the hottest April on record and even though it was late afternoon it was ridiculously warm. The sky overhead was a blue so crisp you'd swear we were still in summer.

The vines were nearly at the end of their growing season. The grapes had been harvested weeks ago and the branches were clinging onto the last of their leaves to store precious energy before winter arrived. They wouldn't normally require watering in April but they were confused with the unseasonal heat, continuing to burst into spring-like greenery. Without a cloud in the sky and wide cracks showing in our clay land, it had seemed a great idea to water them while I spent a few hours mowing the dying grass between the rows – but I forgot to turn the water off afterwards so back I went. The irrigation had become manual since the kangaroos kicked out the wiring for the automated system, which we couldn't afford to replace.

Never do one job at a time, I'd reminded myself, so I had company: the animals needed some exercise.

I ran as fast as I could past the villas and the house because it was the only way to keep my posse by my side. If I didn't distract them like this at the start they had a tendency to stray, and our paying guests would be likely to find an inquisitive hairy face peering in at their villa windows, or worse: an uninvited guest on their couch if they'd left a door open. Winston the goat is the worst culprit, and once Helga the pig reached adolescence she started to display a mind of her own, too. (Wesley, our youngest goat, is more or less a perfect angel.)

Once clear of the danger zone, I slackened to a walk and we slowly climbed the hill.

If you'd said to me ten years ago that one day I'd be taking two goats and a hefty, headstrong sow for a walk, I would have told you to stop smoking crack.

In the distance I could hear the rasp of Jeff's dropsaw. The wine room on the edge of the dam was coming together nicely. The floor and walls were in place; the roof was on but the windows and doors were only empty spaces. Until we could afford to install them, we promoted it as *Enjoy an al fresco wine-tasting overlooking our vast lake.* I took a photo of its progress and hoped we could have it finished by the end of winter when ·my job as part-time labourer would finally come to an end (and without a single argument on site, mind you – after thirteen years together I rarely question Jeff's wisdom . . . out loud).

I trekked on with my hairy companions. After ten minutes or so we reached the centre of the vineyard and the water taps. As I made my way from tap to tap, Helga ran off to explore. Winston and Wesley couldn't believe their luck that fresh green leaves were there for the taking, as many as their barrel guts could fit in. They're not usually allowed there for this very reason but I didn't mind them nibbling a few so close to the vines becoming dormant. As I turned off the third and final tap I felt a sprinkle on my arm and it was only then that I looked up and saw, off in the distance, a clump of dark clouds. They'd descended from nowhere and were beginning to fill the sky in the west, but it's rare we ever get rain on our property so I was confident the brewing storm would pass us by.

Tap job done, we made our way down to the dam to inspect Jeff's handiwork. Winston and Wesley leaned out from the deck to munch on water reeds; Helga had found the carcass of a snake and was chomping on the bones in its tail. My brother Glen is always quick to remind me that a pig will eat you whole and only leave your dentures behind, but I'm the kind of farmer who believes his 'children' are faultless and would save my life given half the chance.

'You've done heaps today,' I said to Jeff, wishing I'd thought to bring us some beers.

'I didn't get to do the strapping of the roof yet, but it's the first thing I'll do in the morning,' he said, but to me it hardly seemed important enough to mention.

The rain went from sprinkle to heavier droplets and since it isn't Wesley and Winston's favourite thing in the world, they took shelter with us in the rudimentary wine room. Seconds later those heavy black clouds opened, releasing bucketloads of rain and hail, then the wind whipped up, blowing it in through the gaps. As the rain pelted down against the aluminium roof Jeff and I built with our bare hands, Helga galloped up the steps and the five of us moved further inside. The wind was stronger than I'd ever felt before – the rain was being swept in horizontally and, even six metres in where we were cowering against the back wall, we were getting soaked. The rain and cloud was so thick we could no longer see the dam just ten metres away. The animals were scared, edgy. Jeff and I couldn't believe how quickly things had turned.

'Woo-hoo!' I screamed, always partial to a little drama.

'Where the hell did this come from?' Jeff shouted over the ferocious noise.

'Thank god we got the roof on!' I yelled back.

At my words, there was an almighty gust and the six-metre-square roof peeled back like a Band-Aid and simply disappeared.

What the fuck? Jeff and I exchanged incredulous looks but we were too shocked to speak. Thunder crashed overhead. Lightning forked. The deafening sound was too much for Helga and she bolted toward the bush, disappearing into the grey blur of wind and rain.

'I'd better go find her!' I screamed at Jeff. 'You stay with the boys!'

I ran out and immediately went from wet to drenched – and I don't mean that in a sexy Mr Darcy kind of way; more like a fallen loser on *Australian Ninja Warrior*. All I could think was *Helga will be lost to me forever; I must find my little piggy!* I charged toward the bush. The trees were blowing at ridiculous angles; lightning illuminated the greyness and splinters of electricity struck dangerously close to struggling tree limbs.

'Helga! Helga!' I yelled desperately into the chaos.

I heard a faint sound and turned around. Winston had come running after me and, some metres behind, a very wet, very unhappy and very scared Wesley followed. I waited for them to catch up to me and reassured them as best I could.

'Helga!' I yelled again, but who was I kidding? I could barely hear my own voice and she was nowhere to be seen.

I decided to get the boys out of harm's way. It made no sense to put all three of their lives in danger. I ran them back to their pen, all the while keeping my eyes desperately peeled for little Helga, frantically calling her name, my heart breaking at the thought of her being lost and terrified.

Just a few years earlier I had been a high-flying marketing executive in Sydney. My career at eBay was going gangbusters and I was living the classic city lifestyle of hard work and even harder play.

One of my 'executive decisions' once saved the billion-dollar company from disaster and I had been the poster boy for corporate success. Now I was crashing through the bush in a storm in search of a missing pig.

How the hell did I end up here?

1

The Holiday Home
from Hell

Net curtains. That's where our tree-change story really begins. According to Jeff, if you had net curtains on your windows, really, you didn't deserve to live. And our dingy excuse for a B&B was positively swarming with them. (What's the collective noun for net curtains, I wonder? A disappointment? A *gasp* of net curtains?)

It was February 2010 and we were staying in the Barossa Valley in South Australia with our best friends, Melanie and Jesus. (Jesus is Bolivian so when you read his name, imagine it with a Spanish accent – *hey-Zeus* – otherwise you'll think I'm talking about the son of God.)

Jesus had organised the weekend away as a surprise for Mel's birthday. And we came along too, of course. Jeff and I are the guys who crashed the hotel room after midnight on their wedding night to order champagne and pizza, so it shouldn't have come as a shock to Mel when we showed up at the airport bar back in Sydney. I guess she was so out of her in-control comfort zone that the sight of us rocking up out of the blue made the poor girl burst into tears.

'Jeez, Mellie, we can head back home if the thought of spending a weekend with us is *that* depressing . . .'

'Oh my god you guys, I can't believe you're here too,' she said, wiping away tears.

'Let's face it, you weren't going to be having any fun with just *him*!' I pointed to Jesus. 'Whoop whoop,' I sounded, and in an instant he was up at the bar ordering us drinks. I'd trained him well.

Poor Mel still had no idea where we were going but that's the kind of crazy shit you do to make great friendships so memorable, and Mel's is the kind of friendship that just keeps on giving – after all, she was the reason Jeff and I met.

Jeff stalked me. That's how he got this glittering prize. He and Mel worked together for a cancer charity and Mel often raved about her best friend (i.e. me) at work, which was fair enough. Old sleuth-ball Jeff managed to work out where I lived when Mel mentioned my apartment was in a curved building in Elizabeth Bay (but there aren't exactly thousands of those, so he isn't as clever as he makes out). It might amaze you to learn that he and I lived on the same street – but that's where all the single gays lived in the early 2000s so that wasn't exactly a miracle either. With minimal further detective work, he gazed up into the windows of that curved building, trying to deduce which apartment was mine. It turned out that a sugges-tively shaped cactus backlit in the living room window sent a beacon to the world: HERE LIVES MEL'S GAY BEST FRIEND. Who knew?

Jeff didn't like to socialise with his workmates, but he went to Mel's thirtieth birthday party in February 2005 because he knew I was to be the MC.

'What do you think of that guy over there?' I asked my friend Kirsti at the party.

'Not really my type,' she said flatly.

'Really? I was just talking to him and he seems really nice. You should go and have a chat to him; I reckon he'd be great for you.'

'Um . . . he's gay.'

'No, he's not. Trust me. I would know.'

'I think we both know your gaydar has been on the blink for years, my dear. Trust *me*: he's gay.'

Next, I sent my friend Andy over to suss Jeff out. Andy's is the truest, longest male friendship I've ever had. He even made sure I wasn't ripped to shreds the night I decided it was a great idea to visit a death metal club . . . while wearing swimming goggles (for no particular reason).

'You want *me* to guess if he's gay? Oh Toddy, you know I'm shit at that sort of stuff.' A few minutes later he came back to report his findings. 'I'm with Kirsti,' he said, but I was still unconvinced because Jeff just talked and moved and held himself like a straight guy.

At the Iguana Bar later I put Jeff through my never-fail straight-detector. You're welcome to play this one at home whenever you please.

'So, Jeff, if you could choose to go home with anyone in this nightclub tonight, who would it be?' (Clever of me, right?)

'I don't get what you mean . . .?' (Dammit, he was out-testing me!)

3

'I mean,' – time for less subtlety – 'if you could choose any one of those girls on the dance floor to take home tonight, which one would it be?'

Give her half a second and Kirsti will tell you that she is always right. Well, on this particular occasion it turned out she actually was.

'I bet you live in that one up there,' Jeff pointed to my window a bit later that evening, after we'd placed an unsubtle bet about who had the best view. From that night on I couldn't get rid of him – and trust me, I wasn't about to make it easy to be in love with the likes of me. Despite stalking me, he did fail the first hurdle of remembering my name the next day, but I decided to give him another chance.

'What are you doing this morning?' he asked before heading off.

'Just reading the papers,' I said with a shrug. It was dangerous territory, I certainly wasn't about to suggest doing something *together.*

'Why don't you grab them and bring them over to mine? I'll make us a cup of tea.'

I couldn't believe my ears: he'd asked me on a second date *the Morning After*, only unlike the movie of the same name I wasn't as glamorous as Jane Fonda, nor was there a corpse in my bed (far from it). But that's just how it was with us from the outset – no games, no second-guessing.

'I've been invited to a wedding in two weeks,' I mentioned in passing.

'I'll come as your plus-one,' he said without flinching or waiting to be asked.

'I invited my friends over for dinner next week,' he said. 'You should come.'

4

And I'll be honest, being the disastrous dater that I was, I wanted to grab a hold of him and shake him! 'Jeff! That's ten whole days away! Ten more days of . . . this . . . and you're still committing to seeing me!' But of course that was all kept internalised and on the surface I was the supremely confident sex god he clearly thought I was.

'Shyness is no aphrodisiac,' he said to me one night, and he's been suffering for it ever since.

Four months into our relationship I had to go to the US for work for a couple of weeks and I felt sure this would be the time Jeff chose to stray.

'Great!' he said enthusiastically. 'I'll move into your flat and renovate it!'

Because I was in a rental and hadn't seen any of Jeff's handiwork I flew out to the US fearing I'd be evicted and return both homeless and single. He assured me he had lots of experience and two weeks later I returned to a fresh and lovely makeover, and a new flatmate. It was the middle of 2005 and less than six months later we'd purchased our first apartment together overlooking Rushcutters Bay – so then we both had the *same* view.

Mel, Jeff and I made a nice little threesome for a year or two, hanging out together in Elizabeth Bay. Somehow I knew Mel was about to meet the right guy.

The Athena Starwoman in me got it right.

When you love someone as much as I love that beautiful woman, you want her to be loved by someone special too. I was always nervous about meeting any boyfriend of Mel's because there wasn't a hope in hell anyone would be good enough for her, in my humble opinion. And there was also a bit of me that was scared some boofhead was going to come along and queer-bash me behind my back. But that was underestimating Mel; she isn't into meatheads.

The night Jeff and I met Jesus mid-2007, he said, 'I bet you didn't think I was going to be so black.'

'I bet you didn't think I was going to be so straight,' I replied, and from that moment our fate was sealed. In marrying Mel, Jesus adopted two more brothers – only I was suddenly the best-looking in his family, if not the most modest.

Jeff has seven sisters back in England (*Well, yes, but seven!*) and at the time my brothers were either overseas or off procreating in suburbia, so Jesus became like a big brother (a much, much older big brother) to both of us. He is always taking the piss out of us and saying and doing inappropriate things. I really couldn't have chosen a more perfect guy to come into my life. I suppose he's a pretty good catch for Mel too.

It wasn't until the plane landed that Mel realised where she was.

'Adelaide? You brought me to bloody *Adelaide* for my birthday?'

'Ease up on the gratitude, Mellie,' I reassured her. 'Don't worry, we're off to the Barossa!'

Dammit if that wasn't one of the nicest weekends of our lives. It was real Hollywood stuff: a sophisticated foursome exploring beautiful vineyards and great restaurants without a worry in the world. I'm sure I heard a bit of Enya on the soundtrack, and an incredibly handsome and muscular leading man was playing the role of Todd.

The sun was shining as we drove along winding country roads. Clear blue skies overhead, beautifully manicured gardens wherever we turned – you get the picture. And the rigid uniformity of vineyards really appealed to the *Rain Man* in Jeff. It was such a shame we'd only thought to book two nights, because we all wanted to stay longer in that little bubble of happiness and relaxation where no one seemed to have a worry in the world and everyone we met looked so bloody content. Maybe it was all just a show, part of that Hollywood film, but I didn't care – I was hooked and never wanted it to end.

I have all of Maggie Beer's cookbooks, love her warm, gentle personality and am incredibly inspired by her story, so one of the must-sees on my list was Maggie's farm in Nuriootpa. There's just something familiar and welcoming from the moment you arrive – beautifully kept groves and orchards, hundreds of pheasant fattening up for harvest, a quaint little shop where you can buy anything Maggie's ever made (it seems) and a lovely large dam at the centre teeming with ducks and other birds. It's all a million miles from anywhere in a haze of peaceful perfection. We had a picnic lunch by the dam watching ducks frolic to more Enya songs in my head.

'I really could live here,' I said with a sigh. 'I think I would like to *be* Maggie Beer.'

'I'm not sure her husband, Colin, would be too happy about that,' Jesus said dryly.

That's how our daytime hours in the Barossa were spent – living idyllically with no schedule, meetings or other mundane chores holding us back. But after tasting delicious wines, spending too much on lunches and visiting cellar doors of exquisite beauty, every evening the dream crashed back to grim reality: we'd somehow managed to pay a shedload of cash to stay in a dreary backyard on a suburban street. Advertised as a 'villa', there was no disguising the fact we were sleeping in a garage converted into two bedrooms, and while maybe all we needed were beds and a roof over our head, this little garage was just awful.

The felt carpets were filthy, their flower patterns faded and frayed. The thin fibro walls were beige, but we couldn't tell if they were painted that colour or were just filmed over with years of other people's grime. The beds were rock-hard; the sheets were see-through, and they felt and smelled like a weeks-old scourer that had sat in the kitchen sink, too disgusting for anyone to contemplate throwing in the bin until Dad cracked the shits and took the fall for everyone. The advertised 'generous breakfast provisions' comprised, per person per day: one rasher of bacon, one egg, 125 millilitres of orange fruit drink, two capsules of milk and one small box of Sultana Bran (the one from the variety pack wanted by no kid, ever).

'I reckon we could do a better job than this,' Jeff said to me the first morning.

'I reckon my nan could do a better job than this – and Jeff, she's been dead for ten years,' I agreed.

'I mean, come on people, it's not hard,' Jeff continued. 'Net curtains have no place in the world – anywhere! And don't get me started on the choice of cushions. It's not that hard to find a lovely cushion to lift things a little.' Jeff never really acts all that gay, but get him started on soft furnishings and he turns into Mr Humphries from *Are You Being Served* . . . 'I'm free!'

Before going out to dinner, we decided to make full use of the amenities and walked to the covered carport to partake in a little hot spa action.

'Ooohhh,' Mel, the first one to climb in, cooed, 'this is sooo nice.'

I stepped in next, turning up my nose against the strange chemical smell that singed a few of my nostril hairs on the way in. As my body sank beneath the surface of the water, my skin felt like it was coated in Vaseline.

'Oh boys, wait till you get in,' I joined my partner in crime. 'It's perfect!

'You're such a bitch,' I whispered to Mel.

'You didn't think I was going to suffer this alone, did you?'

'You two are a pair of shunts,' Jeff said, leaping straight back out again. 'That's the most disgusting thing I've ever done.' I knew he'd done worse but decided to save that challenge for another day.

Within a minute we'd all evacuated the chemical spill and were towelling ourselves with delightfully threadbare cotton, scrubbing away at our contaminated skin as if we were all Meryl Streep in *Silkwood*.

That night at dinner, Jesus said, 'I looked at our host's website and she's fully booked every weekend for the next few months.'

'You've got to be kidding me,' Jeff said dismissively. 'I've stayed in better hostels than that, and for just twenty pounds a night.'

'And at least there you got a few complimentary extras from some of the other guests.'

'Supply and demand,' Mel said, ignoring all the smut, as she so often has to. 'She's got the location and that's all most people care about when they book.'

'And remember: we do have Jeff to thank for choosing such luxury.'

'Piss off! I'm sure she didn't advertise the fact she's hung net curtains on every bloody window . . .'

'We're so missing out on something here,' I said as the mains arrived. 'If she can make that much money from a dirty rundown shithole, imagine what the four of us could do if we put our heads together. I mean, even with Jesus weighing us down . . . heavily.'

'You wanker!'

'I'd get to open my chocolate shop . . .' Mel looked like she'd transported herself there already.

For the rest of the meal I kept daydreaming about a different kind of life. I imagined how freeing it would be to call up work and tell them I was never coming back. We could just stay right there in the Barossa and forge a new path. The funny thing was, I hadn't even been conscious of my dissatisfaction with our Sydney life until the Barossa showed me that Sydney wasn't the only place on the planet I could be happy.

'Hey Knob, can I try some of your pink bits?' Jeff motioned to Jesus's rare quail.

'Only if you let me pack some of your fudge for dessert.'

'Oh my god you two, stop!' Mel cried.

'Inappropriate!' I called. 'Mel, can I try one of your bearded clams?'

'Enough!' And she was right: they were mussels, not clams.

Later back at the 'villa', I said to Jeff: 'We should talk more seriously about doing something like this.'

'Yeah, we should,' he said, but I wasn't sure just how much his heart was in it. And anyway, for the time being we had much bigger fish to fry.

2

Desperately Seeking:
Cushions and Cookbooks

We returned from the Barossa to our house in Annandale, knowing that we were about to launch into a full-scale renovation. No wall or window in the house was to remain untouched.

When we'd moved to Annandale in 2007, we were among the first of our friends to make the change from the smart but expensive Eastern Suburbs to the cheaper and more spacious Inner West. We'd thought we'd always live in apartments but by the time we sold the one overlooking Rushcutters Bay, I was tired of living in such close proximity with others and fed up with our old angry neighbours telling us our music was too loud (believe me, I just don't do loud music) or that our dinner parties (*dinner parties!*) were too raucous.

When we decided to put the Rushcutters Bay apartment on

the market early in 2007, it became the scene of our one and only barney to date. I mean, Jeff and I *never* argue, not even about small things, but like most couples we chose a monumental, universal topic as the catalyst for our near-divorce: chicken balls.

Jeff is incredibly well endowed: his more than adequate proboscis affords him hypersensitive olfactory abilities. Before deciding the Inner West was the place for us, we had gone looking for bigger, more private apartments around Elizabeth Bay, but often he would walk out shaking his head in disgust: 'Could you smell the . . .?' and every time the apparent stench was completely lost on me. Foot odour on a sock at the bottom of the laundry basket? *Really?* Guinea pig urine from the pet of a kid who'd lived in the apartment in the 1970s? *No?* A glass that three weeks earlier had been filled with a Barossa Shiraz and hadn't been allowed to dry in the heat of the dishwasher properly? *Nope, didn't get that either.* But days-old cooking fat was the one that got Jeff's goat the most.

When it came time to sell our apartment, Jeff wanted everything to be 'Jeff-perfect'. Nick, a local real estate agent, was my man for the job. In time he would go on to star in that Nestlé commercial wearing nothing more than an apron and condensed milk smeared all over his body. Perhaps I was an early appreciator of his star quality, sensing it would appeal to the largely gay and single female audience we were marketing our apartment to.

With our apartment on the market, Jeff would have liked to place me inside a plastic bubble – and he really did put plastic sheeting over the new cream carpet beneath Mel's chair one dinner party. Sure enough, as was her habit, within minutes she'd knocked over her glass of wine.

'I'd like to invite my friend Keith over for drinks, show him the results of all of our hard work,' he said one day, and I quickly agreed it would be a lovely thing to do. Keith is someone whose opinion Jeff values more than most because he's quite fastidious in his own home and enjoys the finer things in life.

'I'll make some nice hors d'oeuvres,' I offered. 'Make it a special occasion.'

In my opinion, what followed was not exactly the grandest surprise in the history of the world. Clue One: I immediately began perusing a finger food cookbook. Clue Two: I read my proposed menu to Jeff, including the dish 'chicken balls'. Clue Three: we went shopping and I sent Jeff off to find two litres of vegetable oil. *Two litres!* Clue Four: come the day of the get-together, I was in the kitchen rolling said chicken balls and on the stovetop was a large frying pan filled with said oil. Jeff went up the road to get some forgotten beers and when he came back I was frying my last batch of chicken balls. There was Clue Five.

'What are you doing?' Jeff asked with agitation. Clearly the clues weren't landing with Mr Perceptive.

To say I was mildly surprised would be a tad of an understatement. 'I'm making the . . . um . . . chicken balls?' I said, sure this was some kind of joke.

'I could smell that oil in the hallway downstairs,' he said. 'After everything I told you about oil, I can't believe you're frying when we have an open house in four days' time . . .' and on and on and on he went, but I'd stopped listening.

With greasy tongs in hand, I yelled at him mid-sentence, 'Fuck! Off!'

I stormed into the bedroom and slammed the door. Jeff blared Mary J Blige (what would the neighbours think?) and set about eradicating the apartment of the world's worst smell, and the thought of him faffing about covering up my crime made me angrier and angrier. (As if Mary's voice were not grating enough! I mean, she was no Cyndi Lauper.)

Jeff's version of events is somewhat different . . .

In time, the chicken ball fiasco passed into our folklore and it never fails to make us laugh. To make but a wee final point, the auction of our property smashed the building's sales record despite the alleged faintly lingering scent of chicken balls.

Though we'd made decent money on the apartment it seemed that the only ones we could now afford in the east were shoeboxes with no views. I kept widening our internet searches, prompting Jeff to consider leaving the only area of Sydney he'd ever lived in.

Almost from the moment his stalking plan had come to fruition, way back at the start of 'us', Jeff and I worked out that we share a similar view on life: neither of us believes in the concept of 'forever'. This applies to practically everything – relationships, homes, jobs, dreams, scowls from moronic neighbours . . . we believe in enjoying things in the moment rather than fixating on what everything might look and feel like at some imagined point in the future. So while Annandale was never going to be our 'forever' home, we both knew we would be living there for a few years at least. And after that, who knew?

We settled on a rundown terrace on a one-way alley, which we planned to renovate and turn into our dream home. To celebrate, Jesus – who creates stunning jewellery in his spare time (he designed and made Mel's beyond-fabulous engagement ring) – gave us each a shiny new key ring as a housewarming present. They were stainless steel and shaped like a J on one side and a T on the other.

The beauty of the key ring contrasted nicely with the state of the house. The walls cried when it rained (we had buckets in the bedroom to catch drops), the floors were uneven and see-through in places (there were about eight different levels inside the house), windows were broken and the outdoor sewage pump had a habit of overflowing. None of this daunted us – but then we never looked too far into the future, as if what we might find there would scare the fuck out of us.

For the remainder of 2007 and through to the end of 2008, the house was a revolving door of visitors. Dinner parties, barbecues, cooking for friends, celebrations, drinks, huge bashes, me and Andy's girlfriend Ali on the banister doing impressions of Cher on a cannon singing 'If I Could Turn Back Time' at the top of our lungs (I'd always wanted to live in a house with stairs and now finally I had some), very fashionable Nintendo Wii parties, weekly dinners with Andy and Ali, who were now living nearby ... the list went on. It was as if the house's state of near-dereliction put people at ease and while once we'd feared that becoming Inner Westies would keep people away, that didn't seem to be the case.

For our first Annandale Christmas we had an 'open gate' policy – we spread the word that anyone and everyone was welcome to walk through our gate on the street and join us whenever their family get-togethers made them cross-eyed with boredom and/or anger. By the end of the evening we had an eclectic and energetic mix of friends and we partied until the early hours.

Then our friends started falling pregnant, or moving further out to more affordable suburbs with bigger gardens for the children. That was cool; inevitable really, even for those friends who said they were never having kids. It wasn't until our second open gate Christmas, in 2008, that Jeff and I realised we were not quite the drawcards we thought we were. Not a single person walked through the gate, and we sat in the courtyard with wine in our glasses and huge platters of food, excited by the sound of every approaching car but quickly disappointed when no footsteps followed.

'Merry Fucking Christmas!' I said.

Luckily we still enjoyed each other's company because it sure as hell looked like that was all we were going to get.

For Christmas 2009, Jeff's sister Lovain and niece Hayley visited us from the UK and kindly never complained when they were forced to sleep in a room with holes in the ceiling and inch-thick holes in the window frame that let in an endless torrent of mosquitoes and spiders.

Finally we launched into the full-blown renovation in April 2010, which saw us living in one room upstairs with an open air toilet that could be seen from the street. This resulted in a year out from entertaining, and by the time the house was finished, we could count our childless friends on one hand.

'The same thing happened to me,' our friend Cheryl said one night. We'd developed a routine of having dinner weekly at her place in Petersham – our one social outing now that everyone else was playing happy families. 'All my friends went off and had babies and then when the kids grew up they all came back again. You just have to wait fifteen years or so.'

'So we're in friend prison for a crime we didn't commit?' I asked gloomily.

'To some degree, yes. Unless you're happy spending your Saturdays at birthday parties full of screaming children?'

'See, that's when it's likely I'd commit a crime,' Jeff muttered.

'I had one birthday party as a kid – my twelfth – and look how incredibly well adjusted *I* turned out to be. I don't have an addictive personality,' – I gulped some more wine – 'or anything. These kids of today are going to want Happy Meals and ice-cream cakes every birthday for the rest of their lives.'

'Spoilt rotten the lot of them,' Cheryl agreed. 'Now get up and make me a cup of tea in my new glass stovetop kettle, please. Caffeine-free black tea with that organic Manuka honey in the cupboard. Could you only put one and one-third of a teaspoon of honey in it? Thank you.'

After I'd delivered her tea, Cheryl put her feet up on the couch and picked up George and John Brown to place them on her lap. Those two white dogs are everything to her and picking them up usually means only one thing. I glanced at my phone and saw that it was 9.32pm.

'Oh well,' I said with a stretch, 'we should probably be going – it's way past your bedtime.' Home yet again before the witching hour of 9.40pm. As much as we absolutely loved our evenings with Cheryl, they were a far cry from being splashed by vomiting patrons at the now-demolished Baron's Bar in Kings Cross . . . but then maybe that was a good thing.

Our situation was actually quite different from the grave one Cheryl had prophesised because we *do* have kids, though they're not with us full time. Luckily for Jeff and me, I had donated my sperm to a loving couple in Brisbane who wanted their two children to be genetically related and know who their father is. And luckily for them, my donation turned out to be bounteous – in fact, it was one of the most impressive the staff at the clinic had ever seen. Needless to say, I still have a swagger in my step over that. But whenever any of our friends moan about the challenges of parenting I say smugly, 'Well, you should have outsourced it to a pair of lesbians in a different state, shouldn't you?'

The morning after I'd met Jeff I said to him, 'If you plan on sticking around you need to know you'll soon be a daddy.'

I figured day two was as good as any to break the news. Jane was three months pregnant with what would eventually turn into our daughter, Lucy, and I was already slotted in for a visit with her partner, Vicky, at the end of the year for what would become our son, Charlie. *Hello, I'd like to make a sizable deposit, please.* Weirdly, prospective fatherhood didn't seem to faze Jeff and after settling in Annandale we also adopted a 'child' of our own.

Mid-renovation we'd inherited a black cat named Leroy from the daughter of our neighbour. We'd taken to her other daughter's cat that we'd named Florence after she'd moved into our empty house while we were on holiday in Italy.

Flo used to sleep between my legs (insert predictable pussy joke here) and came running to us whenever we sang a particular harmony, but a car crushed her spine a few months after we'd formally adopted her. Knowing how much we loved her, when our neighbour's other daughter needed to offload her cat, it was Jeff and I who received a pleading note in our letterbox: *No pressure at all but if you do not take Leroy we will be forced to leave him with the Cat Protection Society.* There was an altogether too adorable photo of him attached, a pitch-black feline with a lovely red collar. In a bizarre coincidence, I'd included a black dog named Leroy in my first novel, *Pictures of Us*, and it just felt right that we should have him, mid-renovation and all.

Leroy the cat had attacked one of our neighbour's grandkids so we knew from the outset that he had behavioural problems, but I'd also taken on Jeff so another family member with issues didn't daunt me. Although most of the time he was the sweetest cat ever, over the years he did attack us and some of our friends . . . more than we'd care to number. A couple ended up on antibiotics. It was as if something switched in him: his eyes went big, black and vacant and he just ripped into flesh, prompting my idea for a horror film called *Claws* – but that's probably been done before.

In Annandale he quickly became the king of the street. As soon as he moved in with us he set about firmly cementing his position at the very top of the feline ladder.

One day a neighbour said, 'Is that Leroy? He broke my cat's tail and it cost me a bomb to get him fixed up.'

Another neighbour: 'Is his name Leroy? I woke up in the middle of the night a few weeks ago and he was sitting at the end of my bed, just staring at me.'

And yet another: 'Leroy's an absolute legend. We love him! He chases my wife around the house whenever she wears her fluffy slippers and we can't get enough of it. He's always so gentle and loving.'

And finally (overheard): 'Oh look, isn't that cat cute? She must be very heavily pregnant.'

Post-renovation, the pristine, sterile and mostly white house straight out of the pages of *Home Beautiful* where an unpredictably vicious cat lived was not exactly a comfortable environment for any parent visiting with young children. In hindsight, it wasn't a comfortable environment for anyone, so perhaps that's why friends stayed away in droves from our Annandale designer home.

The three-month renovation stretched on to eleven months but it sure gave us something to focus on other than our respective jobs. For Jeff, there were always fixtures and fittings to shop for, new instructions to give to the builders, daily inspections of the work and our fast-dwindling savings to obsess over. I suppose the chaos we were living in also gave us something to bond over – the lack of running water, privacy and security; frustration over the neighbours' junk filling up our skip bin.

19

Because we had no shower, we were running into work to shower there every weekday. We avoided going home to our one room if we could and, whenever we did, the only thing that dulled the stresses of an over-time, over-budget renovation was eating fast food and drinking too much booze. It was a gruelling (*yet exciting*!) eleven months, but then, when it was all over, it suddenly felt like we had nothing to look forward to and dammit if we weren't plain bored. Our feets was gettin' *real* itchy.

'Where are you going?' I asked Jeff as he got his bike ready one day.

'I can't just sit around here all day; I need to get out.'

'Get out where? Am I that repulsive?'

'Don't be ridiculous. I'm going to buy some cushions.'

'More cushions? For where? It's because I'm fat and ugly and you don't love me any more, isn't it? Isn't it, Jibbuz?' (Jibbuz is a nickname I'd invented for him; just as 'Leroy' changed to Roy to Roybert to Bert to Bertram to Bertie to Bertolucci so 'Jeff' went to Jeffy to Jiffy to Jibby to Jibbuz . . .)

He ignored me, and rightfully so.

'I just need to get out,' he said with a shrug. 'Wanna come?'

Finding more cushions to squash into the house wasn't exactly my idea of fun. Did cushions really need to appear on every chair? On every bed? On top of bookcases? Any available space on the hardwood floor was already piled with cushions. Fuck me if those things weren't breeding while we slept and now he wanted to go and buy some more? I let him go out shopping alone and stayed at home to . . . fester.

We may have had the perfect house and the perfect relationship but my blinding love affair with my job at eBay was on the wane. I had traded my love of the customer and the core idea behind the product for a desire to earn more and take on more responsibility but that ended up making me feel like a soulless sell-out. Some people thrive on becoming a part of the management team, but clearly I wasn't one of them.

It ate away at my energy levels and by the time the weekend rolled around I was mentally exhausted and therefore quite content to sit at home in our large empty house fuelling my own new addiction: I just couldn't stop buying cookbooks. I flicked through most of them only once and rarely cooked from any, but gee they sure did look pretty in colour-coded order on the shelves in our unused dining room. Having a separate dining room had long been a dream of mine as I'd envisaged scores of friends night after night being served amazing morsels from my sparkling white kitchen, with the help of my brand-new KitchenAid mixer, Smeg oven, and five-hundred-dollar Japanese knives. But though Chez Todd was definitely open for business, the bookings were few and far between. I suppose cookbooks became my way of imagining what might have been if I lived in a world where all our friends were available for extravagant dinner parties that lasted until the wee hours of the morning, and I had the energy to host them.

I had been promoted to a stupidly paid director position at eBay and was being groomed as the 2IC but I wasn't able to give the company the half of my soul it demanded. Perhaps a part of me had been left behind in the Barossa earlier in the year and was refusing to join the rest of me in my corporate life. It was toward the end of 2010 that I realised something had to give.

'I don't think I can do this any more,' I said to Jeff one evening as we cracked open the second bottle of wine.

'So quit,' he said, deadpan.

'Are you mental? And do what?'

'Whatever you want to do.'

'I'm shit-scared . . .'

'Of what?'

'I don't know.'

'What's the worst thing that could happen?'

'We lose everything . . .'

'Exactly! But as long as we have each other, we'll be okay. So quit. Go on, I dare you.'

A few weeks later, I took up his dare. It was a slap to the face my boss hadn't been expecting. Bless her, she refused to accept my resignation and asked me to give her a few days to think things over. Eventually she came back with a proposal – I could choose how many hours per week I wanted to work, and base myself anywhere.

Working Tuesday to Thursday meant I found myself with a four-day weekend. It was utter bliss and for the first time in about twenty years I felt I had the time to do something *for myself.* I spent my time running, writing, reading, walking and preparing amazing meals for Jeff. We adjusted to the fall in income by spending less money on eating out and other frivolous expenses and this, coupled with my newfound clarity of mind, prompted us to stop drinking. At the end of 2010 we simply went cold turkey.

So if pristine perfection was keeping friends away, then our newfound sobriety with its quiet meals (and no more Cher impressions and the like) and hosts ready for bed by 9:30pm (just like Cheryl!) didn't help attract many visitors either.

My mind turned again to that feeling we'd shared in the Barossa. I drooled over South Australian properties on the internet, showing Jeff the most interesting ones. At that point I wasn't all that serious about giving our whole life away; I suppose I just wanted to be back on that holiday with three of the people I loved most in the world. But maybe lurking in the back of my mind was the gradual realisation that whatever Jeff and I had imagined our quaint little life together would be like, it was starting to throw us a few curveballs. You can't be a childless gay couple in suburbia and not see your straight friends' lives heading off in a different direction.

But with me working part-time and the standing offer to work from anywhere in the country, suddenly the prospect of a tree change didn't seem so beyond our reach, and our searches for the perfect property intensified. My boss had granted me the ideal stepping-stone between the corporate world and one far, far away.

Maybe Jeff Needs
a Change, Too

While I kept showing Jeff potential properties to buy for our tree change, I needed to make sure he was as excited by the prospect as I was. During the renovation, I'd seen a spark in Jeff I'd never seen before. He genuinely loved speaking with the builders, talking them through his ideas and ensuring each came to realisation as accurately as possible. Then after they'd left us to do the finishing touches, day after day Jeff painted every raw plaster wall in the house four times over. If you ask me, painting walls is what they give you as punishment in hell, but Jeff loved transforming the building into our home. He designed the interiors and spent hours scouring the internet and local shops for pieces that would take a run-down terrace and turn it into a thing of beauty. We flew his mum, Millie, out from England to inspect our handiwork and she couldn't believe the transformation – no one could.

I imagine it's like being an actor at the end of a film, after they call 'it's a wrap!' and the party is over and everyone goes on to the next stage of their life. There was an emptiness in the house that distracted Jeff, and to add to his dissatisfaction the company he worked for was becoming more corporate and Jeff increasingly felt like a fish out of water, ill-versed in the new language and the rules of the game.

After the renovation ended and there was no longer that seemingly endless to-do list, it felt as if our lives had no meaningful purpose, so Jeff did what any reasonable man would do – he transformed into Forrest Gump. If Jeff wasn't buying yet more cushions, he was off running. (Saturdays were running days; Sundays were for cushion shopping.) His little legs carried him on and on and on. We'd do the Bay Run, a nearby harbourside track, 'together' and as I plodded along on my I'm-not-a-runner legs, he'd disappear into the distance, lapping me well before I was even close to my seven-kilometre goal. It was as if Jeff ran on a turbo diesel engine and I had to rely on crappy rechargeable AAs that barely worked. Jeff set himself the challenge of finishing a marathon and, unlike normal people who'd just be content to run forty-two fucking kilometres in whatever time it took, he insisted on getting it done in under three and a half hours. My own goal during that time was to make ten kilometres without vomiting, dying or shitting myself.

Jeff downloaded a marathon-training program and for three or four months he stuck to it like a fly to a horse's rump. (More astute observers may be beginning to get the picture that Jeff can be just a little obsessive.) A run of one hour to start with, then another twenty minutes, then two hours and by the end of his training, he could run for three straight hours without stopping.

One Saturday he asked me to pick him up in Rose Bay, so I sat at home perusing cookbooks and listening to Cyndi Lauper till his text came through. At the designated pick-up place I'd expected to find a ravaged man – a mere shadow of his former self – but there he was, sipping on a coffee, a sprightly spring in his step.

'Did you not just run, like, thirty-five kilometres or something?' I asked in amazement.

'Yeah. Why?'

'I just expected you to look exhausted. You look like you've been for a stroll around the block.'

'Nah, I really caught the bus here,' he joked. 'But I didn't have enough money to catch one back home.'

Come the day of his marathon, I was a bundle of nerves; Jeff was calm and excited. I don't know why, but when I dropped him off on the other side of the Harbour Bridge, I felt like I was dropping my kid to his first day of school, a school where the ritual was for the newbies to be hung and quartered. My stomach was in knots. He'd practically run the distance in training already; he could easily do it again on race day so I had no reason to fear anything. But sending your partner off to push his body to its absolute limit is not exactly something you want to do on a daily basis.

I drove home and looked at some more recipes. *Maybe I'll make him a special carb-laden dinner tonight to celebrate*, I thought. He texted me at the half-way point, roughly on-target for his three and a half hours, so Mum, Dad and I made our way to the Opera House to watch him finish. We were going to have beers by the harbour afterward with our friends Hamish and Mel.

As the first finishers started to cross the line, the crowd of onlookers cheered them on with genuine awe and excitement. It was very emotional to watch these runners conquer one of the greatest endurance tests of the human body.

The race clock told me three hours and ten minutes had elapsed, so I knew we still had about twenty minutes to wait for Jeff. But a few minutes later I thought I glimpsed his cap through the crowd. *No, surely not.* I looked at my fancy Ted Baker watch and double-checked the marathon clock. Three hours and fifteen minutes. And then I saw my very own Forrest Gump come running around the bend.

But something was wrong. Jeff was running – well, staggering – and his lights were on, but the people inside had moved out about a decade ago. Vandals had smashed the windows and they were now boarded up with cheap pine. His face was blank. I leaned out over the railing and made eye-contact, but there was no recognition. And come on, if anything is going to bring an exhausted person to their senses, it's this face. I could hear the blaring of the music through his headphones, the crowd noise was swelling once more and I realised then they were cheering for Jeff . . . who looked like he was about to die.

'Come on Jeffy! You can do it! You're nearly there!' I screamed at him as loudly as I could. But again, there was simply no sign in his face that he knew who I was, where he was, or what he was supposed to do.

His legs began to give out and he faltered. John frigging Farnham was blaring over the loud speaker (and I've fucking hated 'You're the Voice' ever since). Jeff stumbled and nearly fell. Two officials ran to guide him (it's against the rules to carry or bear any of a marathon runner's weight) and then he was out of my sight – I couldn't see the actual finish line as people beyond me had leaned far out over the barricade to cheer him on.

I threw the house keys at Mum and Dad and yelled at them, 'Go home! I'll call you! Sorry about the beers!' *Do not cry do not cry do not cry*, I chanted internally.

It took me ages to get to the finish line because the crowd was thicker there. When I did, I was just in time to see the paramedics swoop on Jeff, who was now lying motionless on the concrete. My heart sank. *This is it, I'm losing him.* They placed an oxygen mask on his face but he was still not moving.

'Can I come?' I asked the driver of the ambulance they'd hurriedly stashed him in.

'Who are you?'

'I'm his ... housemate.' I don't know why I couldn't say partner or boyfriend ... I suppose I didn't want to look like a pathetically worried lover, though I have to admit I was feeling every inch Jackie Kennedy in the front of that ambulance once the sirens started wailing.

I turned around to catch a brief glimpse of what was going on behind me. Jeff was finally moving but the paramedic with him in the back of the ambulance looked worried. Jeff was murmuring something but we couldn't make sense of what he was saying through the oxygen mask. The guy placed ice packs under Jeff's arms and in his groin and I saw him give Jeff an injection of something. *At least he's still alive*, I thought. *There's no need to keep fearing the worst. God, I wish I was wearing big black sunglasses*, I couldn't help thinking as well.

'Is he going to be all right?' I asked as unworriedly as I could.

'Hard to say,' came a voice from the back and then it proceeded to ask me Jeff's name, date of birth, medical history, and so on. For a 'housemate' I sure did know a lot about him!

Jeff mumbled something again. The paramedic in the back still couldn't understand him and encouraged him to stay quiet and conserve his energy.

'You're okay,' he was saying to Jeff. 'We will be at the hospital soon. You've collapsed after the marathon. Remember?'

But Jeff just kept mumbling and maybe it was because the paramedic and the driver next to me weren't used to his Brummy accent but to me what he was saying was as clear as Barbra Streisand's upper register: 'Tell Toddy I love him.'

Jeff was alive and that was the main thing. We would deal with any health issues once he'd been given a thorough check-up at the hospital. I just wanted him back inside himself; I wanted to be able to talk to him, tell him I was there with him and everything was going to be okay.

We got to St Vincent's Hospital and they asked me to wait while they got him out of the ambulance. Then something very strange happened. When they wheeled him on the gurney toward the emergency doors, he saw me and said with great surprise, 'Well, what are you doing here?' and it was clear he was Jeff again.

'What the hell happened?' I asked him, after all the tests had been completed.

'I was doing fine!' he insisted. 'I even remember asking the woman near Circular Quay how far it was to go and she said, "About a kilometre; you're nearly there!" and I remember seeing the people on the sidelines cheering. But then there's this little platform thing and I thought I'd finished but then everyone yelled, "No, keep going!" and then I guess my body just gave out thinking it was done, but needing to find more energy to get to the real bloody finish line.

'So how did I look?' he went on. 'Stupid?'

'Oh no, it was very dramatic!' I relayed the whole scene to him, then asked: 'Did you know what had happened to you?'

'No! I really thought I'd been hit by a car. I thought I was badly injured and maybe I was going to die.'

'You couldn't just finish like a normal person, could you? You had to make me run after you, bawling my eyes out, screaming out your name, chasing the ambulance down the Opera House forecourt waving my black lace hanky . . .'

'Yes, yes,' he said dismissively. 'But what was my time?'

'Three hours and eighteen minutes,' I said, and he beamed like a Hollywood searchlight.

We waited hours for them to give him the all clear. At one point a nurse came through the curtains and asked, 'And how are we today?'

'I'm a bit bored, actually,' I said, and she shook her head at me.

'I meant Jeff!'

Watching the footage of him finishing is still one of the hardest things I've ever had to do. Jeff wants to laugh about it now, and although I can make jokes about the drama, I still can't stand to watch it. I suppose it was the defining moment in our relationship – before the marathon I'd taken Jeff for granted somewhat, as so many of us do our partners, and at even the hint that he might be taken away from me, my whole life came to a standstill. He didn't need to run himself to death to find purpose in life – maybe there was something we could do together to give both our lives more meaning.

So what do a marathon man/cushion addict and cookbook-hoarder do to give their lives meaning? First, they buy an investment property in the bayside suburb of Russell Lea and renovate on next to no budget – but it just doesn't evoke the same feeling as when they were making a home for themselves. They go on holidays to amazing places like Japan and Russia but this only adds fuel to their fire, reminding them that something is missing in their settled-down lives. So with a renewed sense of urgency they return to the possibility of a full-scale lifestyle change. They consider turning their backs on everything they've worked hard to create; they ponder the madness of starting from scratch doing something they've never done before. Nothing is forever, after all.

Jeff and I are, in many respects, polar opposites. Jeff worked in finance and I worked in marketing. He is all numbers-driven and precise; I am all airy-fairy with a vivid imagination. He can fall asleep whenever he chooses; I frequently lie in bed for hours counting different kinds of sheep like past lovers, listing Meryl Streep's Oscar nominations in chronological order or trying to create brand-new recipes (chocolate paté!) only to realise most already exist. He likes superhero films and I seek out quirky independents. He loves Mary J Blige and I am borderline obsessed with Cyndi Lauper and have travelled to seven Australian cities to see her perform twelve or thirteen times. I love to cook; he loves to clean. I stay in touch with all of our friends; he is happy to pick up where things left off months before. I learned how to play corporate games like 'How many ways would you like me to tell you you're great?' and he prefers to say it like it is. I avoid confrontation like a toupee wearer avoids the wind; Jeff will pick you up on something he doesn't believe is right: 'That campaign didn't really drive a million dollars in sales; by my calculations it really only made fifty thousand . . .'

'Yes, but it also made our customers happy and you can't put a price on that, Debbie Downer.'

'I'm just being realistic.'

'No, you're being depressing. And you'll never get a promotion if you present the whole story. It's about creative editing.'

Jeff has a keen eye for design. By now we'd renovated three properties and he'd been doing handyman jobs around the house since he was a young kid in Birmingham. I am more of a people person, and my entire career had more or less been in retail – including helping my father run his small business. I am okay at marketing, strategy, customer service and planning. While at university I unloaded semi-trailers full of plastic pots, so in a competition of who is prepared to work hardest, I will definitely win (until Jeff reminds me he used to scrub clean his father's lorry after a long day hauling scrap metal).

The more we talked about changing our lives, the more we agreed we had the right mix of skills; the right balance of personalities – plus we share the same determination to succeed. We also have a passion for adventure: Jeff left home at twenty to travel Europe on five pounds a day; the first time I left Australia I went on a four-week camping safari in East Africa with Kirsti. (Mind you, I did have Daddy's Gold Amex on hand for emergencies but I wasn't a princess, honest.) If any two people could give a tree-change a go, surely we had the essential ingredients? We'd out-run, out-cushioned and out-cookbooked Annandale.

Remembering the terrible B&B from our jaunt to the Barossa with Mel and Jesus, we decided if that landlord could make a killing despite her net curtains and slimy spa we'd have no trouble at all, given Jeff's flair for interior design and my many, *many* talents. Accommodation, we decided, was going to get us out of the corporate world once and for all.

When we announced our imminent tree change to our friends, there was a mixed reaction.

'Just don't sell your Sydney property because you'll need to come back to it when things fail,' some friends advised.

'Accommodation? But you two don't know the first thing about accommodation,' others objected.

'You're giving up a huge salary to work *that* hard and never know where the next pay cheque is coming from?'

'Why on earth would you want to leave Sydney?'

'I don't think you two should work together, it could ruin your relationship.'

'You won't find like-minded people in the country, you know.'

But then Mel and Jesus said, 'We're so jealous! Do it!'

But the real challenge was finding the ideal location where we'd wow holidaymakers with our breathtaking style, heart-warming wit and incredible good looks. Wherever we chose, tourists had to be spending money there. In New South Wales alone the possibilities were endless: Coffs Harbour, Kangaroo Valley, Berry, the Blue Mountains, the south or central coasts. Or we could go further afield: Far North Queensland or even Maggie Beer-land: the Barossa itself ... nowhere was out of the question. Feverishly we started looking at properties online. Jeff had done his sums so we knew we needed to find something big enough to build three villas on or, better yet, something that already had outbuildings we could easily convert. Jeff relished the idea of doing more renovating whereas I'd be quite happy with running water and a flushing toilet, thanks all the same.

We flew interstate to explore a few different places but none felt right. We kept being drawn back to the Barossa but ultimately it just felt too far away from everyone we knew. Every once in a while we'd also look at properties in the Hunter Valley, a few hours north of Sydney, but I'd always ruled out the Hunter because I found the approach through the main Hunter town, Cessnock, slow and tedious. But perhaps that was about to change ...

After a so-so year, eBay had downgraded the annual company celebrations from Thailand to a two-day 'retreat' in the Hunter Valley. We were given a choice of activities and, being the stressed and delicate little flower I was, I chose a spa treatment at the appealing-sounding Golden Door Spa.

On the day of the treatment, I was first in our group to finish so I made my way through the golden door (yes, there really is one, though I was disappointed that it was only painted gold, not made of gold) and sat on a bench facing the Brokenback Range. It was a warm day and the sky was crystal clear. A soft warm breeze occasionally brought the trees before me to life. The bench was on top of a hill that led straight to the foot of the range, a path paved with a mix of bushland and row after row of grapevines just losing their leaves before the cold of winter arrived. The mountain in front of me was mostly bush but some awe-inspiring rock faces reminded me of just how old this valley was – that it was once beneath the ocean. But the thing that struck me most was how quiet it was. I forgot what my life had become, that I was so unhappy in the corporate world and, for those twenty minutes or so without a man-made sound or a passer-by, I was wholly and beautifully just *in the moment*. Maybe I was simply relaxed from my hour-long massage and the spa and sauna beforehand, or perhaps I was inspired by the rare moment of stillness. Maybe it was a subconscious reminder of Jake and Heath in *Brokeback Mountain* or perhaps it really was Destiny tapping me on the shoulder. But as I sat there drinking in that glorious view, I knew I'd found where I wanted to be.

'But I thought you hated the Hunter,' Jeff said when I got back all refreshed and renewed and bursting to share my epiphany.

'I realise now I don't know it very well. And I heard they're opening a new expressway, which means we wouldn't have to drive through Cessnock! Plus it'll make the drive to Sydney twenty or thirty minutes faster,' I added optimistically. It really did tick all our boxes: the Hunter is to Sydney what the Barossa is to Adelaide. After Sydney, it's the second most-visited tourism destination in New South Wales and its famous wines, delicious food, beautiful scenery, world-class musicians in concert, wedding venues, never-ending calendar of events, countless activities and beautiful year-round weather draw visitors back again and again.

'Come on, let's look up properties and make an appointment to see some really soon.'

A few weeks later as we sat looking at the beautiful view from the Audrey Wilkinson cellar door, we agreed: if we could find a property in the Hunter that had some views (okay, probably not those multi-million-dollar Audrey Wilkinson ones, but *some* views), privacy and an opportunity for accommodation, then the Hunter Valley was where the next chapter of our lives would be written.

4

I Want to Go to Here

At least for the medium-term, we decided to keep the Annandale and Russell Lea properties as investments, but armed with our modest pre-approval from the bank, it soon became obvious I was as delusional as a naïve heroine in a Hitchcock film. I wanted my own slice of Maggie Beer's life, only in the Hunter Valley, but I'd clearly missed the boat – our money wasn't going to stretch anywhere near that far. Maybe we could have three chooks on half an acre but that wasn't quite the dazzling vision I had for our future. In fact, buying a shack in one of the small towns of the Hunter was more realistic than something larger in wine country.

Not the type to give up easily, for the best part of the next eighteen months we harassed the lovely local real estate agent, Shelly. She must have hated receiving my calls: *The delusional gays are back again*. We knew the internet listings were uninspiring, but we still made countless visits to the Hunter Valley, dutifully showing up to meet Shelly at the agreed times. We'd watched enough episodes of *Location, Location, Location* to know what unrealistic house hunters looked like – surely that wasn't what we'd become? *Phil, if you could just move this house onto a thousand acres and charge us no more ...* We could afford reasonably sized homes on larger-than-suburban parcels of land, but everything we saw lacked that elusive *je ne sais quoi*. You know – that thing house-hunters say they 'just feel' when they see the right property.

This wasn't just a home we were searching for, after all; it was a whole new way of life and with a long list of desirable features. I was mid-transformation into Maggie Beer but still hadn't gone through with the irreversible operation. We had become those impossible-to-please customers. If she felt frustrated though, the ever-bubbly Shelly never let on. After too many failed viewings to count, we made the decision to sell the Russell Lea apartment, freeing up the extra cash to buy something more in line with our dreams. That apartment was meant to be our nest egg but maybe people who don't believe in forever shouldn't try to act like sensible folk who make plans for the future. Our grand plans to 'gayify' it into a stunning top-floor apartment with water views, converting it from two to three bedrooms, were flushed down the toilet, but selling it would afford us the change we wanted for the here and now, future be damned.

'We're going to lose money on it,' I said to Jeff. 'That makes me feel like hurling chunks.'

'We don't really have a choice though, Monkey. If we want to move to the Hunter and find a property that's going to give us a reasonable income, it's pretty clear 750k isn't enough.'

We'd looked at so many properties, even blocks of land. But our vision was to create something as far removed from net curtains as possible. We wanted to have our guests feel as if they were staying in a property they would very happily call home, and simply painting over 1970s decor was never going to cut it.

So after we lost around forty thousand on that little Russell Lea folly, the bank happily increased our pre-approval to a million dollars. (Of course had we waited five years that apartment would have increased in value by around fifty per cent but we didn't have a crystal ball and, really, it's not something we like to think about these days!) At that point we intended to keep the Annandale house, rent it out and move to the Hunter full-time.

Even with an increased budget, the search dragged on for another few months. There were more viewings of properties – all ugly, run-down or on main roads – and a constant scouring of real estate sites, but there were only so many brick veneer huts a gay with delusions of grandeur can endure. It was now early 2012 and we were beginning to wonder if the dream would remain just that. It was time to concentrate on more cushions and cookbooks instead – that wasn't such a bad life after all, was it? Maybe I'd even try to run a marathon?

The only listing I'd ever truly liked was way out of our budget but those delusions of grandeur just wouldn't leave me alone. It was a grape and olive farm set on one hundred acres (over forty hectares), with two massive dams, expansive views and wide-open fields. It was altogether very Maggie because of those olives and dams, and it even had a few fruit trees at the front of the house. I imagined people coming to have picnics eating our food, drinking our wine and watching our ducks play in the dam. There was a simple but functional house. I first came across the property mid-2011, not long after my Golden Door moment, when I did one of those dangerous 'no upper limit' searches 'just to see what else is out there'. It's a bizarre form of torture sillier house hunters like me can't help inflicting on ourselves. That first time I saw it, the property was listed at $1.9 million. Then over the following six months or so, the price came down to $1.7, then to $1.3, and by the end of 2011 it had come down to $1.1 million. I wondered why nobody wanted it; why the vendors were slashing the price on an almost monthly basis. Surely other people dreamed of being Maggie Beer, just like me? One day when Jeff had dragged me off to shop for yet more cushions, I decided on a whim to call Shelly while I waited on a wooden bench outside the soft furnishings store.

'Squire Close,' I said to her, 'do you think they'd consider an offer below a million?'

Shelly knew our budget had increased but she also knew there was no chance of us going over our million-dollar cap.

'They're really eager to sell,' she began, 'but they've come down over $800,000 in around eighteen months so they just wouldn't be prepared to go any lower, I'm sorry.'

'I knew it was a long shot, don't worry,' I told her. Back inside the shop, I relayed the conversation to Jeff.

'That's a bummer. Do you prefer this one or this one?' he asked, holding up two basically identical cushions. I shrugged and pointed to the one in his left hand – at the checkout I noticed that he'd chosen the one in his right.

Just over six months later, in July 2012, and with not a single property exciting us, we were on yet another of our trips to the Hunter and treating ourselves to a delicious lunch after several property inspections. Hopelessness was beginning to creep in. We were questioning whether we shouldn't cancel the rest of the afternoon's viewings but as we ate, I got out my phone and again looked up that hundred-acre property just to have a little daydream.

'Oh my god!' I said excitedly to Jeff.

'What?' he asked flatly, thinking this was some sort of prank.

'That property . . . the one with the dams and the olives . . . it now says "offers over one million".'

'It's still too expensive, I don't know why you do this to yourself . . .'

'I can't help it,' I said with a shrug, finding it impossible to hide my excitement. 'Can we?'

'Oh come on, stop it! You're just going to be disappointed.'

'Please . . .'

And less than one hour later we were driving toward the property that had been so flirtatious with me for well over eighteen months, teasing with its evocative photographs, willing me in with its falling price tag. The stalked had become the stalker – only this time the prize on offer was even greater than the treasure Jeff had won.

The approach to Squire Close was down a road called Sweetwater. *Give me some of that sweet water, baby, I got a good taste for this one.* The neighbouring properties were uniformly bordered by lovely rural wooden fencing (rather appealing to a pair of gays) and one of them was a formidable Tuscan-style mansion (ditto); others were beautiful properties in their own right. There were countless rows of grapevines, olive groves and fantastic views of the Brokenback Range. That day, it felt like we'd arrived at a secret doorway into the Hunter Valley, a secret and golden door.

The roads were quiet and deserted and, in an omen too hard to ignore, just as with every other property we'd ever bought together, Squire Close was a cul-de-sac. My heart was racing, my palms began to sweat. My mind was spinning with such excitement and my inner Maggie Beer was about to appear. When you know something is right, *you just know.*

The gate to the property was locked but I stopped the car, lowered the windows and we sat listening to the sounds of nature around us. In front of us was an olive grove (just like Maggie's!) but that was all you could see from the road. It was just row after row of beautiful silver-green foliage and, up along the driveway, lovely deciduous trees that had lost nearly all of their auburn leaves. My mental list was being ticked: tourism (vineyards), serenity, privacy, space and beauty . . .

'This is it,' I said aloud though more to myself than to Jeff. I didn't look at him for fear he would not be as in love with it as I was. I had no hesitation about that property whatsoever. I'd known it all the times I'd looked at it longingly on the internet; I knew it that day I called Shelly to ask whether they'd accept an offer under a million dollars; I had known it at lunch; I knew it driving along the approach roads – and I couldn't even see a cactus in the window.

'Get us this property, Toddy,' Jeff said suddenly, without a trace of *It's too expensive stop doing this to yourself.* 'Whatever you need to do, negotiate your arse off and get it for us. I want to go to here.'

And we hadn't even placed a foot on it.

Olives and Grapes
and Dams, Oh My!

Once Shelly's business partner Cain had agreed to meet us at the property, we cancelled all three of the afternoon's other viewings. We'd known all along they weren't the right ones for us and there's nothing quite like popping all your yet-to-be-purchased chickens' eggs into your already-filled-with-cushions basket.

As if we hadn't been excited enough waiting for Cain to unlock the gate, the completely awesome view at the crest of the olive grove totally blew us away. We had stopped at the top of the hill to get into Cain's four-wheel drive, pretending we hadn't noticed his chuckle at our very un-country and totally useless Barina that hadn't coped very well with the rough driveway and certainly wouldn't have made it cross-country through the vineyard. As far as we could see, there was not a single man-made structure. It was a far cry from the stinky bins lining our cramped one-way alley in Annandale. Vast fields of grazing land and dense bushland gave way to the simple, breathtaking beauty of the Barrington Tops. Over to the left lay the Great Dividing Range, with the Brokenback Range behind us on its eastern tip. Large black dots on the landscape revealed themselves as big fat heifers grazing on the long dry grass.

As we silently took in this magnificence, I didn't dare look at Jeff: I feared a little bit of wee would come out or I would burst into uncontrollable fits of schoolgirl giggles. Instead, I was concentrating on making Cain feel we were lukewarm about the property, all the better for negotiation.

A mob of kangaroos lay relaxing in the shade of the olive groves and bounded out of our way to allow the four-wheel drive to pass.

'I ordered those in especially,' Cain said.

He drove us up into the vineyard first, fifteen acres of vines, about 150 rows. Vines stretched out in both directions as we drove down the central aisle. If either of us was feeling daunted by the idea of running a vineyard, we didn't let on. In my mind I was thinking, *Holy shit, there's a tonne of work to do here and I never wanted to be a grapegrower but we don't need to keep them; we could use the land for something else. No, this is too big for us, it's beautiful but too big. This is crazy, there's no way in hell we can manage all of this. There must be a million snakes in that long grass. Bushfires! Bushfires! What about the bushfires?* Normal people would have shat their pants at the thought of managing or even clearing out the vines (*Terribly sorry, Cain . . . I've just sullied myself*), but with my blinkers on, all I cared about was how perfect the rest of the property felt. One enormous dam commanded the centre of the property at the base of where two hills met – on one was the house, on the other were the grapes. Next to it was another large dam, home to a beautiful selection of ghost gums, scores of native ducks and a clump of casuarinas that whispered in the softly blowing wind. Cain also told us there was a third dam between the two olive groves. The olive trees were a beautiful silvery hue, lush and well established and the house looked out at them. There was just so much openness compared to our tiny little plot in Annandale and the air was noticeably clearer, but the most awesome thing was the sky – the vast never ending sky that swamped us completely. We barely caught glimpses of it out of our windows at Annandale. The whole scene gave me an enormous feeling of relief and relaxation. Could it really become ours?

The house itself was nothing special. In fact, that was severely over-selling it. It was adequate at best, with three bedrooms and an open-plan living and dining room with big views out over the property and mountains beyond. Cain had also organised for another couple to view the property at the same time as us; Chinese investors interested in the vineyard side of things. We knew Chinese dollars were buying up large chunks of the Hunter Valley wine region and feared our comparatively measly budget would be easily trumped. Apparently the house was not grand enough for them and they left after only a few minutes, but for me it had a few of the items on my 'nice to have' list: views, verandahs, walk-in pantry, en suite, walk-in robe. It was in desperate need of a clean and refresh; it was tired and grubby, having served as the family's weekend working farmhouse for many years – no one was here to clean when they visited Block Eight. This should have been a reminder of how much backbreaking work was in front of us but I was still too busy stifling giggles to worry about things like the bare-naked facts. I also knew the house was the least of our issues as I happened to know a guy who was an excellent painter and had a keen eye for transforming properties for next to nix. He was cheaper than cheap and brought with him an arsenal of lovely cushions.

Cain explained that the name Block Eight came about when the Hardie family subdivided the original fourteen hundred acres of Sweetwater Ridge. They'd subsequently built their Tuscan-inspired mansion completed with materials imported directly from Italy, as you do when you're the Hardie family. We were told the original purchasers of each of the new plots had been given the opportunity to name their properties (Sunset Hill, The Old Vineyard, The Meadows, etc.) but when it came to get a name in by the deadline, the owners of the eighth block in Sweetwater Ridge did not, and Block Eight stuck.

At the property inspection, Cain left Jeff and me to explore the house alone and in one of the bedrooms we mouthed excitedly to each other so Cain wouldn't overhear. We could not believe how completely perfect Block Eight was for our vision of the future. Job done: we'd become Maggie and Colin.

'It needs a lot of work,' I said seriously to Cain, stating the obvious. 'And the house isn't as big as what we're used to so we'll have to think about that . . .' and then I went on to ask him a series of questions to make it sound like we were having severe doubts, or at least as if we thought the asking price was too high. Having got to know Cain well over subsequent years I have no doubt he could see through my facile negotiation tactics – and besides, it was Shelly who would be handling any sale, not him. But I knew he'd be informing her of everything we said and did so she would be in the best position to negotiate for the vendors.

As we drove away that afternoon, our years-long mood of hopelessness had melted away and in its place was a lightness and buoyancy we hadn't felt since we were in the Barossa on that perfect weekend getaway with Mel and Jesus. I was plain silly with giddiness. I just had to work out how I was going to negotiate for the best price, because even though we had no idea what we were in for, we did at least know that every single dollar would make a difference in helping us achieve our dream.

Over the following days we finalised our plan. We were so in love with Block Eight that we decided we would shut down our Sydney life altogether. This meant we decided to sell the Annandale property after all, Jeff would ask to work remotely and while I would commute for the time being, when the time was right I would ask to do the same. Once our new business was established we would both finally quit. We got all our finances in order with the bank. In those situations it helps to have contacts. On paper Block Eight is a commercial property – it is large, rural and has about twenty-five acres of crops on it. But the contact we had in the bank helped us pitch it internally and the fact that neither crop had produced significant income in recent years (and let's face it, the vineyard was rundown and looked like shit) and there was only one dwelling on the property meant the powers-that-be agreed to give us residential loan approval which meant a better interest rate and a longer term to pay it off so our repayments would be manageable. Of course, the fact that a behemoth like a bank would dismiss the crops as useless because there was no recent evidence of income should have raised a few alarm bells, but by that stage I was tone-deaf. *Ringing? What ringing?* Then it came time to negotiate.

I called Shelly to say we liked the property but we needed to hold back a chunk of cash for renovations. My initial offer was $915,000.

'There's no way they're going to go for that,' ever-the-optimist Jeff said, 'that's almost half what they originally wanted for it.'

'We'll see . . .'

We were in the middle of a meeting with a real estate agent in the Annandale house, getting everything in line for its sale, just in case we got Block Eight, when my phone rang. I was shitting my pants. The vendors rejected the offer but said they would sell for $950,000. It was unusual to get a counteroffer and it felt like we were getting close. I asked Shelly to leave it with me. After an hour or so I called her back and said we would meet them near the middle and I offered $935,000, a figure Shelly didn't sound confident about but said she'd discuss with the vendors. It was, after all, roughly the same amount you would have paid for a smallish two-bedroom apartment in the stylish beachside suburb of Bondi at the time. This all happened without me telling Jeff. In my heart I knew we were going to get it and while he didn't really enjoy receiving surprises, I thought I'd make an exception for this one.

Part way through our chat with our old estate agent, Nick, in Annandale (yes, we got an Eastern Suburbs agent to sell our Inner West home even though we had a great relationship with several local agents who probably had thousands of interested buyers on their books), my phone rang again. I excused myself from the kitchen table and went outside to take the call.

'Congratulations,' Shelly began . . . and the rest of the conversation was lost on me. I just couldn't believe it: we'd got a $1.9 million dollar property for less than half price!

Whether it was because no one else was stupid enough to buy it, or because it was worth far less than what we'd paid, I didn't care. I have to admit to myself that I'm a stickler for stability, a nice predictable ride over smooth ground with no bumps or sudden turns. So when it dawned on me that we'd just bought a farm almost three hours out of Sydney, I had a brief moment of complete terror. What the fuck was I doing? This shit was about to get real! I'd lived in the city for nearly twenty years.

Strangely, once the bile subsided, I felt elated. It was only then that I realised perhaps I had wanted this move my whole life, long before Jeff and the property purchases and my serious corporate roles. I remembered that in my hermit-like twenties before I came out and discovered what real friendships were, I'd written a crappy novel about a hermit-like twenty year old with no real friends who drops out of society and goes to live self-sufficiently on a farm. Maybe there was a bit of Nostradamus in me; though, thankfully (unlike the book), I wouldn't need to wait for the handsome masculine farmhand to wander onto the farm – that role had already been filled by Jeff. (Come to think of it, there was also a scene where a woman takes some of the main character's sperm and becomes pregnant with his child – now that's *spookily* prophetic!)

The meeting with Nick went on for another forty-five minutes. Some might accuse me of never wanting it to end . . . *Another cup of tea, Nick? Glass of wine? One more tour of the house? No? Did I point out the moth-motif lightshade over the dining room table? Oh, have I shown you my cookbook collection?* It was nearly an hour of me bursting at the seams to tell Jeff but also revelling in the fact that I had this secret and I was going to have some fun getting it out.

'So they rejected our offer of $915,000,' I said, after Nick had vacated the premises. 'Shelly sounded unimpressed and made me feel like we were a million miles off the mark. Actually, she sounded like I was a million dollars off what the vendors really wanted to sell for.'

'Damn,' he said, dejected.

I was loving every minute of this!

'What do you think we should do? I'm over it,' I said. 'I just don't think I could be bothered playing this stupid price-guessing game when the property's never gonna be ours.' Though I was the only boy who took drama in Year 11, I'm not much of an actor unless the atmosphere is just right.

'Well we have to offer more,' Jeff almost pleaded, 'Just one more offer and see what they say. And as your dad always says "what's meant for you won't go past you".'

'How about I offer $935,000? Would you want it if it cost that much?'

'Hell, yeah . . .'

'I don't know if we can afford that much though,' I toyed some more. 'I reckon maybe we should just forget about it, as much as that gives me the shits.'

'No, make another offer, it can't hurt! Whatever happened to your "there's no harm in asking" philosophy?'

'What about 950? As our absolute top offer, not a cent more?'

'Yeah okay, let's give that a shot.'

I could have played like that all day.

'Hmm, what about 935? As a middle point, just to test the water?'

'Whatever you think,' Jeff said impatiently. 'You're the negotiation expert.'

'So you'd pay 935?'

'Man, it would be such a bargain if we could get it for that . . .'

'935? You think?'

'Yeah, don't you?'

'Well that's exactly what we've paid for it!'

'What?'

I went on to explain and we jumped for joy, arms around each other's shoulders, bounding around the kitchen like a pair of lunatics.

'I can't believe you kept it a secret from me!' he grinned.

'Sorry, Nick was here. I just had . . . other things on my mind.'

We raced to the computer and looked at the images of Block Eight, pinching ourselves that it would soon be ours, where we were to live! We looked at Google Maps, trying to work out just how big a hundred acres was. Jeff printed up the image and used the same scale to lay it out over a map of Annandale.

'Let's walk it out after dinner.'

It took us nearly an hour to walk its perimeter.

'This can't be right,' I said to Jeff not even a third of the way into our walk. 'You've stuffed up the scale. There's no way we own a property that could fit this many houses on it.'

But it was. The land we owned in Annandale can fit over 2000 times on Block Eight. It is as big as the frigging Vatican and the smoke had gone up, people: there was a new leader in town.

'How many olive trees did you say we had?' Jeff called me one day at work a few days later. By then the contracts had been signed and the lawyers and bankers were doing their mysterious work.

'I think about one or two hundred?'

'Try again.'

'Four hundred?'

'There's about a thousand!'

'No way! How do you know that?'

'I'm looking at Google Maps and I counted every single one.'

Of course he had.

From a four-by-four metre courtyard with about eight pot plants (that I wasn't very good at keeping alive) to over a thousand fifteen-year-old olives trees, and with about 150 rows at about 100 metres each I guessed there were around 15,000 grapevines . . . things were beginning to get interesting.

How Hard Can It Be?

During the settlement period of around two months, Shelly called to ask if we were interested in buying the vendors' farm equipment, currently stored in the shed. They wanted $100,000 for a tractor, gator ('What's a gator?' I asked Jeff, who just shrugged so I googled it to find out it was a four-wheel all-terrain vehicle like a large turbo-charged golf buggy), ride-on mower, grape bins, pallet racking and a stack of other equipment. At that point we still hadn't decided what to do with the crops and as we didn't know the first thing about running a farm on such a large scale we told him he was dreaming! With that beautiful little thing called hindsight that decision could have saved us a bomb and, though we didn't know it at the time, it wouldn't take long to see we were more than a little out of our depth.

As the settlement date of the end of September 2012 drew near I searched the internet for bottles of Brokenwood 2006 Belford Block Eight Semillon, to our knowledge the only single-vineyard wine ever produced from our (*our!*) grapes. Website after website showed that it was sold out, and little wonder, given the rave reviews it'd received. Finally on about page eight of Google, I came across a site that had some for sale so I ordered three dozen, only to be told they had just nine bottles in stock.

According to the plan, Jeff asked his employer to let him work remotely. Over the preceding months he'd created a manual for his role and set up an intranet that meant he could work from anywhere but, despite this, they refused. So after much consideration of our financial situation, he resigned. Our last remaining connection to Sydney would be my three days a week in the office.

By late September, we'd managed to convince enough of our friends to join us to give the Annandale house her final party (Jeff's fortieth combined with a house-cooling – we partied the day it sold at auction), and the following week we left Leroy with Jeff's mum, Millie, who was visiting from Birmingham, to hire a truck and take the first load of our possessions to Block Eight. We stopped along the way to buy a new charcoal barbecue and ingredients to make dinner on the deck that overlooked our new domain. To celebrate, we opened one of the last remaining bottles of Brokenwood 2006 Belford Block Eight Semillon in existence, the first from our own vineyard and only our second bottle of wine in as many years. (The other was the bottle we shared when I took Jeff to Tetsuya's for his birthday dinner.)

Perhaps it was a combination of the excitement at finally moving in, or maybe the sight of those vines in the distance but we couldn't help feeling this Semillon was one of the most delicious wines either of us had ever tasted. It had a smooth, buttery texture and an almost butterscotch-like taste. There was just the slightest hint of acidity at the front of my palate but at the back a touch of sweetness. Believe me when I say I've tasted more than a few wines over the years and nothing compared.

'If our wine can be this good, how could we possibly pull out all of those vines?' I asked Jeff while waving the glass of Semillon toward our vines.

'We can't,' Jeff agreed.

'So we're farmers now?'

'Seriously Toddy, how hard can it be?'

How. Hard. Can. It. Be? Five very simple, single syllable words. But it's the question mark at the end that gives the game away. In that little symbol there is a galaxy of uncertainties.

'You don't need ten years at uni to be a farmer,' I scoffed. I had it all planned out – I'd be the brains, naturally; Jeff the brawn.

Jeff joined in my singing of Pet Shop Boys' 'Let's Make Lots of Money' (though really, with Jeff's voice, he should have left all the singing to me) but then he suddenly stopped.

'You really think you're more intelligent than me, don't you?'

'Yes. Yes I do.'

'Piss off!'

'It's okay to be going out with someone smarter than yourself, you know. There's no shame in loving someone for their brilliance and punching above your weight. You go okay.'

'You're not smarter than me!'

'Than I. And yes, I am.'

'I'd say we're equals.'

'In most areas. But in brains and looks, I've got the upper hand.'

'Now I *know* you're not being serious. Have you looked at this face lately?'

'Which one?'

'Yeah, good one. You're very lucky to have me, you know!'

'Every morning, Jibbuz . . . every single morning I wake up and I look at you and I just cannot believe how lucky I am.' I increased the pitch of my voice an octave and continued with tongue firmly in cheek, 'I pinch myself and I think: *I'm just the luckiest person in the whole wide world.*'

Little did we know we'd just dived headfirst off a very high cliff and we'd forgotten to tie on our bungee cords. Who was smarter or better looking probably shouldn't have been the main topic of conversation.

The next morning we went exploring before driving the van back to Sydney to reload. I've always loved the feeling of exploring a new home – only now we had one hundred acres to absorb.

First we made our way up into the vineyard. As we passed the main dam, we noticed a school of enormous silver perch in the shallows, each as big as a rugby ball. We climbed the small ridge that keeps the dam from hijacking water that flows through a natural creek then walked up the hill toward the perfectly straight rows of vines. Being late September, the vines had only just burst their buds. To a novice like me the new growth looked like delicate little orchids: dainty yellow-green leaves with a stamen-like formation in the middle. Each was bent lightly by the strong breeze blowing down the length of the rows. For as far as the eye could see, these little green 'flowers' danced in the wind and it had the overall effect of a vast field of butterflies, gently flapping their wings before taking off in massive co-ordinated flight. The vision was awe-inspiring.

We walked to the back of the property where natural bushland formed our north-eastern border. It had taken us about ten minutes to walk this far and from the back corner of the property we were treated to a stunning vista of the

Barrington Tops, looking out over our burgeoning grapevines, over the neighbour's open paddocks with grazing heifers to the mountains beyond. Looking west we could also see the Brokenback Range in all its glory.

We continued down the left side of the vineyard. From here, the small sign at the top of the post told us the Chardonnay vines looked the most advanced in growth. Its rows ended at the central aisle then the Semillon took over, up over a slight hill that gave the impression of an emerald ocean wave. It may have been the wind, but I got tears in my eyes.

'I just can't believe it,' I said to Jeff.

'I was about to say the exact same thing,' he said and squeezed my hand. 'This is the most beautiful property I have ever seen.'

We cut across the main field to the west of the house and watched grey kangaroos scatter before we got too close. The olive trees reminded us of our holiday in Italy in 2009, back when Flo the cat took it upon herself to move into our house in Annandale.

'Leroy is going to love it here,' Jeff said with a chuckle. 'He's going to be the king of the castle.'

Between the two olive groves we came to the small dam that Cain had told us about and we sat on its bank listening to the scores of birds around us. A magpie called and then two ducks flew in to land on the khaki water in front of us.

'Jesus, you couldn't get any more *On Golden Pond* if you wanted.' I again tried hard not to cry; I was just so overwhelmed by the beauty of it all.

'Never seen it,' Jeff said with a shrug, so my Katharine Hepburn impression that followed was met with a completely blank face.

'We better get back to Mum and Roy,' Jeff said after we sat in silence for a few minutes more.

'Let's just check out the shed first,' I suggested and it took us another ten minutes to walk across the field, past the house and into the shed we'd never been inside before.

It was more of a warehouse, really. The previous owners had stripped it of everything except one long tool bench and it must have measured twenty metres long and eight metres wide. It contained a large mezzanine and another bathroom and toilet.

'What are we going to fill this with?' Jeff yelled at me across the space.

'Wine,' I answered simply.

We got back to Sydney late Sunday. Jeff went to work one last time on the Monday to hand over to his replacements, while I spent most of the day cramming as many of our possessions into the truck as I could, filling every last nook and cranny, mostly with Jeff's cushions. I couldn't help but count – they numbered ninety-three to be exact. Unfortunately the cookbooks were all in boxes so I couldn't count those.

We were due at Mel and Jesus's for dinner. Mel, although heavily pregnant with their first child, Sophia, wanted to cook for Jeff's mum. Mel's crunchy uncooked semolina orange cake is the stuff of legend but in truth she is a much better cook than her more talked-about dishes will have you believe. Millie likes things plain, none of the fancy million-flavour meals I tend to cook, so she was looking forward to catching up with Mel and 'Elvis' (Jesus was not a name she could quite get used to).

'I think we should drive to the property after dinner,' I said to the others on our way to Mel and Jesus's.

'Mum isn't ready yet,' Jeff said, anticipating his mother's reaction.

'Toddy, you're bleedin' joking, ent ya?' she asked warily.

56

'Come on, Millie, pack your bags, you're off to the Hunter!' I said like a game show host and this sent my 'mother in law' into a blind panic.

After Mel's surprisingly competent roast chicken dinner we returned to Annandale to retrieve Leroy and made the long drive to our new home. I was alone in the moving truck; Jeff, Millie and Leroy followed behind in the Barina. It would take us until around midnight to get to Block Eight but I couldn't wait – it just felt stupid to be cooped up in Annandale any longer than we needed to when we had the fresh open space of Block Eight waiting for us.

We were all exhausted when we arrived, and Millie and Jeff were freezing. While my ride in the truck had been full of music and solo singalongs, unfortunately Leroy wasn't used to such long drives and had shat in his cat carrier inside the Barina. There ain't quite a stink like a hot cat turd. Jeff and his mum had weighed up whether to pull over and clean it all up, but with only thirty minutes to go, they decided that it was best to just get to Block Eight and deal with it then. The smell had been so bad they rode the rest of the way with their windows down, the crisp September night air made even colder by the speed of the car. Millie's teeth were chattering.

First, we cleaned up Leroy, who was a little out of sorts. Next, I reversed the truck up to the back door and we began unloading a few essentials like the fridge, perishables and a bed for Millie to sleep in. We were cold and tired, and I think they were both fully pissed off with me for taking them on this crazy trip in the middle of the night. When Millie tripped over the vacuum cleaner I thought, *She's going to break her bloody leg.*

'Oh bleedin' hell,' Millie said from the floor.

'Mum!' Jeff yelled. And then the two of them burst out laughing. It was the tension-breaker we needed and after making

Millie's bed we sat on the back deck drinking beers and looking out over the property.

'I still can't believe it,' I said. 'I just can't believe this is where we live now.'

'Look at the stars,' Jeff said, gazing up to the sky, as Millie slapped away bug after bug after bug.

Gradually we were getting used to the scale of things, or at least that's what we thought. It is so much easier to under-estimate things when you're in the dark.

One of my little quirks (okay, maybe it's not so little and perhaps I have too many to count) is that whenever I move house I like to stay up all night and unpack as much as I possibly can. There's just something so comforting in making a new place immediately your own. Jeff and Millie went to bed and I stayed up having another few glasses of wine, picking my way through the boxes we'd piled up the day before, deciding which pieces of our former life I was going to force into the new jigsaw it had become. By about three I had managed to unpack most of the kitchen and when I went to bed Jeff's soft snores told me he was truly content.

Up again at six, I continued with my unpacking as quietly as I could, not realising until I heard her cough that Millie had risen at dawn and was on the back deck having her tea and cigarettes while admiring the view. I went out to see if she wanted more tea.

'Toddy,' she said, 'I just love it here, I do.'

'Every time we've moved, you've been with us.'

'Oh, I have too, haven't I?'

'You're our good luck charm, Millie. We love that you've been a part of this.'

Later that morning, we asked Millie to choose a spot to plant the three Japanese maple trees we'd brought with us from Annandale. With wine-red leaves in autumn, the potted statement trees had dwarfed the back deck of that house and we thought they'd make a similar impact on our property, visible from just about every corner of the open fields, and of course they would always remind us of Millie. Jeff dressed her up in a straw hat and gumboots and off she went with a shovel to dig some holes for the trees, down on the main ridge of the dam. I carried the trees down one by one and helped Millie get them into the ground, then we watered them with buckets filled with water from the dam. When we trudged back up to the house, we expected to turn back and see their lovely shocks of purplish red but from the front deck their two-metre high forms simply disappeared in the distance and we could barely make them out. It was another early lesson in the scale of the property and a reminder that a lot of our Annandale life simply wouldn't fit in here.

While I got ready to go back to work, Jeff went on the internet to find the nearest Bunnings and took Millie to grab a few supplies. It was a hardware store, not home décor, so I didn't exactly feel like I was missing out. I continued unpacking while they were gone and with all the doors and windows of the house open still could not believe just how quiet our new home was. I have to admit, after a while that silence began to irk me somewhat and, as my too-many-horror-films mind took over, I had to put on some music to distract it.

Most people say you have to keep a cat indoors for three or so days when you move house but already I could tell Leroy was going stir-crazy being cooped up inside. When Jeff and Millie returned with the car packed full of supplies we discussed the pros and cons of letting him go exploring.

'There's no way he's going to stray,' Jeff said.

'He spent most of last night under my bed,' Millie added. 'He'll be too scared to go too far.'

'I really don't know . . .' I said hesitantly. 'What if he runs off? We'll never find him . . . out there . . .' I pointed to the Great Cat Unknown.

'I think he'll be fine,' Jeff said and Millie said, 'Me too,' and so it was decided.

Jeff put Leroy in the walking harness we'd bought for this very occasion and instantly you could see the look of distaste on his face. When his paws hit the back deck, he just threw himself on the ground and did a kind of '80s breakdance move, writhing in circles.

'Oh he hates that,' I stated the obvious.

'C'mon Roy,' Jeff said. 'Let's get this stupid thing off you.'

He quickly removed the harness and set Leroy back down. Leroy sniffed the air several times, took in a long recon look of the property, then walked down the back steps to continue his sniffing mission. We could tell by his body language that he was curious and happy. He'd never known so much open space in all his life, and the only grass he'd ever touched in the past couple of years was the tiny patch in our Annandale courtyard. And off he went to explore – not very far, and coming back every half an hour or so to nibble some biscuits and make sure Jeff was still inside.

After lunch we took Millie on a walk to the bush next to the main dam, where we discovered the creek that runs through the property. We got to it through a casuarina forest, and again their lovely whispers welcomed us as we walked over millions of their dried needles, the sunlight dappled by their branches.

'We should build a nature walk all over the property,' I suggested helpfully. 'A few kilometres of boardwalk through all these secret little spots – people would really love it and then we could run along it too.'

'We could take guests on guided walks,' Jeff suggested.

Millie stopped dead in her tracks: 'What the bleedin' hell was that?' Her eyes popped with fear.

'A cicada, Millie.'

'A what?'

'A cicada? Kind of like a big cricket,' I explained. 'That noise is them rubbing their back legs together.'

Millie nodded as though she knew what I meant but I could tell perhaps it was time to get her safely back to the house where she could swat away flies and mosquitoes – bugs she knew.

I could have walked for days on end but that would have to wait, and would come in due course. For now, I needed to get ready to go back to work.

It was after midnight and I couldn't sleep. Not because it wasn't quiet or dark enough (we insisted on sleeping with all the curtains drawn because the thought that 'anyone' could roam onto the property and peer in at us without us knowing was just too plain terrifying). Even with the gate on the street securely locked I couldn't sleep, my mind was dreading what was to happen tomorrow, and the next day, and the next, until I returned to Block Eight.

I sat bolt upright in bed. 'Jeff,' I whispered, nudging him awake. 'Jeff?' He groaned and came-to. 'Did you lock the gate?'

Like drawing the curtains, failure to complete the task, we were sure, would result in our horrific deaths.

'Shit, no!' he said.

'Come on, you'll have to come with me,' I said throwing on the day's dirty clothes.

We drove down to the gate. I reversed the car back up the drive so the high beams could shine toward the padlock and onto the road to illuminate any imminent threats. I jumped out quickly, ran to the gates and closed them, then pushed the padlock together, checking it twice for safety.

'Thanks,' I said in a whisper to Jeff. 'I couldn't have slept knowing it was open to just anyone,' and then I reversed back into the olive grove before driving back to the house.

Rather than a daily commute, I would be spending every Tuesday and Wednesday night for the following six weeks (the settlement period) at Annandale. I'd left myself a mattress on the floor, a television, a handful of towels and one plate, one cutlery set, one glass . . .

If waking at five wasn't taxing enough, then the three and a half hour drive followed by a one hour wait at the rental place to return the van certainly didn't help, and then while I sat at my desk typing away on the latest presentation to show international execs, all I could think about was being back at Block Eight; wishing I was with Jeff, Leroy and Millie, exploring, enjoying the peace and quiet and wondering what project would be at the top of the list. By the time I made it back to Annandale later that night, I was a mere shell; I was pretty much at rock bottom. I grabbed a pre-made meal from the local supermarket and a bottle of wine and went back to another shell – the home that was formerly ours. It echoed with loneliness and never in my life did I crave company more than I did that first night. I missed Jeff and Leroy more than I could ever imagine and the thought that this would be my life for the foreseeable future filled me with utter dread.

I called Jeff. 'How was your day?' I asked.

'Good. I gave Mum the job of walking to the letterbox each day so she went down today and I think it took her about fifteen minutes each way. I've made a list of all the things I want to do to the house, starting with paint, but what were you thinking of for wallpaper in the living room again?'

'You know, just anything like Ina's.' One of my discoveries during my days off work was Ina Garten's cooking show, *The Barefoot Contessa*, and I loved her house in the Hamptons almost as much as I loved watching her cook. I made Jeff watch episode after episode, pausing to point out the features I loved most in her house.

'How was your day, Monkey?' he asked.

I wanted to cry, silly me. I wanted to tell him I was exhausted and lonely and . . . scared. The very first night we'd moved into Annandale I'd had a nightmare about a woman dressed in Victorian clothing and I convinced myself that I'd seen a ghost and now that I was there all alone she was going to come and rip my head off for destroying what was once her home. 'Oh good, the usual,' I said instead. 'Will you be scared up there without me after Millie goes home?'

'Hell yes!' he said. 'Closing that gate last night scared the shit out of me.'

And there it was – we were both scared. *It is a means to an end*, I told myself, but in truth I wanted that end to come faster than immediately.

Our Baptism of Fire

Each Thursday, I left work a little before 5pm to catch the train from the city to Tuggerah on the Central Coast, a journey that took around one hour and forty-five minutes. Jeff would collect me at the station and then we would drive the one hour to our house. I was bursting with excitement those nights, so happy to be home, so eager to see what Jeff and Millie had accomplished while I was gone, and itching to set to work on the property the following day.

Jeff and his mum transformed the house. In the first two weeks, it was fully repainted, had new door handles, cupboards were removed to build new bookcases to house my precious cookbooks, art was hung, cushions were staged (naturally), the deck was re-stained and the outside of the house was painted top to bottom. Jeff had drawn up plans for the kitchen renovation

(I wanted two ovens so I had more space to bake and sterilise jars for preserves) and had employed a local company to fit it within about a month. New carpet had been ordered and together we ripped up the old stained cream stuff, preferring to live on raw floorboards while we waited for the new dark plush pile to come.

The living room had been papered just like Ina's house, in a two-tone pale cream stripe, barely noticeable to the naked eye. We travelled into Newcastle and ordered an open fireplace, to be installed early in the new year. We may have created the perfect home in Annandale, but to me this was more *us*; more to be 'lived in' than admired. Hell, we might even attract friends with kids to Block Eight – Mel was due to pop any day.

In Annandale we'd had three square metres of lawn, which I'd laboriously cut with scissors or gardening shears. Knowing how ill-equipped we were at Block Eight, Dad had kindly loaned us his Aldi electric mower and it took Jeff about two hours to mow the green circumference around the house using three extension leads end to end.

Despite the lack of rain, the grass on our property was very long. It looked more like hay – yellow and crunchy, but so dense it made getting around the property on foot difficult. We had no practical farm vehicle like a gator to get around in, so we were constantly trudging through knee-high – sometimes waist-high – grass. There was also the issue of brown and red-bellied black snakes: we'd seen a few of those, suggesting they weren't exactly rare. Walking around with my face in my phone was a city trait I quickly grew out of, as one day I'd come face to face with a long brown snake while texting Mel. After shitting my pants I walked backward away from it and my legs shook for another hour or so.

To minimise the risk of snakes venturing close to the house and environs, I telephoned a local grass-cutting company and asked the owner if he would be able to come out and slash the open fields at Block Eight. He went onto Google Maps and looked over our land as I explained which areas needed mowing. In all, it probably amounted to around twelve hectares and I figured that two or three times a year ought to do it.

'Yep, the boys and I could come out and take care of that for you,' he said.

'How long would it take?' I asked.

'A couple of days,' he said. 'Three at most.'

'And how much? I mean, if we were to get you out a couple of times a year to do it for us, how much would you charge to be our regular grass cutter?'

'Around three thousand . . .'

'Per year?' I asked, thinking it a fairly reasonable price, if a little inflated due to my clear lack of experience plus the inflated cost for me sounding gay.

He chuckled. 'No mate, per mow.'

And this didn't even include mowing between the vines, the olive groves or around the house. Needless to say, I passed.

The most important job on my to-do list was to get the vegie patch up and running. The previous owners had removed five acres of merlot grapes but had left the pine pole infrastructure behind, so Jeff got out his pencil and pad and designed a series of vegetable garden beds that would utilise the abandoned posts. Using Jeff's fancy new chainsaw, we chopped down scores of the posts, piling them in the back of the Barina to take back to the shed. For weeks we worked on those lovely beds, making over twenty in all, proud of ourselves for frugally recycling rather than shelling out any of the savings we'd earmarked to build the accommodation.

Just before Millie left, we placed all twenty beds in prime position near the kitchen window so I could look out over the garden while I cooked. We built a rabbit- and roo-proof fence around the enclosure . . . and only then realised we now owned a vegetable garden that was bigger than our whole property in Annandale. Well, it would be, in time; for now, I had trays full of seedlings that would soon be transplanted into beds full of fresh organic soil.

Saying goodbye to Millie was particularly hard. She had become a part of Block Eight; would forever be linked to those early days of uncertainty and the excitement of exploring it for the first time. At the airport we all cried, though Millie always says she'll miss Leroy the most.

Leroy soon settled into his new life. He developed a penchant for fluffy bunnies and tiny mice. We'd leave the bedroom window open at night (with curtains tightly closed, of course) to allow him to jump in and out at his leisure. One night he brought us a rabbit then proceeded to chase it around the room. Uncle Paul and Aunty Marie were visiting and sleeping in the room next to ours, so I hate to think what they thought all the bumps and noises were.

Jeff eventually managed to get a hold of the tiny rabbit with the intention of setting him free through the window, which we would then close to keep Leroy inside. Leroy seemed to have forgotten about his initial catch and when he saw the fluff ball in Jeff's hands, got all excited and wanted to play. In the ensuing confusion, Jeff forgot the curtains were closed and went to toss the rabbit out the window but misjudged things and smashed the rabbit's skull against the window frame. He eventually got the rabbit outside but it was dazed and confused and once Leroy saw it looking a little stunned, he pounced on it again. A few weeks previously, Leroy had seen a goanna devour a baby rabbit whole, its body slowly disappearing down its throat, the poor rabbit squealing in tremendous pain. It was all rather dramatic and Leroy had been fascinated by the whole spectacle, wide-eyed (and possibly mouth agape with drool) so once he got a hold of the one Jeff had failed to set free, sadly, he knew exactly what to do.

When I came home the following Thursday night, Jeff took me into the shed to show me his surprise. He'd built the most beautiful little chookhouse and had painted it bright red. The soon-to-come chooks had drop-down doors to keep them safe from foxes at night and a little ramp up to their laying boxes which would in time keep us eternally stocked with eggs.

With a beach ball in her belly, Mel and Jesus visited us for the first time and it was just like being back in the Barossa again, only now we could share it whenever we chose.

Jesus insisted on getting to work and helped Jeff build the chook run, which was the first large-scale fence we built, mastered over a weekend with Jesus sweating half his body weight. We knew nothing of plumb lines so it turned out a little dog-legged but the chooks would have that lovely little red house thanks to Jeff, so I learned to take the mastery with the experimentation and never complained about the latter.

A few weeks later Jeff and I went outside to watch a storm roll in over the property, admiring the silhouette of the enormous ironbark tree about fifty metres from our front door. A rural sky is so vast that nature takes on a whole other dimension and its sheer force is much more impressive. It really brings home that we are just tiny playthings at its mercy. The thunder was so loud it rattled the walls of the house and menacing streaks of lightning flashed the black sky alight. Every fork was discernible. We lounged on deckchairs on the deck sharing a bottle of wine, having turned off the television to enjoy nature's show instead. The thunder became even louder, and the lightning seemed to have descended in altitude and was looking for a place to land.

'Do you think we're safe here?' I asked Jeff.

'Of course we're safe, what could possibly happen?'

On the word 'happen', thunder and lightning joined formidable forces and a fork pierced through the sky, striking the centuries-old ironbark near the house and arched onto the telegraph pole that takes power down to our pump house. Sparks flew through the air and the *Bang!* of impact sent me jumping up off my seat, landing practically in Jeff's lap – though skilfully without spilling a single drop of wine.

'We're not fucking safe at all!' I screamed, running back inside the house.

'Bring the bottle inside would ya, darl?' I poked my head around the frame of the front door a moment later. 'And I think I may have left a nugget or two on the chair.'

The storm brought no rain, so the next day I went to turn the irrigation on to water my vegetable seedlings, but nothing happened. The lightning strike had shorted the power, and the surge had completely destroyed the pump we relied on to get water to our crops and to all four corners of the property. It took weeks to have the pump's electric pad replaced and cost us two thousand dollars to boot, as I hadn't thought to insure it when we moved in. The saddest impact of the storm took a few more years to emerge – the lovely lone ironbark that filled so much of the view from the house had been sizzled and over time it lost all its leaves and then, one by one, its limbs began to fall.

By late October, four weeks into our tree change, the vineyard was a vibrant sheet of green in the middle of what was otherwise a brown, cracked, parched landscape, thanks to the fact that we'd had practically no rain since moving in. I called Shelly the real estate agent to see if she knew anyone who could help us make a decision about the grapes. Shelly had visited us with a bottle of wine to see how we were settling in, and was always on hand to answer my stupid city-boy questions, never showing the slightest judgement when I asked: *What's the code on the shed lock again? I've forgotten. Do you know who might want to buy our grapes?* and *Do you know if we're allowed to tar our driveway without council approval?* My calls never ever went through to voicemail and even as I write this, six years later, I know I can pick up the phone any day to call Shelly or Cain, and they'll be on the end of the line dispensing advice, sharing a laugh and – without fail – asking how Jeff and I are going. It was important to have them in our lives – especially as advisers were few and far between.

Surprisingly, we hadn't met any of the neighbours. We'd assumed that in the country our arrival would be met with bottles of wine, just-baked apple pies and handmade macramé potholders, but in over six weeks we hadn't heard or seen anything of the people on our road. The neighbouring property was used as a weekender, but it seemed only rarely visited; across the road was more or less the same story, so for a kilometre it felt as if we had our own private road – passing another car on it was a rarity.

Shelly gave me the number of a local winemaker and grape-growing consultant named Jenny, who agreed to meet us up at the vines to discuss options for the vineyard's future. Fortunately for us, she was not only familiar with it (having consulted with the previous owners on an ongoing basis) but had also been part of the team to plant the vines in the first place.

We could tell from the instant we met her that Jenny was no-nonsense and didn't suffer (farming) fools gladly. Her hair was a shock of pink, she wore riding boots and faded jeans and a long-sleeved woollen jumper despite the heat. She was probably in her early fifties but had a spark in her eye that suggested perhaps her sense of humour and joie de vivre were much younger, though when she spoke her voice had the unmistakable authority of an ex-teacher.

By early summer that sea of green had produced fruit and there were more grapes than we could possibly wrap our heads around. We thought there might even be an opportunity for us to sell the fruit and make a little extra cash. (*A quick buck for no work? Ha ha, who was I kidding?*)

'You can't harvest these grapes,' Jenny said with a slight laugh when I relayed my brilliant idea.

'Why not?'

'Well, the vines weren't pruned which means there are too many grapes and not enough energy in the plant to produce great-tasting fruit. Also, by the looks of things you probably haven't been watering them?'

'No . . .' Jeff muttered, like a kid in detention.

'It's stuffed, your irrigation. Look, there's a break in the line,' Jenny pointed to a tear in the thin black pipe, 'and there's another. So you'll want to get that fixed as a priority. Not watering impacts the quality of the fruit too. And you probably haven't fertilised them or sprayed them?'

'No . . .' Jeff said again, this time barely above a whisper.

'So you could try to sell them on but believe me, when anyone looks at them they're not going to be keen.'

After we had chatted about the history of the vines, Jenny asked: 'Do you boys have horticulture experience?'

'Not much,' Jeff said.

'None,' I corrected him. 'My dad worked in the nursery industry, though, so I've always loved plants,' I added helpfully and was embarrassed when Jenny chuckled in response.

'And I take it that means you have no experience with viticulture?'

'No, but we love drinking wine!' This had become one of our fallback lines since taking over the property. Our city friends thought it was witty and charming; country people thought it was naïve and plain stupid.

'Okay, so the way I see it then, you have three options.' Jenny wasn't exactly in hysterics. 'You can bulldoze the lot and return the land back to grazing, then decide if you want to raise cattle on it in the future. You could get in a team of people to manage the vineyard for you, but that can be expensive. Or you could manage it yourself but by the sound of it I'm not sure you'll have the patience, time or equipment to make that work. If you choose option two or three, you can then try to sell the fruit to someone or you could go down the path of making your own wine with one of the contract winemakers in the Valley.'

'We tasted the 2006 Brokenwood and thought it was stunning,' I said, hinting option one was not really a possibility – and instantly regretted my choice of adjective: 'Stunning' wasn't a word real farmers used if the knowing little grin on Jenny's face was anything to go by.

'They're good vines,' Jenny agreed, 'and with the right maintenance they can make good wine again.'

'Would you be willing to consult with us on an ongoing basis? If we decide to make a go of it, I mean?' Jeff asked.

'Yes, of course I can help!' she assured us.

'So what do we do with the fruit this year?' I asked.

'You could pull it all off. In fact, you *should* pull it all off, it'll be healthier for the vines in the long run.'

'What, and just throw it on the ground?'

'Yep.'

Jenny left, saying to give her a call around March, after the season was over. Then she'd talk us through what we needed to do to get some decent fruit off the vines the following year, stressing that we should concentrate on the Semillon.

'We can't really let all that fruit go to waste this year, can we?' I asked Jeff.

'Well, what did you have in mind?'

Clearly he'd temporarily forgotten that I planned on being Maggie Beer! Over the next few days I tried my hand at making verjuice, a Maggie staple: the juice of unripe grapes that can be used in place of wine and vinegar in cooking. Sadly, my attempt was cloudy and tasteless and soon oxidised, turning an unappetising brown.

'Verjuice *schmerjuice*,' I said with a shrug, 'next year those suckers will be giving us some wine.'

What's That in the Dam?

When you work for a fancy US internet company like I did, one of the perks is a four-week sabbatical to celebrate every five years of service. Because I was part-time, and had decided to take mine over the Christmas and New Year break, my second sabbatical (recognising ten years) stretched out over nine glorious weeks. It gave me a taste of what working full-time on Block Eight would be like, although I hadn't been prepared for just how challenging it might get.

About day three of my sabbatical, in early November 2012, I was walking by the main dam when I noticed something strange not far from the edge. I couldn't make out what it was from a distance. It was not moving. It turned out to be something dead. A very large, very dead kangaroo. I rushed home to report.

'You know that black thing in the dam?' I said. Jeff nodded. 'It's actually a dead kangaroo.'

'Gross,' he said and kept on painting our front door a shiny black gloss.

'Do you think we need to get it out?' I asked.

I mean, it was dead.

'Why?'

'Because we use that water for our crops and vegies – maybe a dead kangaroo might infect the water or introduce some hideous disease or something? What if we ever wanted to swim in there?'

'Swim in it? No way! Why don't you google it?'

Googling answers to questions that highlighted our ineptitude was a daily occurrence in those early days. *How do dams get filled? What is PID? Are red-bellied black snakes deadly? How many grapes does it take to make a bottle of wine? How many bottles of wine per acre? What is the most popular tractor in Australia? Do you need a DA for a cellar door in Singleton Council?* And the list went on and on.

I tried many different configurations using some or all of the words 'dead', 'kangaroo', 'dam', 'taint', 'remove' and 'water', but for once Google didn't have an answer. Even if it wasn't a danger to anyone, my brother-in-law James and his family from Canada were due for Christmas in a couple of weeks and they'd shown me such a great time when I'd been in their country a few years before, I wanted to do everything to make their first Australian trip perfect. *To the left you'll see the lovely living kangaroos grazing in our olive groves but please don't look to your right where you'll see a stinking decaying corpse that I couldn't be arsed to get out of the dam. Oh yes, feel free to swim in the dam whenever you like and eat those lovely vegetables that get watered from it . . .*

'Google doesn't say anything about it,' I told Jeff. 'Maybe I should remove it just to be on the safe side? Any suggestions?'

Jeff's bright idea was to send me down there with a three-metre length of structural pine. Structural pine was Jeff's answer to most things. He figured I'd be able to sort of hook it over the rump of the roo then guide it, floating nicely, back to the edge, where I could then simply pull it out onto dry land. It all seemed so easy and he couldn't see what all my fuss was about.

The dam is about one hundred and fifty metres from the house and it was deceptive just how big that body was, as well as how far into the dam it was. With each step I knew the plank slung across my shoulders was going to be useless but I kept telling myself to believe it would work. *Jeff says it'll work so it'll work.*

Sure enough, even as I stood on the edge of the dam and cast out my wooden fishing line, it fell pathetically short. It wasn't even a third of the way toward the corpse. I walked back to the house but refused to admit defeat.

The next solution was mine. I made Jeff stop painting and asked him to go and buy us a rubber blow-up boat. A few hours later and wearing gumboots, we carried our brand-new boat down to the dam. Getting into the boat was the easiest part, which even this gumby surprisingly managed to do without falling into the muddy water. We rowed out to the dead roo and, as we got close, the stench overwhelmed us. I mean, never in my life had I smelled something so vile. It went right up into your nostrils and down into your gut like you'd taken a big chunky bite of it. I heaved against it, turning my head so Jeff wouldn't see.

I told Jeff to hold on to its tail so I could row us back to shore. I just couldn't believe he agreed to the plan and watched in horror as he leaned out of the boat and took a hold of the animal's tail. *It probably would have been a good idea to bring gloves as well as rope*, I thought. I rowed as hard as I could but all we did was go around in circles.

'Row harder!' he called.

'I am!' I snapped back.

'Its fur is coming off in my hands! It's melting off the bone! Why aren't you rowing?' he yelled at me.

The sight of that rotten tail in Jeff's hands really made me gag: *He's touching it! He's really got his hands around it!* Ants crawled up his arms. I could see more skin than fur.

'Keep holding it,' I said as cheerfully as I could. 'It won't be long now!'

I could feel the roo was stuck on reeds and I just didn't have the strength to pull it free by rowing all by myself.

'Change of plan,' I said. 'It's stuck on reeds and I need you to help me row. You'll need to tie the boat's rope around its neck.'

'What? You can't be serious!'

'Just do it, Jeff; you just have to do it. It's no big deal.' *No big deal that you have to get your arms around its neck and your face close to its head. No big deal it's slowly coming apart in the water.*

Jeff was kneeling on the bottom of the boat and had to reach far out over its edge, his face down close to that melting skin. I heaved again. *His face just touched it! I'm sure his face just touched it!*

'You're nearly there!' I said encouragingly. 'So close!'

He nearly gave up but thank Christ he didn't, though he was constantly brushing away the ants on his arms. After four or five goes at it, he finally got the rope around the kangaroo's neck. I couldn't look at Jeff because I was so worried that a piece of the roo had come loose and would be stuck to his face. My stomach hurled at the thought and I retched again.

Jeff came to sit next to me in the boat but I still couldn't look at him or his hands and with double the strength in rowing we gradually freed the body from the reeds and slowly guided it to shore.

I got out of the boat just as the real rancidity hit the air. If I'd thought it stank before, nothing could prepare me for the smack to the face of it once it was out of the water. I heaved a few more times. It was without doubt the worst smell I have ever smelled.

'Where are you going?' he yelled at me.

'I . . . I can't. Jeff, I'm sorry! Ugh,' I heaved audibly. 'Don't hate me but I just can't do it. Ugh!' I heaved again. 'You'll have to p-pull it out on your own.' I reefed off my shirt and held it over my nose and mouth and crouched down to put my head between my legs.

Jeff muttered some swearwords and a few other choice things under his breath but from my safe distance I watched him use all his strength to haul the carcass onto dry land.

Jeff went a bit funny then. A look came over his face, his voice changed. 'I'm going to be disturbed by this for months,' he said. 'I feel like we've murdered someone and now I'm moving the body.'

I knew this would mean many weeks of a panicked Jeff waking up in the middle of the night, sitting bolt upright convinced he was covered in spiders (and one night it was lucky me 'covered in spiders' and the ever-helpful Jeff in his half-sleep/half-nightmare state thought it best to beat them off my chest . . . such a pleasant way to wake in the dead of night), or ants or perhaps the kangaroo had come to accuse him of foul play but despite this, and those moments of his pure terror that were yet to come, I just couldn't bring myself to touch that dead thing, or get my face so close to its flesh.

We'd already seen what foxes, crows, goannas and ants could do to strip a skeleton bare – a dead kangaroo we'd seen on a walk with visiting friends had all but disappeared within a few weeks – so we decided to leave it by the edge of the dam, hoping it would be gone before our international guests arrived.

We were ready to call it a day, both feeling overwhelmed and dirty, but then out of the corner of my eye I saw something else in the dam, a black thing about fifty metres from where we had retrieved the kangaroo.

'What do you think that is?' I asked, pointing.

'Don't know . . .' Jeff said dismissively.

'Don't you think we should . . .?' I ventured.

'Oh you've got to be kidding me!' He threw his hands in the air and marched back to the boat.

The other dead thing in the dam turned out to be a fully-grown adult swan. So now we both had our T-shirts around our noses and out we rowed again, this time without any rope (it was still tied around the kangaroo and Jeff refused to take it off again), which meant Jeff would have to grab hold of the dead bird's neck with his bare hands.

Quite happily, I was doing all the rowing; Jeff was doing all the dead-animal handling.

'I can feel its vertebrae in my hands!' he squirmed while leaning over the edge of the boat.

I kept saying silly little encouragements like, 'It's fine, no big deal, it has to be done,' all to keep his mind on the job but at the same time I couldn't help but think, *Oh my god, I cannot believe he's touching that!*

Later that night at dinner I struggled to watch him pick up a chicken leg and eat it with his fingers, the same fingers that only a few hours before had flesh dripping through them.

'I'm just not very hungry tonight,' I said and pushed my plate aside in favour of another glass of wine.

*

Another day on Block Eight, another newbie error: 'Gee, the water's running slow today,' I said, standing over the kitchen sink.

It was a few days before Christmas and we had a house full of Canadians – lots of showers, dishwasher loads, water running from most taps at one time or another and it was the worst time in the world for the water to slow down when we needed it most.

We'd been living on the property for three months and hadn't once thought about where the house water came from; it just isn't something city folk ever have to think about: water just comes from water mains!

Jeff went looking for those water mains to see if somehow they had been turned off but after walking the perimeter of the house a few times he couldn't find anything.

'What about that pump in the shed?' I prompted. 'What do you think that's for?'

I went and inspected the pump but could see nothing wrong with it (with all my experience with those kinds of things). Then we walked the ten minutes down to the road to see if we could find a water main down there, but again there was nothing even remotely familiar-looking.

As we were walking back toward the house, now with a curious James in tow, he said, 'Erm . . . do you think those might have something to do with it?' He pointed at the two enormous concrete tanks next to the shed.

Jeff and I looked at each other, aghast, and ran into the shed.

To be sure, the previous owners had given us a twenty-minute run-down on how things worked on the property during a handover session back in August but it had been overwhelming, rushed, and we'd taken no notes. I'd pretended I knew exactly what the husband was talking about because I didn't want to appear stupid or out of my depth (though of course I was feeling totally stupid and out of my depth). I did recall him saying something about the pump in the shed, but I'd assumed rainwater captured in the tanks was a backup.

Inside the shed, we traced the water pipe back from the pump to its source . . . the concrete tanks on the outside.

'Do you think that's our only source of water?' Jeff asked in astonishment. I just shrugged.

My next step was to check the water level in the tanks. I climbed up the ladder and removed the heavy concrete cover of the tank. Way down the bottom I could see a trace of water; a few inches at best. Even as I knew it would not be the case, I silently insisted to myself that the next tank would be full; that there was nothing for us to worry about. But after climbing up and removing its cover I saw that it too was empty.

As silly as it might sound, there wasn't a single internet search term we could think of that gave a set of results for businesses that would bring us water in bulk. It took us over an hour to finally stumble across 'water cartage'.

When you live in a rural area of Australia reliant on water cartage, there's no such thing as an H2O emergency. Everyone is in the same (drydocked) boat and normal people – *knowledgeable* people – plan their water requirements well in advance. Few are stupid enough to ever let their tanks run dry. My pathetically pleading phone calls were dismissed: *Too busy; don't do the dirt road; existing customers only; not until next week.* We would have to put our guests up in a hotel and dance for rain.

I made one last call and finally someone took pity on me, or more likely saw some dollar signs, and we were promised a small load of water within a couple of hours – for two hundred and fifty dollars. But all I cared about was that disaster had been averted. The boys who delivered the water sniggered behind my back and really took the piss out of me – and then I looked down and saw that I was wearing a pair of Crocs with white pull-up socks. Nothing says *I'm a serious straight farmer* like a maiden-in-distress phone call and a pair of Crocs 'n' socks.

The next day I called around again and found a guy called Phil, who was willing to become our regular water carter for a hundred and forty dollars per load, and a few days later he came and filled those tanks to the top. Lesson learned – or so it should have been. Jeff decided it was best to leave a piece of structural pine at the tanks so we could dip it in any time and get a precise level reading.

At dusk on the very next day, with apparently full tanks, I was again confused: 'Gee, the water's running slow again today.'

'Maybe we've used it all. Have you checked the tanks?'

'Jeff, come on, there's no way in hell we've used 45,000 litres in under two days! I mean, I know I like my showers but it just doesn't take that long to rinse and repeat a centimetre of hair.'

'Still, you'd better go check the levels. Use the structural pine.'

As soon as I approached the tanks I saw the torrent of water running down the hill. The ground had turned to mud; leaves and mulch had been completely washed away. Jeff's structural pine level reader had fallen over in strong winds and had cracked open the pipes, effectively emptying all 45,000 litres onto the ground. I raced back to the house and sounded the alarm but by then it was too late.

'You and your fella must shower a lot,' Phil the water guy said when I called to ask him for yet more water. As I hadn't mentioned Jeff to him at all I figured the Hunter grapevine worked just as well as any other, perhaps better. I explained our mistake with the plank of wood and pointed at the fresh pipe from Bunnings that Jeff had used to replace where the crack had been.

'You sure you ladies know what you're doing out here?' he asked.

'Nothing much aside from discos and cake-baking.' I laughed off his dig and went about my business.

Two days later I went to water my vegetable seedlings and had that familiar sinking feeling when I again saw the ground flooded with water. I'd left the tap turned on but the hose nozzle off and overnight the pressure had built and it had burst the hose off the wall. A few thousand litres of water had been lost but at least there was no need to call Phil out for another emergency – thank god.

It was the same when it came to the water in our dams. Where did it come from? We simply didn't know. Jenny had said that we should fix the irrigation, only we thought it was a specialist skill and didn't even think we could do it ourselves. After paying two handsome studs a fortune to fix our vineyard irrigation, which drew on the large dam, we asked them if they knew where the dam water came from but they just looked at us as if we were crazy. After all, we were the guys who'd just paid them two thousand dollars to walk up and down the rows of vines and plug holes in the irrigation with materials you could readily buy at Bunnings (as we learnt later).

Jenny eventually solved the mystery of where our water came from. It turned out we were part of a scheme called PID (Private Irrigation District) that pumps water from the Hunter River all over the valley. It hadn't been in our contract for sale when we purchased the property but we are legally bound to spend five thousand dollars a year in order to get our allocation of 7.5 million litres of water, and if we want more water, we pay more. We have to pay the five thousand regardless of whether we use all of our allocation and this was another nice little surprise to take a further chunk out of our must-only-use-for-villas savings.

9

Girls (and Boys) Just Want to Have Fun

While some of the big picture plans for the property (like water and wine) were gradually coming together, I still had dreams of living off the land as much as possible. We had so much unused space, so much water in our dams, it felt that anything was possible. Plant a seed and harvest more food than any two people could ever eat in a season. Throw in a line, and the critters would practically beg to be caught and cooked.

One of the greatest and most infamous challenges at Block Eight in the early days was whether we had any yabbies in the dam between the olive groves and, if so, who was going to be the first to catch one. The previous owners told us the small dam was teeming with the lobster-like things and as they are one of Maggie Beer's favourite Christmas ingredients, well then, I just needed to catch them and cook them up for myself. I had visions of a long table under the shade of the olive grove on Christmas Day, forty or fifty people passing around share plates – all made from ingredients grown or raised right here on Block Eight. But instead, Jeff and I drove to my parents' house on the Central Coast and had a less bucolic (but still delicious) meal with our Canadian visitors.

Try as I might, those fancy little crustaceans outsmarted me every time I tried to catch them. Not even Jeff and his sister Carole (who was visiting with her partner Tom from the UK) in that dead-roo rubber boat could catch anything by trawling behind it with a large net. I googled ways to catch them, went out and bought an array of fancy (and bloody expensive) traps and nets, but every time I threw in some bait, it was gobbled up and I was left as far from becoming Maggie Beer as I had been when tending to my pot plants in Annandale. I posted on social media about it at the time and before long, thousands of people joined in the challenge to catch a yabby. And when I say thousands, I mean three. Three people. It all came to a head during January 2013, when we hosted relays of friends and family during the traditional Aussie summer holiday.

'I used to catch them in the dams outside Tumut all the time as a kid,' my dad told me. 'Those were the days . . .' and then he went on reminiscing about sliding down hills covered in pine needles or over slippery rocks in the river.

'But the yabbies, Dad,' I brought him back to the here and now. 'How did you catch the yabbies?'

'We just dropped in a piece of string with a bit of sausage tied to the end and whoosh,' he made an impressive sound, 'there was always a yabby on the end of it.'

I dragged him down to the dam, preparing myself to be impressed by the simpler technology of yesteryear. Of course! I had been over-thinking, over-engineering it when clearly a piece of string was all that was required all along.

Dad perched himself on the esky I'd packed with drinks and snacks ready for a long fruitful session, and threw in his line. And we waited. And waited. And waited some more.

'I don't think they like the bacon. Are you sure you don't have any beef sausages? Or chicken sausages?'

'They're yabbies, Dad, not rabbis.'

He just gave me a look. After a few minutes, I asked: 'Any nibbles?'

'Nothin',' he said, defeated. 'But my back's killing me.'

After about nine minutes the former Tumut Yabby Champion had sadly retired for good.

'Must've been the bacon,' he said, as we walked back to the house, our heads hung low in defeat.

'Maybe they've evolved into some sort of super-yabby,' I suggested, whereupon I received another of Dad's looks.

The next batter up was Vicky, one of our kids' mothers. They were all down visiting Block Eight for the school holidays. To say Vicky is competitive would be a bit of an understatement. She loves getting the kids involved, too, so we all went down to the small olive dam one afternoon and she spent some time arranging the meat in the trap just so. Vicky had even bought a pair of nylon stockings with her, as she'd seen on YouTube that this was one piece of equipment that was non-negotiable. After fifteen minutes Vicky pulled the trap back in and the kids and I very excitedly crowded around. Nothing.

'I reckon you need to leave the trap in longer. A few hours at least.'

'Oh, that's what you reckon, is it?' Vicky resisted anyone else's input.

Later that day as the sun went down, Vicky and I took a beer and went to check the nets. We were miffed that Charlie and Lucy had lost all interest in what had become the greatest challenge of the twenty-first century. And don't you know, she'd bloody well gone and caught some. Not just any yabby; like Henry Fonda and his fish in *On Golden Pond*, among her catch she'd clearly caught Walter, the daddy of all yabbies.

'I'd like you to measure and weigh him, thank you!' she said.

Vicky was pronounced World Yabby Champion. For the rest of their holidays we took Charlie and Lucy on adventure walks around the property and gave them little patches of land so they felt they too had ownership in our tree change. We discovered a hidden casuarina grove leading down to a deep creek bed on the far north-west of the property and all agreed we would never tell anyone where to find it. They loved collecting fresh chicken eggs each morning from the five chooks we'd recently purchased from a local hatchery, having named the birds for us via a mail ballot system we'd sent them for fun.

I took the kids up into the vineyard and we picked bucket after bucket of Semillon and Shiraz grapes. They helped me crush them all with bare feet then I boiled the fruit up with sugar – I was going to make my very own cheese pastes. The kitchen was a sugary war zone, my skin was stained, Charlie and Lucy were bored witless once the novelty of squashing grapes had worn off and the boiled, seed-filled fruity sludge that resulted never set. I threw away all the Semillon 'paste' and proudly bottled my first Shiraz 'sauce' but really it was just pink liquid sugar.

'So maybe we'd better make wine with all that fruit next year instead?' Jeff joked.

After our Brisbane family returned home, I'd assumed the yabby challenge had come to a close. But for some who couldn't be bothered fishing, the story continued. Like my lovely friend Ming, who visited one day and brought with him some fresh Balmain bugs.

'I asked at every shop in the fish markets and this is the closest they had,' he said.

Then a few days after Vicky's crowning, our friends Kieran and Bec came to set up a tent and stay on the property with their young sons, Connor and Lucas. Kieran and Vicky share a lot of common traits (read: there was no way on earth he was going to be outdone).

Using his mother-in-law's kefte as bait, Kieran had also brought his own yabby traps. By nightfall his haul was in and it contained a few impressive-looking samples – could Vicky's reign be very short? The following evening we had a yabby feast with lashings of garlicky butter and I isolated the largest yabby and sent a photo to Vicky.

Against a ruler please. And please advise weight. Vicky texted back.

Vicky's whopper was declared the winner.

'They shrink when they're cooked,' Kieran complained and so the jury was still out, unless you were Vicky.

Over the following years, it was parents like Vicky and Jane, Bec and Kieran, and Mel and Jesus (not to mention Jeff and me) who went all-out to show our children everything Block Eight could be, providing exciting adventures born from the kids' imaginations with the aid of an enthusiastic adult. White-water rafting, fishing, fire building, melting marshmallows, the world's longest slip and slide, building a phenomenal shelter in the bush, learning how to drive, making dolmades out of our grape leaves, foraging for the makings of Christmas tree ornaments, making horror films, school-holiday Olympics . . . the list went on. That so many kids will continue to have incredibly fond memories fills both Jeff and me with joy.

*

But the kids weren't the only ones who enjoyed Block Eight to the full. Many of our friends visited for a relaxing break.

One of our mates, Keith, visited from Sydney and asked if he could take photos down by the dam. Sure, no problem was the reply.

'I've always wanted a photo of me from behind, naked in front of a dam wearing only these boots,' he said. But of course he did. An hour or so later he came back and excitedly showed Jeff the photos his boyfriend had taken. 'Oh skip over that one,' he flicked his iPhone screen, 'you can see my balls in that one.'

'Could you actually see his dangle berries?' I asked Jeff later.

'Trust me, Toddy, that was not exactly on my bucket list.'

Another time, a mate of Jeff's was visiting from the UK while I was in Sydney working.

'Can I take a swim in your dam?' he asked Jeff. Sure, no problem was the reply.

Jeff had forgotten that he was a naturist and he stripped off right in front of a blushing, bashful host.

'Trust me, Toddy,' Jeff said later, 'seeing my mate's bald yabby is not exactly on my bucket list.'

Other friends were visiting from out of state.

'Can we take a walk in the olive grove?' they asked Jeff. Sure, no problem was the reply.

An hour later they returned all flushed. 'Oh my god, you two did it in the olive grove, didn't you?' Jeff joked.

They just laughed awkwardly.

'Trust me, Toddy,' Jeff said later, 'picturing my mates humping on that patch of grass I mow every few weeks isn't exactly on my bucket list.'

Which begged the question, really – wasn't there even one naked friend on Jeff's list?

We loved filling the place with friends. In those early months, our property's seclusion remained a bit confronting for a pair of city slickers like us. It felt is if we were completely isolated, so each night we religiously went down the driveway to ensure that front gate was firmly locked, then we'd close all the new blinds in the house so no axe-wielding maniac could look at us from a distance.

We shared a passion for 1980s horror films with my oldest friend Nicole (we had a mutual pet name for each other – 'Pet'). In our vernacular they were called 'gew' nights because in the movies, any woman getting stabbed to death produces in the throes of terror a shocking sound of panic that goes a little something like *Gew! Gew!*

Quite alone on the pitch-black property, we thought it the perfect atmosphere for introducing Pet to one of the scariest modern films we'd seen, *The Strangers*. All the lights were turned off, the blinds were raised to invite axe murderers, and we were soon all scared shitless.

'Pause!' I said. 'I just need to use the loo.'

I walked down the dark hallway and closed the toilet door, then silently opened the back door in the laundry. I crept to the back deck of the house then once at the living room window I hammered my fists on the glass, yelling in a deep voice to seal the deal.

And that, my friends, was one of the most memorable gew nights ever!

Getting My Maggie On

Another thing I wanted to do – getting my Maggie well and truly on – was create a signature dish to serve friends when they visited. I wanted it to be representative of the Hunter, and of Block Eight specifically. I settled on a one-pot chicken dish using locally sourced organic birds. It was butterflied and served on a bed of vegetables – creamy potatoes, leeks, mushrooms, whole green olives and lemon slices topped with a whole bunch of thyme and two half bulbs of garlic. It was then smothered with a whole bottle of Semillon, lemon juice and some chicken stock and in less than two hours guests' mouths were well and truly watering. In time we would grow or make most of the ingredients . . . except the bird.

I loved nothing better than strolling out into my vegie patch and picking fresh produce. The radishes were the first things to ripen and we ate them fresh out of the ground with a little salt, and used them in every salad we made. Enormous bushes of herbs were regularly pillaged and I made jar after jar of mint jelly, mint sauce, chilli paste, harissa, my own version of Tabasco – herbs went bananas.

Week by week the vegetables developed and it filled me with so much satisfaction to watch those tiny seeds sprout, then grow into strong seedlings before I transplanted them into our garden beds. The first purple flowers of the eggplants were a revelation, I picked and pickled green tomatoes into a relish and baby beetroots were plucked from the earth to be eaten 'carpaccio', roasted with other vegetables or pickled and turned into relishes and sliced salad ingredients. Every mouthful was so brimming with vitality and flavour that eating store-bought vegetables by contrast was completely disappointing. To think we'd been missing out on this freshness and intensity of taste all our lives!

We were fortunate that the previous owners had planted fig, lime and orange trees right near the house and with the vegetable patch proving bounteous, my dream of becoming the Hunter's version of Maggie was in full swing. It was a whole new way of cooking, learning to deal with large quantities of one ingredient and finding ways to use as much as possible.

For instance, the lime tree. That bastard of a tree just produces and produces and produces. It seems there isn't a day that tree doesn't have a fresh lime appearing – they're there in summer, in winter and if you don't pick them fast enough they fall to the ground and rot. What would Maggie do with five trillion limes? I created a treacly, toffee-like lime marmalade that friends regularly begged for. My lime cordial was a triumph, my Indian lime pickles were a personal favourite of our friend Mary-Jayne, and my lime granita made the perfect palate cleanser for a special meal. I made lime tarts, a delicious lime curd, experimented with lime-infused vodka, bought a dehydrator to make dried lime slices (but didn't leave them in for long enough so they soon went mouldy), put sliced lime into water bottles, froze the juice, tried my hand at salt-preserved limes, gave away boxes and boxes of the things . . . and still I couldn't stay on top of them. Cor blimey, I had citrus coming out of every pore and frankly won't mind if I never see one of the buggers ever again.

Of course, not everything was a success – the pickled watermelon rind was vile, the parsnip and orange marmalade vomit-inducing and the pumpkin butter so rich it instantly clogged the arteries. I still desperately wanted to create our own Shiraz or Chardonnay paste to serve with local cheeses and while we certainly had no shortage of grapes, no matter how hard I tried, I could not get it to the right thick-paste consistency. Some of my preservation attempts also failed – lids popped, food fizzed, bubbles appeared where they should never have been. (Attention all family and friends: if you have any unopened jars of Block Eight preserves from the early days it's definitely best to dispose of them at your earliest convenience.)

I did eventually master the arts of jam-setting and pickling, however. After spending hours sweating away in physical labour outside: shovelling chook poo, planting fruit trees in the new orchard, mowing the lawns and digging up the dying gardens around the house – to name but a few of my outdoor activities – I'd come inside, scrub up, then spend more hours chopping fruit and vegetables into tiny pieces and toiling over a hot stove, risking third-degree burns from spattering saucepans.

It reminded me of being on school holidays with my nan: she'd have us on the linoleum floor of her kitchen shoulder-deep in white buckets full of fruit and sugar; the crystals coarse against our skin, the sugary smell a kind of heaven. As the whole house filled with the scent of boiling toffee later that night,

I'd go to bed on a Willy Wonka dream cloud. Never in a million years would I have imagined that I'd end up making my own jams on a farm in the Hunter Valley! Thanks to my cousin John I even inherited two of Nan's handwritten recipes and regularly make them from produce grown in my own garden.

One day when I was about ten, Mum called from the office to explain she would be late for the first time ever, and would I mind making the spaghetti bolognaise for dinner? I asked her how to do it and she talked me through the steps over the phone. While it may not have been perfect, that night her appreciation fuelled me on to help her out some more. No one had ever helped Mum make dinner before so I decided to do it for her every night. I followed the recipes in the four or five cookbooks she kept in the pantry, I followed instructions on packets and I experimented. Give or take a few nights, I've made the evening meal ever since. They say you need ten thousand hours to attain a high level of skill. Well, let's just say that cooking now comes fairly easily to me, but it's never a perfect pursuit.

The kitchen at Block Eight became a battleground: Todd versus toffee. Usually the toffee won but I did rack up a few victories. Among our friends, my burnt fig jam (not as good as Maggie's but still delicious) was a big hit, particularly when I added vanilla seeds. Vicky and her mother, Nita, proclaimed my orange marmalade as one of the best ever.

I pitched a television show called *The Preservation Kitchen* to a producer friend but it went nowhere; I created my own little cookbook of my winning recipes, which I added to by hand (just like Nan did); and I even branched out into retail with a stand inside one of the local shops.

Poor Jeff was chief taste-tester but time and again he was cornered.

'I preferred the last batch,' he'd offer warily.

'Yeah well, that means me chopping every single lime into thirty six tiny pieces so that won't be happening again, will it?' I'd snap. 'What about the taste?'

'It's good,' he'd say, backing quietly out of the kitchen.

I presume he saw a lot of it as a poor use of time when there was so much outdoor stuff to do but letting our bountiful harvest go to waste wasn't something I was ever going to let happen. Cooking was my release from some of the more menial and strenuous work on the property, just as cooking had always been my relief from the stresses of corporate life – I had always loved nothing more than coming home after a busy day to spend an hour or two whipping up a treat for Jeffrey.

'I don't see the point in eating out any more,' he said to me one day. 'Every meal I get at home is better than just about any I've eaten in any restaurant.'

It felt nice to be appreciated.

'Except that disgusting angel hair pasta you made that time,' he continued.

It also would've felt nice to pour a glass of wine over his head, but I would never have wasted it.

11

Crop It Sweet

I barely blinked an eye when Jeff suddenly declared his new favourite film was *The Money Pit*, that '80s classic starring Tom Hanks and Shelley Long about a couple who get duped into buying a nicely presented but actually decrepit mansion with the idea of renovating it back to its former glory.

As the title not so subtly suggests, things don't exactly go according to plan . . . I heard the original subtitle was 'How two gays bought a hundred acres and thought they could manage it with an electric mower and a pair of garden shears.'

Before we moved to Block Eight, we'd been determined to bulldoze all those grapevines – but that was before we tasted that bottle of Brokenwood Semillon. Living on the property, the beauty of the vineyard also changed our minds and we knew it made sense to give guests a real taste of the

Hunter – after all, they'd come to immerse themselves in all things wine – what could be more perfect than to stay amid the grapevines?

Primed with Jenny the grape-growing expert's advice about the vines, we decided to find a winemaker. As luck would have it, my old mate Andy was very good friends with a Hunter Valley local named Natalie, and Natalie's husband just happened to be a contract winemaker named Daniel Binet. After my first faltering, awkward *I'm not sure if you're open to the idea* call to Dan, we briefly met up at the end of January, despite Dan being in the middle of harvest. With enthusiasm and patience he agreed to become our winemaker. In time, we would have our very own Block Eight-branded wine.

'I fucking love that you boys are willing to give this a go,' Dan said over a beer after he'd walked with us through the vineyard inspecting and tasting grapes. 'We can do some really cool stuff with your wine because you two don't strike me as stuck up Sydney wankers who only want to win awards and show off to their mates.'

'Do you reckon the wine will be any good?' I asked. 'Given that the vines haven't been looked after this year, I mean?'

'Mate, you give me good fruit, and I'll give you good wine. It's not fucking rocket science, you know? But if you give me shit fruit . . . there's nothing I can do about that. It'll just be good for vinegar.'

Even this piqued my excitement because I would've quite liked our very own wine vinegar.

'We're in,' Jeff and I said in unison.

'Good. Well, you just listen to JB [Jenny] and do what she says and I reckon you'll be tasting your first wine in about June of next year. Mate, if anyone knows anything about grapes, it's JB. You're in good hands there. She's fucking taught the whole

Valley how to grow grapes. Your fruit's not shit, not even this year, so next year it'll be a ripper.'

'Would you want to buy some of it this year?'

'Mate, I said "not shit". I didn't say it was good.' And we caught on to his infectious laugh.

Dan stayed for more beers and rang Natalie to come and get him. We talked a lot about the state of the wine industry and I shamelessly bombarded him with question after question, fascinated by how much he knew and impressed by how willing he was to share that knowledge with a pair of wannabes like us.

Natalie arrived and embraced Jeff and me with warm, genuine hugs and we shared the bottle of wine she'd brought from their own cellar door. It was an incredibly light, delicately sweet sparkling Moscato and from my very first mouthful I knew we were in good hands.

'Dan, this is seriously good,' I said, trying not to blow too much smoke up his arse.

'Next time, we do the gin,' he said, and he left, promising us there would be many more nights like this in the future. And there were. Dan and Natalie were the first friends we made in the Hunter, and once Jeff proved to be a willing, obedient and more than capable student, Jenny soon took us under her wing and our relationship quickly morphed from business into one of genuine mutual affection.

So our plans for the grapes were set. Once the fruit had all fallen off, been eaten by the birds, or just plain left to shrivel up, we would consult again with Jenny and from March onwards, Jeff would focus on bringing them back to health. By 2014 we would have fruit as perfect as possible to put into Dan's more than capable hands. It felt as if we'd taken a step closer to becoming real farmers. But there were also a thousand olive trees to consider.

So a week later Peter, who owned the local olive-processing plant, and his offsider came to talk to us about our olives. We all trooped into the groves to inspect the trees. They looked incredibly healthy to me – trunks as thick as watermelons, silvery leaves that looked strong and vibrant – and amazingly the irrigation looked to be completely intact.

There is a serenity inside an olive grove. Their mass casts wide shadows yet still allows you to see the big full sky overhead. Strolling among them is humbling, as if they are proud of their strength and vigour and unashamed of their unconventional beauty. They have insignificant flowers and their colours are not vibrant or particularly remarkable, yet the sun creates so many hues you find yourself marvelling every few steps.

Peter told us the top grove consisted of Frantoio olives for oil and the bottom was Manzanilla for pickling – who knew there were different types of olives? And who knew all olives went from green to purple to black as they ripened?

Then Peter got down to practicalities: it was a similar story to the grapes: the olives needed pruning, de-suckering, watering, fertilising and spraying for bugs.

'Do all of that,' we were told, 'and in the future you might get a crop, but without putting in the work you'll get nothing.' And then the pair went on to give us some extra, unsolicited advice, like: 'You're being very optimistic about those deckchairs, you two,' and: 'That vegetable garden fence you've built won't keep kangaroos out. They're going to destroy the lot.' (But in time it turned out they were wrong on both counts.)

Vines plus groves plus unkempt fields meant yet another expense to add to the growing list: we needed a tractor.

After the sale of the Annandale house we had every intention of keeping aside a chunk of the profits to build the accommodation that would give us an income from Block Eight. But when we started pricing up tractors we quickly realised that money was not going to stretch very far. We didn't want the problems that might lurk in second-hand machinery and new tractors could cost anything up to $200,000 for the most complex models – and besides, we had already spent $2000 repairing the irrigation in the vineyard, another $2000 repairing the irrigation pump and $30,000 renovating the house. Based on Jeff's research, we knew we needed a minimum of $100,000 to build the three villas. On a property of our size, the scale of every single expense and repair was tenfold what we thought it was going to be and all of that added up to one simple thing: we had run out of cash. We had become Shelley and Tom.

Building for Our Future

We still needed a tractor, so late January saw us shopping for that most macho of farm machinery. Of all the makes available, I'm ashamed to admit that I chose the most expensive, John Deere, because it was the only tractor brand I had ever heard of. But I didn't know it in the 'I know my tractors' sense; I knew it thanks to my years managing the Collectables classification at eBay. John Deere caps and replicas were quite the collectors' items – so surely, I reasoned, their machines were worth the money! We explained to the salesman exactly what we needed a tractor for and attachment after attachment was added to our order. Salesmen must dream of days that boys like Jeff and me walk onto the lot.

'Why do you insist on talking like that to them?' Jeff asked when we were safely back inside the car.

'Like what?'

'All blokey and Australian!'

'Do I?'

'Oh come on, you know you do!'

'Oh Jeff, so much to learn. In these parts, there are three kinds of pricing. You've got your retail – that's for just any loser who walks in off the street. Then you've got your lo-tail. That's a special price for locals. Then finally you've got your gay-tail. That's the premium price poofters like us have to pay.'

'You can speak as ocker as you like, they still know we're gay, you know? They're not going to give you a discount because you're a gay guy trying to sound straight.'

'Tryin'? Stone the flamin' crows, mate, if this don't sound straight to ya, you're as queer as a flamin' three-dollar bill!'

'You're so ridiculous.'

The day the tractor was dropped off to Block Eight in February, the delivery guy took us through the various buttons, levers and features . . . in about six minutes.

'She's all yours,' he said referring to all that shiny green and yellow newness. 'Now hop up and show me you can drive it and then I can get out of here.'

'No way,' I said pathetically. 'I can't even drive a manual car let alone a tractor! I mean, I once drove my cousin Barb home from squash when she was drunk but she was changing the gears for me and then one day my friend Mel wanted to teach me but after the first bunny hop I got right back out of that car and vowed never ever to drive a manual, ever again . . .' My voice trailed off.

But before I knew it, Jeff was up on the seat. Jeff, who'd only received his first ever driving licence five months before, was driving a tractor and he didn't stall or bunny hop it once! The crashes into trees and vine posts came shortly after, as did the smashing off of the indicator lights, but no serious damage was done.

Once the delivery guy left I felt brave enough to follow Jeff's example so I too jumped up into the seat. Jeff showed me what to do – put one foot down on the brake, one on the wet clutch, turn on the ignition, move the gear stick into A1 (the slowest gear for a shy wee thing like me), move the direction lever into forward, lower the park brake, ease my foot off the brake and clutch, then slowly. . . ever so slowly, push my right foot down on the tiny accelerator pedal. And I was off! Jeff stood next to me and encouraged me to go faster, showed me how to change gears to increase my speed. *See? I can do it!* I felt like driving down the street after the delivery guy, *Hey, I'm not such a loser after all!*

We invited Mum and Dad up from the coast and let them have a little test drive of the big green machine too. Forget the law degree, the two kids, the eight books and the high-flying corporate career, I swear my dad has never been as proud of me as the day he watched me driving that big butch farm equipment in my sparkling steel-toed boots and brand-new John Deere cap (yes, you get a free cap when you spend $70,000 on one of their machines!). Mum managed to ram it into a vineyard post but we decided to keep that a secret from Dad.

'Please don't hate me,' I said to Jeff one day shortly after my debut on the tractor. 'But I've run over three grapevines.'

'Please don't hate me,' I said a few days later, 'but I've run into one of the flame trees and it's nearly chopped in half.'

While I slowly grew more adept at handling the tractor, 'Please don't hate me' became a kind of currency for me, a precursor to the inevitable lecture that would come from Jeff, about how to treat equipment with respect. Of course I pretended to listen but always thought I knew better myself and in time my ignorance would shine through.

We put that tractor through its paces for most of autumn. With the shiny new slasher attachment we took turns driving it over all the open fields at Block Eight, mowing all that dry, waist-high grass. In all, it took us over eighteen hours to do the fields and suddenly the usability of our land was revealed to us. Whole acres we'd previously thought pointless became open fields of possibility, especially the hill that led down toward the natural dam where all the ducks liked to play.

With the ground now visible, Block Eight took on more of a park-like beauty. It was easier (and safer) to stroll to all four corners of the property and only then could we truly start to plan for the next stage of our business: where were we going to build our villas?

For me, the most obvious choice was just in front of the olive grove, that flat parcel of land that captured a stunning view to the mountains far into the distance. After a hard day's work, Jeff and I would often head up there, sit on the grass drinking beers and just revel in the beauty and silence, instantly transporting me back to my Golden Door epiphany – the moment, without doubt, that led us to Block Eight.

Jeff spent weeks researching what type of building would be best for accommodation. We considered pods, prefabricated builds, trucking whole Queenslanders in on the back of semi-trailers; we even thought about theming each of our buildings with a different type of garden (the Japanese room, the English country garden, the Arizonian desert). I wanted sandstone huts but was once again dreaming way beyond our means. But the idea of keeping in harmony with our environment struck a chord with each of us and when Jeff came up with the idea of constructing classic Australian sheds it felt perfect for our hot, dry, rural location. On the outside they would sit flawlessly in our landscape and on the inside Jeff would go to town designing something luxurious to take our guests' breath away.

Design settled, it was then time to submit plans to council. We employed a consultant to guide us through the process, having nearly gone postal several times during the council stage of our renovation in Annandale but, like all bureaucracies, our local council had its rules too. We were informed that we couldn't build within fifty metres of any crop – which ruled out our chosen space right in front of the olives and also anywhere near the grapes. We also had to consider bushfire-risk zones, protected fauna and flora, and the natural flood zone of that creek that ran right through the middle of our property on the rare occasions it rained heavily enough. Then there was the considerable cost of getting electricity, water, sewage treatment and roads to wherever we built so after all that was weighed up we only really had one choice – overlooking our natural dam. But now that we had mowed the field that led to it, we both could see just how perfect this position was, and imagined our guests having coffee on their back decks each morning, watching the birds on the dam, those lovely ghost gums and how, on sunny days, the water sometimes danced as if its surface was sprinkled with gold dust. Our plans were drawn, our DA submitted and council pointed out that we would require an accessible villa, which had to be built first so we decided to add a fourth one by converting part of our machinery shed (my mum's suggestion). Then we were slugged with a $14,000 development cost to council and a $25,000 bill to create internal roads ... which meant we then had just enough money to install the shed shells *and that was all.* Thank god I still had my job in Sydney because it was our only source of income.

My friends were beyond generous for letting me stay in their spare rooms, but I insisted on travelling light, so lived out of a small backpack and never left anything behind. Bodily functions became something to fear and hide, and getting ill (like the time at Andy and Ali's after I'd eaten bad sushi for lunch) really had a way of bringing me closer than my friends had ever truly wanted. Oh it wasn't all bad. I had delicious meals and wonderful chats in Cheryl's Petersham home, wines and laughs with Andy and Ali, plus quality time reading books with their son, Sam (I was Aunty Todd), and way too many wines (followed by a fifteen kilometre hungover jog the next day) whenever I stayed at Pet's. Plus the benefit of Sophia cuddles at Mel and Jesus's.

But work was financing our tree change so it was a necessary evil. Without that income Block Eight would have failed and we would have returned to Sydney with our tails between our legs, forced to start our careers over again and deal with those knowing, told-you-so looks from the naysayers.

Some people thought we were mad for even giving it a go; others suggested that we'd be back in Sydney within twelve months; that we'd completely underestimated the effort required to make a success of the place. I was warned about accounting, saving, spending, exhaustion, the perils of small business, a dying tourism industry, the impossibility of making good wine, the dangers of equipment, losing touch with my network, becoming seen as unemployable ... but a handful of people did believe in us, and they know that once we put our mind to something there is no way in hell Jeff and I give up without a fight.

In those early days most people asked me how Jeff was coping with 'my' decision to move to the country, assuming I'd somehow railroaded him into it. But if they knew Jeff at all, they'd know he never does anything against his will. He applied himself to learning whatever was required to get the property to optimum production, and while I continued with my necessary corporate treading of water, Jeff threw himself into every aspect of our future.

With the plans for the villas going through the approval stage, it was time for us to get the grapevines ready for spring. Since we'd moved onto Block Eight, we'd watched them grow long green canes that overflowed into the rows, we'd eaten the plump juicy fruit to see what it tasted like and then we'd watched the birds feast on it before whatever was left shrivelled up in the last heat of summer. Then during April and May, the leaves gradually turned brown, fell to the ground (Where did they all go, we wondered? Was there a gargantuan pile of shed grape leaves in some wind-swept corner of the Valley?) and what was left behind was a tangled mess of long stubborn limbs.

In June 2013 it was time for us to prune more than 12,000 grapevines (by then I'd done a more thorough count). Jenny came to show us how it was done. Basically, every vine has six main parts and each plays a crucial role in developing fruit for wine. The roots are obvious enough, then there is the trunk. The trunk rises to a crown or head and on either side of the crown are arms, or cordons. From the cordons there are a collection of spurs, spaced about a hand's width apart. A spur is created when you cut back the cane (or limb) of each season's growth. When you look at the spurs closely you can see tiny buds – two usually at the spur's base, then after an internode of about an inch or so, another two. In essence, you need to ensure you cut the spur just after the buds at the top of the first internode. Each bud will more or less develop into a bunch of grapes. This way you ensure the vine puts all its energy into a controlled number of bunches so you get a concentration of flavour and quality. So simple, right?

Jenny ran us threw a few vines then told us to have a crack. *Snip, snip, snip, snip* I went like Edward Scissorhands.

'Jesus Christ, you're a fast learner,' Jenny said, sounding mightily impressed.

She watched us do a few more vines before declaring that we had got the hang of it, and were the best students she'd ever taught.

'If in doubt, cut it out,' she reminded us before we all trudged back down the hill with her lovely border collie dog Archie and went and had a cup of tea and some of the cookies I'd baked for her.

I put the call out to the entire staff distribution list at work: did a weekend working in a vineyard sound appealing? Jeff and I would provide all meals and alcohol and all people needed to do in return was snip a few vines and pitch their tents (we even went out and bought thirty tents in preparation).

Thankfully my colleagues proved a ready and willing labour source, as did our friends. There was a real sense of camaraderie on the property that weekend. People were genuinely keen to help us in our new venture and share in its success. We purchased gloves and pruning shears for everyone, but those vines were old and hadn't been pruned in a while, and their woody canes were thick and difficult to cut. Everyone complained of sore hands and fingers . . . but with the aid of those thirty or so beautiful people we managed to prune well over half the vineyard on those couple of days.

With the additional tireless help of our great friends Mervyn and Ron, Jeff took care of the other five thousand or so vines while I was at work. (Merv is the father of my first boss in the book industry, Meredith, and they live not too far away in Lemon Tree Passage, north of Newcastle.) Those two men have given us so much of their time over the years that they own a piece of Block Eight, along with a piece of our very grateful hearts.

We seemed to have the pruning mastered but we still made mistakes, or got led into making them.

When spring came and those hundreds of thousands of buds once again looked like a blanket of butterflies, it was time for Jeff to spray their delicate growth to protect them from bugs and disease. Despite telling the tractor salesman earlier in the year exactly what we needed the machine for (including the spraying of chemicals), he neglected to advise us that it would be best to purchase a tractor with an enclosed cab. Jeff was handling some fairly dangerous chemicals and while a cab would have safeguarded him against harm, once you bought a tractor without a cab, you couldn't add one on later. So for the time being, he dressed from head to toe in Hazmat gear, a vision in white, regularly coming off the tractor smelling strongly of sulphur.

One of the world's greatest arachnophobes before we moved, Jeff would get up at four in the morning and drive the tractor through the dark (answering his question of why a tractor needed headlights), ducking beneath countless spider webs while snatching spiders from his face. After finishing his five-hour spray I'd welcome him inside for breakfast, when the white suit and goggles always made me think of the Oompa Loompas.

Throughout the hot summer of 2013, water continued to be a problem for us. In October, Phil the water guy came to deliver us another few loads of his precious commodity – plus an extra load of commentary thrown in for free.

'It's no secret,' he was saying to me this time. 'Where do you think this water I bring ya comes from?'

I could have just answered, 'From the water mains on the outskirts of town that you're authorised to tap into,' but I knew what answer he was expecting and played along in the role of gormless townie. Anything for an easy life, that's me.

'Erm, from the sky?'

'Exactly! And if it doesn't rain, we don't get any. It's that simple.'

While Phil went on, I reflected that a handful of the local suppliers seemed to delight in either pointing out our ignorance or trying to take advantage of it. Luckily, Jeff's acute sense of right and wrong meant he always challenged this.

When one of the very expensive sprayers we bought for the tractor broke during the last of one of Jeff's sprays at the end of April as he tried to keep the vines free of disease, the retailer sent a mechanic to repair it. He looked about twelve.

'I've never seen one like this before,' he began – and that really isn't what you want to hear from someone who's been sent to mend your $12,000 sprayer.

He worked away on it for an hour, tinkering and swearing, muttering under his breath and then, rather proud of himself, declared that it was fixed. Jeff turned on the sprayer and opened the valves, and it still wasn't working properly.

'That's not fixed,' Jeff said patiently. 'They should be spraying like this . . .' and he showed the guy what he meant. After another two hours, the guy finally succeeded, mostly because Jeff talked him through how it needed to be done.

When the bill came in for the service, we'd been charged a call-out fee, the first hour's consultation and then an escalating rate for the second and (even higher) third hours.

Jeff instantly called the retailer to complain, pointing out that it was his own fault for sending a mechanic unfamiliar with the equipment he was supposed to fix. The guy argued; Jeff stood his ground; finally the retailer snapped.

'I tell you what, mate! I'll charge you for just one hour but you're never to come back into my shop ever again and if you ever want your machinery fixed don't bother calling us.' And he slammed down the phone.

So every time Jeff says he's off to the local industrial area of Rutherford I worry which shop-owner he's going to offend next – I suspect his face features on a poster above cash registers around town with the words: NEVER SERVE THIS MAN. HE IS AN ARSEHOLE.

That is, of course, unless he's going to one of the furniture stores, where they know him by name, greet him warmly, refer to him as one of their best customers and frequently give him generous discounts. Perhaps the cushion sellers of the Inner West spread the news that Jeff is one to keep onside. In those stores there's probably also a photo of Jeff behind the counter, only it reads: JEFF. VIP. SHOW CUSHIONS.

Unlike Jeff, whatever the situation I always play Mr Nice Guy, even when the locals insist on testing me.

'Where's your fella?' Phil asked now.

'That's him up in the vines, spraying.' I pointed.

'What's he spraying?'

I shrugged. Jeff had undertaken his chemical-handling course and although I knew it was either sulphur, copper, weed killer or bug killer, on any given day I was never interested enough to know which was in use. He wasn't all that interested in my jams, after all. Phil looked about the shed and saw a chemical container on the ground.

'See that there, mate? See what it says?'

'Poison?' I asked cautiously.

'Exactly! One drop of that shit on his skin, mate, and your fella is a goner. Dead. One drop and that'll kill him, mate!'

'He knows what he's doing,' I offered, but Phil was unconvinced.

'I dunno with you boys . . .'

At least we'd graduated from 'ladies'.

111

Not even Phil could dampen our excitement at the development of the grapes. When they are dormant throughout winter there is nothing much to see, but then from bud burst in spring, the tiny grey-green leaves appear before a small shoot develops – the stage that had got me all goose-bumpy with orchids and butterflies the previous year. The growth comes on so quickly, by the middle of spring there is a sea of green leaves, and soon after tiny flowers appear. They look like a dwarf grape bunch, sparsely spread, then the white wispy flowers turn into tiny hard green balls and these are the beginning of the grapes – green for many weeks before the plant decides to invest all of its energy into producing fruit and (in a process called veraison) the grapes turn from green to red (Shiraz), yellowish (Chardonnay) or a lime-green (Semillon). That we would be harvesting our first fruit in the new year was a milestone in our journey we could barely wait for.

13

The First Sip

By late October 2013, council had approved our villa plans. We paid a company $45,000 to erect the three sheds and it was time to find a builder to fit out their interiors, plus work on the accessible villa inside our machinery shed. Despite my valiant attempts to appear macho in company with 'real men', I'm really not great at communicating with actual blokes and I was amazed when Jeff took it upon himself to go and chat to the builders he'd seen working on one of our neighbours' properties. After a brief chat, they agreed to move onto our job next.

Pete reminded me of a young Paul Hogan. He was short and buff, and had Hogan's humour to boot. His crew consisted of his young son, Cassh, and an older carpenter called Colin. Where possible, I avoided them, leaving all that blokey builder talk to Jeff. I'm ashamed to admit that I didn't want them to know we were gay, because I always worry that people will take advantage of Jeff and charge him more than they would any straight guy. But Jeff quickly showed them that he knew what he was talking about, and often worked with them in the shed, toiling away with one of his new tools, asking questions and learning as much as he could.

I couldn't pretend I didn't exist so when Jeff asked me to make 'the boys' a Friday lunch of hamburgers, I knew it was probably the easiest way for me to win them over. Ina Garten had taught me to put a small knob of butter inside the burger patty and as a result they were lush and juicy. I made an array of toppings, and took over a massive tray of wedges as a side.

'Christ mate, that's a good burger,' Pete said.

'Oh this old thing? I throw these together every Friday,' I joked.

And quick as a whip Pete said, 'I'll be here!'

Over the following weeks I continued to take the boys treats, happy to play the role of 'farmer's wife' when fuck me it was obvious I would have been utterly useless doing any of the building work, unless they asked me for an extra bit of muscle to lift a heavy beam or move a pile of wood, which sometimes they did.

In December 2013, the end of our first calendar year at Block Eight, I turned forty. At my thirtieth I surprised everyone with a rendition of Stephen Sondheim's 'I'm Still Here' with lyrics I created myself, suggesting that if my family and friends thought I was about to behave like a mature thirty year old, they were sadly mistaken. I made everyone wear black to mourn the death of my youth, but then changed half-way through the night into a sparkly gold-sequined jacket to sing my song.

I wanted to do something equally memorable for my fortieth. You know, being so shy and withdrawn is often crippling but

I was willing to make an exception for one more night of 'It's all about me!'

Jeff and I set to work on our secret project a few months ahead of the actual date in December. Mostly it involved a lot of wine, but when the mood took us, we went off and filmed a little video to play on the night of my party.

'So what costumes do you want to wear?' Jeff emailed me at work one day.

I sent him a list of eight scenes from movies I would be re-enacting. His passion for cushions may be palpable but another of Jeff's little-known qualities is an ability to scour op-shops for the perfect copycat outfit. It's never a precise copy, but he has this uncanny knack of choosing clothes that make a person or scene instantly recognisable. (And let's face it, one of the worst disappointments ever is rocking up to a fancy dress party and finding yourself having to explain who you are meant to be.) 'COSTUME SHOPS ARE A COP-OUT' will probably be Jeff's epitaph. Oh, that and 'WASHING LIQUID IS THE ONLY CLEANER ANYONE EVER NEEDS.'

Sure enough, I came home from work the following day to Jeff's phenomenally accurate costumes complete with wigs. For months we filmed scene after scene and we both wound up literally on the floor clutching our bellies more times than I can count.

For my fortieth I invited forty people to sample a nine-course degustation menu and some of the best wines the Hunter has to offer. We started off at sunset down by the dam, drinking Dan's Moscato and looking up at the beautiful healthy green of the vineyard, knowing that within a few months we would be drinking our own wine! Afterwards, we moved up to the shed, which was mid-conversion. Jeff had cloaked the walls in hessian, and Glen and James, who were out from Canada, beautifully dressed the two long tables that Jeff had made by hand. The meal was phenomenal (I'd done all the preparation and hired a chef to finish off the cooking and help me serve, and a waiter to pour the drinks). Everyone had a printed menu and their place names were written on pieces of grape wood. Cheryl and Dad gave lovely impromptu speeches and when I stood up and proclaimed how very lucky I felt, I very nearly burst into appreciative tears. But the video was still to come.

'There is one person who was not able to make it here tonight . . .' I began, 'someone most of you will recognise has been an integral part of my life, who has kept me company for more hours than many of you in this room, and without this person I would have had a very different life . . .'

The video began to play. In Jeff's choice of clothes and wigs, my resemblance to each character was uncanny. I did them all: *Evil Angels, Out of Africa, Sophie's Choice, The French Lieutenant's Woman, Mamma Mia, The Devil Wears Prada, Julie & Julia, The Iron Lady* . . . the most recognisable of Meryl Streep's films and, if I may say so, my audience found it absolutely hysterical. Aside from the wardrobe, the other significant role in the film was played by Block Eight. That a property could look like the desert around Uluru one day, a Greek island the next, and a fog-heavy pier at Lyme Regis in the dead of winter was truly remarkable.

In early January 2014, Dan visited us again to inspect the crops. In one of those extreme strokes of ridiculous good fortune, it turned out that the 2014 Hunter wine season was one of the best on record because we'd had lots of lovely sunshine, very little rain and the birds and caterpillars had more or less left us alone. *Growing grapes really is a cinch,* we thought naïvely.

Dan tasted the Chardonnay grapes first.

'Man, these are good,' he said, before spitting out the pips. He squeezed grape juice onto his refractometer, an instrument that measures the sugar levels in the juice. Sugar not only helps determine taste, but the sugar percentage will be the alcohol percentage once yeast is added to convert the former to the latter. You don't want to make a weak wine, but you don't want to make rocket fuel either.

'There's not a lot of fruit on them though,' he continued, 'and that makes sense because of what you told me about them being left untouched by the previous owners. I reckon you'd get a few tonnes though so why don't you get some mates around and pull these off yourself, and we'll make a nice little vintage out of it. I reckon they'll be ready in about two or three weeks, but bring me another sample next week.'

We walked over to the Semillon next and again he tasted some grapes and read their sugar level. 'I've always known how good this fruit is,' he said with a smile on his face. 'Fuck me, that's gonna make a delicious wine. We'll do two sorts – a dry style and a slightly sweeter style. Chicks love the sweet stuff but you want a serious one too so you can cellar it and then sell it for a fortune later.'

Up over the back of the hill, we made our way finally to the Shiraz.

'Jenny says this will be shit fruit and has never made a good wine,' I tell Dan.

He tasted and tested. 'Nope, she's wrong. It's coming along nicely too.'

We drove back to the house in Dan's ute, gave him a cup of tea and introduced him to our kids.

'Getting the grapes to harvest day is just the start,' Dan said and then proceeded to rattle off everything we needed to organise within the next two weeks: *call Janell for hand pickers and to hire extra equipment for the harvest or call Jan if you want machine harvest. Call this person to order some barrels – we want maybe American oak for the Chardonnay, medium toast, but while you're at it, grab some French too. And you could try Flex Cube for the Shiraz so let's get that organised. You'll need to call Bluey to come collect the grapes on harvest day, here's his number. Do you have bins? We'll need maybe four for the Chardonnay, say eight for the Semillon and about six for the Shiraz. You don't have bins? Okay, call your neighbours and borrow theirs. What do you mean you don't talk to your neighbours? Okay, does your tractor have forks? Because you will need to fork the bins onto the truck . . . What? No forks? Okay . . . well you could buy a hand-driven forklift for a few grand or . . . And you should set up a meeting with Russell and Suzanna at Hunter Bottling because you need to slot in well in advance and then you'll have to pre-order your bottles, boxes, caps . . .*

Our heads were spinning.

'Holy shitballs!' Vicky said. She and Jane had brought the kids down for the school holidays and she'd accompanied us around the vineyard.

I felt like vomiting. Jeff and I had agreed that his job would be to get the grapes to harvest. I would take over from there and get the grapes picked then turned into wine and bottled, then (hopefully) sold. I so desperately wanted to quit and convince Jeff that we were kidding ourselves if we thought we could do this. Maybe it would be best to ask Dan if he knew someone who wanted to buy the fruit and they could come and pick it themselves, I thought in a panic. But I let all the information swim around my head and after a few hours sat down and composed an email to Dan. Once I'd got the names of all the people we needed, I sat on the phone and managed to get our harvest and bottling plan into action. Every single

individual involved in the process was beyond generous accom-
modating my lack of knowledge and not one of them made
me feel stupid, called me 'girlie' or posed a trick question. In
particular, Suzanna at the bottling company was so patient
and kind, talking us through every single option for packaging.
She was incredibly patient with us when we didn't know any
of the terminology and would use phrases like 'that thing that
goes under the other thing'. She and her partner Russell (who
co-owns the company) even came to Block Eight to inspect our
tractor and advise on how much weight they thought it could
take so that when it came time for delivery we wouldn't struggle
to remove the pallets from their truck. To this day, whenever
we see Suzanna and Russell we are greeted with genuine warm
hugs and they always have time for a good old chat. With each
change in process (a new bottle size, a change in materials) they
and their staff hold my hand and show understanding and not
a hint of annoyance.

Australia Day, 26 January, was the date chosen by Dan to
harvest our Chardonnay. Like the prune-off, we again put the
call out to our friends but since it was a public holiday, we
received only a modest response. Meredith and her husband,
Lachlan, came, of course, as did Mel and Jesus (and their local
friends Bec and Jim). With Meredith's mum Lis, brother Tom,
and Ron and Merv we had a neat little crew to harvest our first
ever crop. Cheryl was on hand to do all the cooking to feed
us regularly. It was a beautiful, momentous day. It was hot and
calm in the vines, no breeze to speak of. We'd bought everyone
buckets and pincers to remove the fruit and Tom served as
bucket boy, running back and forth to pour the fruit into the
bin we'd placed on the back of Merv's ute.

Our arms were sticky and dirty, our skin burnt despite the
sunscreen we'd applied, our backs ached and after twelve hours

of continual hand-picking, we'd only collected 800 kilos from the five-acre plot (an optimum yield from a vineyard of that size might be anywhere up to about twelve tonnes). Generous Dan, knowing it was our first harvest and that Jeff loved Chardonnay, agreed to waive his minimum quantity and those grapes were crushed the very same day'to make our first ever barrel of wine – but we were forced to wait over a year for it to mature, and to get our first taste.

By mid-February all the grapes were picked (shirtless European backpacker pickers being one of the highlights of the season – *sure it's safe to swim in the dam, in you go!)* and we would end up with around twelve thousand bottles of wine. In a bumper season this would skyrocket to around thirty thousand bottles and while we were pretty good at drinking the profits away, not even Jeff and I would be able to put a dent in that. At a rough cost of four to five dollars a bottle and at least seven or eight months before we could sell the Semillon, and over twelve months before the Shiraz and Chardonnay could be sold, it also became apparent that, without putting too fine a point on it, our financial situation read: fucked. As my mate Scott reminded me, 'How do you get a million dollars out of a vineyard? You first put in five million.'

But with our first wine just months away, it was time to give this business some personality. Two friends of mine, Chris and Verity, had just started their own design agency, Pixel Eight. We didn't consider asking anyone else to help us create our brand and it was pure coincidence we both featured the lucky number eight in our names. From the moment we saw their vision of what Block Eight could become we were blown away. Because they know us, and had visited us and heard our dreams, they instinctively knew how to encapsulate that in our brand. What really won me over was Chris saying, 'I imagined you were publishing a cookbook and I worked my way back from there.' Had he been pitching to Jeff I have no doubt the words 'cushion', 'interior design' and 'structural pine' would have been used. (As part of our brand, Chris designed the heart frame included at the beginning of each chapter in this book.) Things were becoming tangible, and seeing our first wine labels and business cards and launching our website meant that momentum was well underway.

In March, finances were on my mind again: we were slapped with a $70,000 personal tax bill we hadn't been expecting and for the first time ever in our relationship Jeff and I had no spare cash. Thank Christ we'd already paid for the villa shells and at least using an accountant meant we'd lodged our tax return almost a year past the end of the financial year it was due.

I'd lie in bed wide-eyed at night listening to Jeff snore as I went over Meryl Streep films in my mind. Deciding sleep was impossible I'd get up and watch *Crossing Over* re-runs until early morning; sobbing as distraught loved ones believed they were talking to the spirit of their family member. ('Something in the stomach region, I see blood, older father figure beginning with S . . .' it was all just so accurate!) It began to look like I'd applied a permanent layer of black eye shadow beneath my eyes, which were also delightfully puffy.

Tired and petrified about losing it all, it was easy for my mind to be distracted. I was on edge, irritable and moody.

While it's true that Jeff and I never really argue, that is mostly because I always take the moral high ground and simply walk off whenever he gets on one of his soapboxes. For the record, I am *never* annoying. Whatever he'd done to annoy *me* on this particular day I don't recall, but as he was making lunch for Millie (who was on another of her visits) and me, I thought to myself, *there's no way I'm going to sit across from you at the lunch table without screaming my head off,* so I decided instead to go and mow some grass, which meant attaching the slasher to the tractor.

'You'd better be careful with that tractor,' my Aunty Marie had said shortly after we got it, 'those things have a habit of rolling over and it'll kill you! People die on them things all the friggin' time!'

'Yes, yes,' I said dismissively. Like *she* would know.

But the tractor is a very big, very heavy machine. With the benefit of hindsight, it probably wasn't a sensible thing to do, the day I decided to go mowing on an empty stomach and tired and overly emotional then annoyed by some silly thing Jeff had said without thinking. It was so unlike me to overreact, after all.

In order to get the slasher on the back of the tractor I first needed to remove the counterweight – basically a big metal cube that weighs something like seven hundred kilograms. I'd done it scores of times by now; I didn't even need to really think about what I was doing – and so I didn't think at all.

One bolt removed, connecting arm disengaged . . . it all happened so quickly. Without any warning, the weight crashed suddenly to the ground, breaking through the wooden pallet I'd rested it so carefully on. My hand was somewhere in the process of removing the second and final bolt from the arm when that seven hundred kilograms came down with an almighty crash. At the sound, I'd instinctively moved my hand, but not fast enough or perhaps not in the right direction so the back of my palm bore the brunt of that dead weight as I pulled it clear of the tractor arm. Had I not, it would have been wedged there.

'That smarts,' I said aloud, before the real pain took hold.

Hot diggity if that wasn't the worst pain in the whole entire world! I felt the blood drain from my face, I couldn't move my

fingers and then my legs began to tremble and weaken. I had
to get out of the shed before I fainted. I clutched my right wrist
with my left hand and carried what felt like a dead thing back
to the house. I channelled Hugh Grant in *Four Weddings and a
Funeral* – *Fuck. Fuck. Fuck. Fuckety fuck*, I kept muttering under
my breath.

I walked as casually as I could into the house, past Jeff and
Millie who were just sitting down to eat and went straight to the
bedroom where I threw myself down on the mattress (face up,
there was no way I was going to put any pressure on my hand).
I held my hand bolt upright in the air; I just had no idea what
else to do. The pain was so intense it could only mean every
single bone in my hand had been shattered. Despite my little
spat of a few minutes before, Jeff rushed into the room. He must
have sensed something was up by the way I walked past white
as a sheet and without making any eye contact or saying a word.

'Toddy, what have you done?'

No 'please don't hate me' this time: 'I just crushed my hand
in the counterweight.'

Within minutes we were on our way to sit in the grim
interiors of Cessnock Hospital, where there wasn't a cushion
in sight.

'Please can we not fight ever again,' I said through tears. 'Oh
my god, this hurts so fucking much!'

The triage nurse gave me an aspirin (a fucking aspirin!) and
told me to wait for the doctor. After what felt like hours, I was
seen by a guy who didn't feel all that worried about the plight
of what I thought was my *very important* right hand, and then I
was given an X-ray. As it turned out, I was extremely fortunate –
I had only caused tissue damage, there were no broken bones.

Once I'd recovered, I could again concentrate on our financial
plight. I hated having no money and worse still, none was due

to come in from the property or the wine for quite some time. We had only one choice and that was to go into more joyous debt by refinancing our close-to-maxed-out mortgage; thereby taking another huge step back from independence.

I called every single financial institution and talked through our situation. Hours and hours on the phone, but the story was always the same: 'We won't refinance your mortgage without forcing you onto commercial terms'. Banks had tightened their lending rules in the eighteen months we'd been on the property and it now seemed that with one hundred acres and two crops there was no way we were getting residential refinance, and we almost certainly didn't have enough equity in the property to satisfy the even tighter controls of a commercial loan. If I mentioned the fact that we wanted money to build a villa for accommodation I was immediately put through to the commercial lending team, at which point I'd hang up the phone in defeat. All of this meant not only were we unlikely to get refinance on a residential loan, if any application were made and we were forced to be seen as commercial clients we would be precluded from any loan at all. Even if we could afford commercial repayments, we only had my part-time income (though it was still better than average). We were labelled risky business. No, *we* were labelled risky – our business was non-existent. We were inching ever closer to failure and we hadn't even started building accommodation; we hadn't sold a single grape or bottle of wine and yet there we were with an astronomical winemaking bill breathing down our necks.

Jeff and I actually toyed with the idea of abandoning the plan to open villas. We figured that if we were able to pay all of the bills to make it and then sell all our wine at a thirty-dollar retail price we would have a healthy little income (in an optimum year) of close to a million dollars. But the more winemaking professionals we spoke to, the more it became obvious that pipedream would not be handed to us on a silver platter: considerable marketing and promotion expense was required, the opening of a cellar door (a costly exercise in itself with endless red tape from the local council), free tasting giveaways and even then a huge chunk of our stock would have to be sold at knockdown prices to wholesale buyers and foreign importers. We just didn't have the money to promote our wine or build a cellar door to realise sales at full retail price.

We briefly considered asking my family to invest in the business but we also knew what that double-edged sword looked like: *Maybe you should furnish the next villa from Fantastic Furniture to save a bit of money? Do you really need a fireplace in every villa? Why not give guests Coon cheese instead of locally made stuff?* Crowdfunding sites were just starting to get traction but we knew the amount of money we needed wouldn't be raised as fast as we needed it.

'Hey guess what?' Jeff asked one Thursday evening in late March as I drove us home from the Tuggerah train station. I shrugged. 'I've started sleeping with the blinds open!'

I quickly looked at him in disbelief before turning back to the road. 'You aren't scared?'

'Nah, of what? We'll do it tonight. You'll see, it's beautiful looking out there into the darkness and then being woken up by the sun.'

'Well if you're already doing it then I'm happy to do it too.'

'So, you know, I've been thinking . . .'

'Uh-oh,' I responded the way I always did to one of Jeff's *I've been thinking* lines.

'We're sitting on a little goldmine here and I think we'd be stupid not to cash in on it.'

'It's prostitution, isn't it?' I sighed.

'What? No? Don't be stupid! I said we needed to make money, not pay people to have sex with you.'

'Sorry, my mistake. What's the big idea then?'

'This house. Pete the builder suggested it to me. I've been doing some research and I reckon we could easily get a thousand dollars a weekend renting it out,' he said.

'And what would we do? Go stay at Mum and Dad's? Come to think of it, couch surfing two nights a week is nowhere near enough for me, I'd love to do more of it,' I said facetiously.

'No, we can move into the first villa as soon as the walls are up inside. We'd just have to crash there Friday and Saturday nights but I reckon that's worth it for fifty grand a year, don't you?'

It was hard to argue against Jeff. So once agreed, he set me to work weaving my masterful marketing spiel. After listing the house on a couple of travel websites, our first booking, for Easter, came in very fast, a precursor to suggest that Jeff was once again right, though of course I never said that aloud to him.

We had a few weeks to depersonalise our home – removing all photographs, clothes and other personal or valuable belongings along with any risqué art and my favourite cookbooks. *That one's going into storage! That one too! That one too! Yes, and that one.* Almost immediately our home ceased evoking any feeling of belonging to us – it was merely a place we lived in between guest bookings.

Our first guests were an Indian family based in Sydney who'd never been to the Hunter Valley before. When we met them shortly after they'd checked in they could not stop raving about how beautiful our property was and how amazing it was that so many kangaroos lazed in our olive groves, and they thanked us for all the personal touches in the house like the breakfast hamper, local wines, freshly baked cookies we'd left as well as the impressive collection of novels and cookbooks. They asked us a lot about our story – how we ended up here, why we chose the Hunter, what our plans were for the future – and after their stay they left us the most beautiful, gracious note thanking us for one of the most memorable holidays of their lives. It humbled us to know that we'd given them such a happy experience and we genuinely looked forward to doing the same again and again.

Of course, we'd left the gate unlocked for our guests so they'd feel more welcome on the property. The evening of their departure, I sat bolt upright in bed.

'What?' Jeff sat upright too, woken by my sudden movement.

'Did you lock the gate tonight?'

'No . . . did you?'

'No.' I sighed. 'Should we just leave it?'

'Yeah,' Jeff said and lay back down. We never did lock that gate again and within a few weeks we removed the padlock altogether.

On the weekends when the house was rented, we moved into the side of the shed where the new villa was to be. We shoved an old mattress on top of one of the tables Jeff had made for my fortieth birthday party so the crawly critters couldn't get us, and we had a tent flyscreen as our only protection from spiders and flying bugs. It was hot and dusty – and I don't mean that in a sexy cowboy kind of way; there wasn't anything remotely comfortable or enticing about it. We did our best to make it bearable but really it was basic camping. Leroy was not a massive fan, regularly pawing at the zip in the screen to be let in, then out, then in again so most of the night was spent tending to his needs, not in something as useless as human sleep.

Still, that first payday from holiday rental was a memorable one and those guests gave us a glowing review, so at last we felt we were on the right track. Before long, available weekends were scarce and the almost-weekly income allowed us to clear some of the backlog of bills.

To celebrate our first booking, Jesus had created some stunning key rings that we would eventually use in every villa as well as the house. Reminiscent of those he made us for the Annandale house, but of bronze, there's a B on one side, an E on the other and our business name etched along the edge of the letters. They're heavy, stylish and impressive, and his creativity heralded the end of our address as just our home, and the beginning of our business.

I wasn't ashamed of talking about our financial situation so most of our social circle knew how desperate it had become. Pet suggested I reach out to her dad, my 'Uncle' Rod, a mortgage broker. After yet another lender had turned us down I called Uncle Rod and explained the situation, how much money we needed to get out of trouble and which lenders I'd called and been refused by. All we wanted was enough cash to get the first villa open by October, then hopefully income would start coming in to pay for the ongoing costs of running a property as large as Block Eight and help meet some of those impending wine-making bills. We'd at least managed to pay the pickers for harvest and Dan's monthly bill was just being covered, but within two or so months bottling would need to take place and this meant much more expense.

'Don't give up hope, Pet,' Uncle Rod said encouragingly, 'there will be a way out of this.'

'I don't believe in miracles,' I said, resigned to having already lost the fight.

'Well, luckily for you, I do. Leave it with me.'

While we waited for news on the loan situation, Jeff oversaw the erection of the villas and, once that was complete, decided to search for a winter job while there wasn't as much hands-on stuff to do at Block Eight. Pete and Cassh were left to do the build without Jeff (or Colin who'd since moved on) so progress would be slower. Despite Jeff's considerable experience in finance, he lacked the degree that many of the advertised jobs required and even when he seemed to have the perfect skills, very few ever bothered responding to his application. It looked as though I would have to ask eBay if I could return to full-time work (what clearer sign was there that I had failed in my tree change?), and I would also have to look for a cheap room in a shared house close to the city so I could stay there four nights a week. Internally the thought of either made me want to curl into a ball and cry like a young actress winning her first Oscar but I presented a brave face to Jeff: *Of course I'll share a flea-riddled cesspit in Glebe with a bunch of bong-head Arts students, honey – anything we need for us to survive at Block Eight, I'll do it. Did you want me to try my hand at prostitution while I'm in the city? May as well earn a few extra bucks.*

Even with the uncertainty of our financial situation, in late June we experienced one of the greatest highs imaginable. Thanks to a modest bonus from work we were able to funnel funds into bottling our first ever wine, the 2014 Reserve Semillon. Chris had designed a label shaped in an abstract number eight and it featured the silver perch from our main dam. On bottling day we raced to the factory and watched our wine fill the empty green bottles we'd chosen. They were then topped with grey metal screw caps before being shunted into another machine where our perfect new labels were applied. Suzanna handed us one of the very first bottles from the production line, knowing just how momentous an occasion this was for us.

When you bottle wine, the enzymes are affected by the process and you're supposed to wait four or so weeks before you drink it – as if! That very night we cracked open our debut – we were beside ourselves with pride and as usual tears welled in my eyes. *Sure, we might be facing bankruptcy but look at this! Look at what these two clever little Sydneysiders have achieved in just under two years with no prior experience and armed with only passion!*

The moment the wine hit my lips I knew we were onto a winner. It had echoes of the 2006 Brokenwood wine we'd drunk on the deck our first night – citrus acidity, a fullness in the mouth, a dry flinty finish and just the subtlest note of sweetness at its end. We sipped at it like it was the last bottle of wine remaining on earth and we stretched it out over dinner, pairing it with my Block Eight butterflied chicken dish.

'We did it!' Jeff raised his glass to mine.

'I don't know how, but we sure as hell did.'

'It's called determination, Toddy. There wasn't a chance we'd be making bad wine and I can tell you now, there isn't a chance this business is going to fail. We will find a way to make it work.'

In July 2014 we held our second annual prune-off and this time we had our very own Semillon to bribe about sixty people into helping us out. The generosity of our friends and colleagues was overwhelming, however pruning is a precise science and we had to ensure it was done properly as the quality of the workmanship could drastically impact our yield. We also had the cost of keeping everyone fed and watered and the worry of keeping them warm enough at night as they slept inside our un-insulated villa shells.

There was another outcome, too: by the end of the second prune-off my hands were completely numb. I'd wake in the middle of the night and find the numbness had spread all the way up my arms. Carpal tunnel syndrome was diagnosed in both hands, requiring an operation that put me out of action for a few weeks. So, as wonderful as the prune-offs had been in many ways, we made the tough decision not to hold any more after that second one. From that year on, it became my carpal-tunnel-free job to prune the entire vineyard with a very expensive pair of electric shears, a feat that took around four hours each morning for sixty days.

A few calls from Uncle Rod throughout July brought the same disappointing news – no one was prepared to lend us more money against our residential mortgage. Jeff got a part-time job in Newcastle and, though it would alleviate some of the stress, there was still a huge financial gap and I was stepping ever closer to returning to full-time employment.

Every time I saw Uncle Rod's name on my phone, I steeled myself for more bad news from him, but then in August there came a call I'd never expected.

'Todd, mate, we've got it!' he exclaimed with glee one Thursday morning and I could not believe what I was hearing.

'Uncle Rod, you told me to believe in the impossible but I couldn't and you proved me wrong,' I said, sounding very much like Dorothy in *The Wizard of Oz* waking from her dream. 'Thank you so much for not giving up, I can't tell you how much I appreciate all that you have done for us.' *And you were there. And you were there . . .*

'My pleasure, Pet. Your Aunty Anne and I want to see you guys successful.' They'd been at both prune-offs with Pet and felt very much a part of our journey.

'How much wine do you want? You name it, Uncle Rod, it's yours . . .'

He thought a minute. 'Actually, Pet mentioned you were thinking of getting a pig. I think it's only fair that it's named after me.'

The refinance on the loan would be enough – just – to finish building our first villa whose budget had spiralled way beyond our initial estimate.

I got home from the city that evening to Jeff having finally mastered *boeuf bourguignon* (man, we went through quite a few bowls of dry salty dead cow to get to that outcome) opening a bottle of local Shiraz to go with it.

'Here's to the loan,' I said, raising my glass to his.

Running one hundred acres is hard work, particularly when you're both employed part-time elsewhere. Hour after sweaty hour is applied to the tasks at hand. The scale of everything can do anyone's head in – but somehow with each other for support we never lost sight of the dream, knowing that blood, sweat and tears would be mandatory payment to get us there.

Welcome to Unemployment

By early September 2014 we were edging closer to opening our first villa – the converted side of the shed. We had very high expectations: we'd spent a lot of money on the conversion and still more on designing the interior and furnishing it. Jeff would disappear for hours on end then come home and painstakingly reveal every single item he'd bought, expecting me to comprehend his grand vision. *Oh, that's nice. Oh . . . right. Okay . . .* I'd say all the right things but really had no appreciation for how one thing would work alongside another. To me, nothing appeared to match. But I should never have doubted him.

Now, Jeff may not have known how to drive a tractor or where our water came from when we first came here, but the gay sure knows how to design an interior space! We had an opening date of late October 2014 for the converted shed, which we named Orchard View for its sweeping views over the citrus grove, and it felt as if we were finally achieving what we'd moved to Block Eight to do.

At the same time, things at work didn't feel right and, during a review with my boss in early September, we agreed that I would accept a voluntary redundancy package. In no time, the wheels were in motion: by 11 September I would be unemployed for the first time since I was seventeen.

I'd never been more scared in my life. (Okay, maybe aside from the time when I was four and the bogeyman character my cousins had created, Heart, came to get me when we were on holidays. My Uncle John crept outside and tapped on my window: '*Toddy . . . Toddy . . . Toddy Ally-ander . . . . It's Heart . . .*' Scaring the bejesus out of each other must be a bit of a family trait.) But once I could rationalise some of that fear, I knew deep down I was also relieved to have been set free and brimming with excitement at the prospect of being at Block Eight full time. This, after all, had been the plan all along.

Redundancy packages from any US-based company tend to be better than those based in Australia but Jeff had spent the money before it even landed in our account. Old Mr Sensible Finance Guy wasn't about to let Dreamy Airy Fairy Spendthrift get his mitts on it, so there were no fancy holidays, no new sports cars and none of the plastic surgery I'd been longing for most of my adult life. (Just a suck here and a tuck there, nothing too drastic.) Instead, Jeff pre-paid one year of our mortgage, and the rest was earmarked for the completion of the second villa and the bottling of our next wine, the Estate Semillon. With me out of work and Jeff's award wage being part-time, we were now desperate for the accommodation to generate as much income as possible.

In late September we'd received the first bottle of Estate Semillon. If tasting our first ever wine had been momentous, the fact that this was our second certainly didn't reduce our excitement or sense of achievement. Dan had created a beautifully balanced wine, sweeter certainly but well-rounded and smooth on the palate. At the time I definitely preferred the Estate (this time with a yabby on the label!), but that was possibly because it was new and fresh and we'd definitely grown accustomed to drinking the Reserve (and eating into our profits, though, as we saw it, drinking our own was always cheaper than buying someone else's). But eventually the wines became like our offspring, or perhaps works of art – it was impossible to choose a favourite and you learnt to love each equally.

Orchard View opened for bookings in mid-October on several online sites and I sat back and waited for the cash register to start ringing. We expected it to be as popular as the main house, given we knew that the Hunter is a magnet for romantic getaways and in Orchard View we'd created the ultimate love nest for couples. It had a king-sized bed, private little outdoor verandah, fully equipped kitchen, heated flooring in the bathroom – every mod con. We'd really spared no expense and had assumed that the bookings would come thick and fast. So we waited for those bookings. We waited some more. But after four or so weeks there was not a single booking for November. Then no one came in early December. I was beside myself with worry so Jeff surprised me by taking me for a drive in the Barina into the Barrington Tops National Park.

The Barina, needless to say, is not four-wheel drive, is automatic, and does not have improved suspension or extra width tyres. It's about as Annandale as any car can get. Originally we'd gone shopping for four-wheel drives but I'd found my one and only second-hand-car-buying experience too stressful and had settled on the cheapest new sedan we could find. We walked onto the lot in Rosebery and said, 'we'll take that Barina there, thanks' without so much as a test drive or opening a single door. It was without doubt the fastest lot sale in history, as the salesman exclaimed once we had signed the relevant papers. It went on to be a lemon of the tallest order – the speedometer didn't work so you had to guess your speed and month after month after month Holden failed to fix the problem, then the blinkers didn't work, and then once they were, the odometer didn't work and then once that was fixed, the speedometer stopped working again. She has managed to transport a Noah's Ark's worth of animals and building materials during her employ, however, so we got our money's worth in the end.

The Barrington Tops trip was a spur of the moment thing, so Jeff hadn't thought it necessary to pack water, lunch or any snacks at all, let alone check that the car was up for the three-hour long and (as it turned out very) rough drive. Hell, Jeff hadn't even worked out a route, assuming Siri could get us there without any internet connection in the boondocks.

After three hours of driving (it sure was purty) – the last thirty minutes over very bumpy rocky roads – our car got a flat tyre. No sweat, we may have been idiots but we still knew how to change a tyre – we were bona fide blokes, after all. But then when I lowered the jack and the car sat on the newly changed spare tyre, it too went down very quickly. There was as much air in that tyre as there was in one of my profiteroles (the only thing I haven't quite mastered in the kitchen ... along with angel hair pasta). We asked for help around the entrance to the national park but no one had a pump, not even the park rangers, who sniggered at our stupid car.

Our only option was to drive back into the nearest town, about forty minutes or so on the flat tyre, and along the way we kept a constant look out for a local who might be able to help us.

'Jeez, look at these places,' I said to Jeff. 'Jeffrey Dahmer would feel right at home on one of these farms.'

'They just look Australian to me.'

'Do they? Do they Jeff? Do they really Jeff?' I asked drolly, like Homer Simpson often asked Lisa. 'So you'd be happy to drive up to one and ask for help?'

'No way!'

'Good, because I wouldn't let you. You'd be shot within a few seconds and then I'd be held captive in the basement and forced to do all the washing and cooking for some toothless hick.'

'Sounds right up your alley if you ask me.'

'Yes, but at least you have all your teeth.'

As luck would have it, we came across a man and woman (a woman! A nice, safe, human of the female variety) working on their tractor. We pulled our car into their driveway and I told Jeff he needed to do all of the talking but as soon as we got out of the car, instinct kicked in. I figured it was better coming from my ocker self than in Jeff's still potent Brummy.

'How ya goin'?' I asked. (All gs were dropped from any -ing word in the following conversation because g is for gay, after all.) 'Sorry to bother you but we were drivin' down the road and we got a flat tyre. We were wonderin' if youse had a pump to help us blow it up?'

They took pity on the fools and the woman drove her quad bike up to her shed and came back with a battery-powered pump.

While the tyre was inflating I said: 'Nice fertile land, here – what kinda cattle are you raisin'? Dairy or beef?'

When she talked about the cattle I then went on to explain that we too were farmers and owned a hundred acres 'just down the road. We're growin' grapes and olives . . .' She didn't really seem to give a damn.

We were nearly out of there without being lynched when Jeff said, 'You know, I really love the way you've painted your fence like that. Would you mind if I asked what colour it is?'

The woman looked at him queerly. 'Black.'

As we drove off, I burst out laughing. 'Oh my fucking god! Ooh, is that a Dulux shade?' I mimicked him.

'Oh fuck off,' he said with a laugh, 'Is that eatin' beef?' he put on his best (and by that I mean the worst) Australian accent.

We laughed all the way to Dungog where we had really bland toasties in a run-down shithole of a café for my birthday lunch, but it is still destined to be one I will never forget. *I just love what you've done to your fence!* It was good to laugh in the face of our failed launch of Orchard View but on the drive back home I got a surprise birthday present – finally, a booking trickled in.

The booking was for 1 January for three nights, so on New Year's Eve, Jeff and I decided to drive into Newcastle to treat ourselves to a few beers at a local pub to watch the clock tick over. We were forty minutes from home, and ten minutes from Newcastle when I received a message from the guest asking if he could come early, in the next two hours. It meant an extra few hundred dollars for us so of course I said yes and within a minute we'd abandoned plans to celebrate, turned the car around and were headed back to Block Eight to finish cleaning and preparing the villa for the guest's arrival.

James was our first ever villa guest – he came without a human companion but we were so desperate for cash we even allowed him to bring his dog with him, having previously made a blanket rule that no pets would ever be allowed to be brought onto the property. To this day he is the only person we've ever made an exception for. James is a personal trainer in Bondi and a part-time model/actor and he was looking for the perfect escape from the mayhem of a city New Year's Eve to carefully plan his business for the coming year. After meeting him at the door, he closed himself inside and we never saw him or his dog for the next three days. Upon leaving, James came to say goodbye and we started talking. He thanked me and said this was the most perfect escape he'd ever been on and asked how I ended up at Block Eight and within minutes we worked out that he used to date an ex-colleague of mine. James returned to us several times and always holds a special place in our hearts as the man who broke our villa-booking drought but alas, his did not begin a tsunami of bookings.

'I think we've made a terrible mistake,' I said to Mel on the phone one day in late January 2015 while I was up in the vines de-suckering shoots. It's backbreaking work, bending down to pick off new shoots that appear anywhere near the base or lower trunk of the vine, and walking kilometres in the heat, stooping up to twelve thousand times, depending on how many vines have suckers. As I paused to speak to Mel, I pressed on the small of my back, trying to ease the ache.

'How so?' Mel pressed.

'We've only had a single booking for the new villa and nothing more for the foreseeable future. I can't believe it, but I think I'm going to have to suck it up and go crawling back to the corporate world with my tongue out ready to lick more arse. Young, Gen-Y, self-entitled arse.' I brushed sweat out of my eyes and bent down to the next shoot with a slight groan.

'You're rushing into things,' she said calmly. 'You have other things to lick! You have a lot of wine to sell – how seriously have you tried to shift that? You could write more books – anything! A friend of mine teaches up there and makes a lot of money from it. Just don't assume your only option is to head straight back into a world you no longer want to be a part of. You were so happy to get out of it, you'll be miserable returning to it again so quickly.'

We talked some more and she gave me some great ideas. Abandoning the de-suckering, I rushed back to the house, called up all the internet listings for the villa and breathed new life into the descriptions, just like Mel said I should. I experimented with the lead image and pricing. I listed the villa on two more sites. We invested more money in having a fireplace installed to take advantage of early bookings for the winter season. Over the following three weeks another booking came in, and then another.

In late February, we received our Button Chardonnay to taste. Now back in the day, when I first started drinking wine, Chardonnay was very *de rigueur* and I drank it by the bucketload, but since then my palate morphed to prefer Sauvignon Blanc, then again towards Riesling and Pinot Gris, and since moving to the Hunter and making our own, Semillon. I'd distanced myself from the oakiness of Chardonnay in the intervening years so was nervous to try ours. We'd bought a new American oak barrel to mature the wine in and it adds a traditionally coarse oaky taste to the wine, hence my anxiety. When the sole pallet of wine arrived from Hunter Bottling, it struck us just how precious a drop this was. It had been made despite the odds: severely unkempt vines, just five hundred kilos of fruit that most winemakers would have mixed with something else and that our band of loyal friends working tirelessly to pick ... its scent certainly packed an oaky punch but the taste was buttery and mellow, thick on the palate and a butterscotch aftertaste that blew my mind. I knew I wasn't supposed to play favourites, but I had fallen in love. Knowing this wine would never be sold commercially because its small volume prevented Dan from performing all the necessary filtering only added to the sense that it was a special drop, and we shared it lovingly with our friends and former colleagues.

Now that we had three excellent wines to sell, I followed Mel's advice and turned to the wine to try to raise some funds. I drained my corporate network dry. I mean, I scoured LinkedIn like a junkie licking powder from the top of a toilet cistern. Anyone who had the remotest connection to the wine or hospitality industry was emailed; from my own contacts I emailed people whose names I barely recognised – perhaps I'd met them once at a speaking event or else they'd come into the office pitching one of their own ideas to me. *Do you need wine?* I asked every single person I knew to buy a case, and most did. The money slowly started coming in but we were far from in the clear.

In March 2015, Shelly called me to advise we were getting new next-door neighbours at The Meadows. We knew the house and vineyard next to us was for sale, but we hadn't expected it to be sold so quickly – in just three months (it usually takes up to twelve months to sell a larger Hunter property). Unlike our previous neighbours, who we'd never actually met due to their infrequent visits, Shelly said the new owners were moving in permanently so there'd be a bit more action on our street and perhaps, I thought, we mightn't feel so alone. Shelly gave me their names and I immediately jumped onto Google, learning Natalie and Andrew were mortgage brokers and financial advisors.

As no one had welcomed us to the neighbourhood, I was absolutely determined to reach out to Natalie and Andrew shortly after they arrived. But when you're busy mowing, rotating vegie crops, pickling, writing (I was putting the finishing touches on a novel), well, life sort of gets in the way of your best intentions. I came home from the supermarket one day and found a brief note of introduction in the mailbox. I called her immediately.

'Hi Natalie, it's Todd from next door. I'm so sorry, I was going to call you and welcome you but you beat me to it.'

'I thought we'd say hi and let you know we've moved in . . .'

'You guys will have to come over for drinks,' I said, excited to be speaking to people our own age, a couple who had moved from Sydney to dive headfirst into an adventure so similar to ours. We would have so much information to share with them and also have someone to bond over similar trials and tribulations. 'How does next week sound? Friday at eight?'

'I'll check with Andrew and get back to you ASAP,' she said. Her voice was warm and rich; I immediately liked the sound of her.

I chose 8pm because I figured it was too soon to sit across from each other at dinner. We'd have our respective meals at home then have a few drinks, and because we'd started later, the neighbours would be under no pressure to stay longer than they wanted.

They arrived with a bottle of Champagne and three other bottles of wine. I'd already placed four bottles of wine in the fridge. We hosted them in the house and from the second they sat down we were off – no awkward silences, no major alarm bells of differing world views, just four people chatting through their histories and their plans for the future. They had two daughters, aged three and four, and two dogs, and their plan was to eventually open a wedding venue . . . which would feed perfectly into our business plan, a funnelling of guests well in advance (as weddings were generally booked). I thought they'd stay until

10pm at the latest, but the conversation continued unabated, the wine kept being poured, and a little after 2am they said their goodbyes. A few weeks later we went to their house, met the kids, dogs and Natalie's parents, and more or less from that day on our friendship has grown in strength and vitality.

In many respects, Jeff and I were right back where we'd started almost a year previously, living in an unfinished villa (though this time it was one of the new sheds, which we named Barrington View) with no running water, no toilet and only a handful of electrical outlets. While the redundancy package would help us get this villa finished, we still needed the income from the house and Orchard View so we had no other choice but to live through the renovation. As winter 2015 approached we rugged up in three layers of clothing to keep ourselves warm.

'Are you cold, Toddy?' Jeff asked while we were watching a DVD.

I breathed out vapour. 'Is it normal for my balls to be sitting at the back of my throat?'

Jeff had developed a new love affair as he'd finalised the designs for the villas: recycling wooden fences. Jeff took the palings and nailed them wherever there was a spare wall, so he was constantly on the lookout for free palings. No wall on the property was safe from Jeff and his nails. If Leroy hadn't moved for more than an hour I gave him a little shove just in case Jeff thought he'd look better dressed in recycled hardwood. If someone was pulling down a fence on any road we drove down, Jeff would swerve the car over and ask to remove their palings for them. There was an almost constant scouring of Gumtree and, if he made a find, the next day we'd be on our way to the other side of Newcastle in a hire truck to stack palings dumped in someone's front yard, a new Colourbond fence gleaming behind us as we worked. According to Jeff, Colourbond was the outdoor equivalent of net curtains. Our friend Merv seemed to spend his spare time patrolling the streets of his suburb looking for palings for Jeff too – in fact, it felt like Jeff had a whole army of people on the lookout for fence palings. But then one day in spring Jeff found the mother lode. A guy in Singleton wanted someone to pull down an entire yard full of wooden fence.

'He wants a quote,' Jeff said like Darryl Kerrigan from *The Castle*.

'I reckon a grand is fair,' I offered.

Jeff went off to make his call and returned a few minutes later. I was practically rubbing my hands together in his absence – that grand was sure going to come in handy for two destitute farmers.

'The fence is ours,' he said, all chipper and proud of himself.

'Did you ask for a grand? Or more?' I thought he might have been cheeky and try to hide a bit of cash from me just in case I hadn't let go of the liposuction dream.

'I didn't . . . I told him we would remove it for free.'

'Ha, ha, yeah, sure you did!'

'I did, honestly. It's just that we're getting all those palings for free, it didn't feel right to ask for money as well. Can you hire a truck for next week?'

To say I was against doing it for free from the outset would be a little misleading. There were a lot of things I was prepared to do for free but chopping down some guy's fence was not one of them. I hired the truck as requested, not even flinching at the two-hundred-dollar-per-day charge, nor the knowledge that I would need to put in about eighty dollars' worth of diesel. We got to the guy's yard and were shown the side gate.

Leroy surveys his new domain,
ready to defend us and our pets.
(Jeff Ross)

Jeff and my favourite view on the property
and the reason we fell in love with Block Eight.
(Melanie Luque)

Helga at Sugarloaf Animal Hospital just after
her operation – my favourite photo of her.
(Dr Mark Simpson, Sugarloaf Animal Hospital)

Rodney and Billy
loved to jump up
on their fence for
food and scratches.
(Todd Alexander)

Jeff *(left)* and I take Helga and the kids on a family walk.
(Melissa Evans, Left of the Middle Photography)

Winston walks
the steep drive
at his new home.
(Jeff Ross)

'There she is, fellas.'

That was no suburban backyard, let me tell you. There must have been about five hundred metres of fencing. And no, it was no cricket pitch either. The backyard must have been at about a sixty-degree slope and it was bordered on three sides by dense bushland, lovely snake-hidey, thorn-wieldy, slippery-from-recent-rain bush. I took a deep breath. I couldn't look at Jeff. I took another deep breath. I would not look at him for the rest of the day if I could help it.

Within minutes it was obvious the two hammers we'd brought were not sufficient tools for the job. Jeff left me to dismantle the fence by hand and went to fetch himself a new chainsaw, and three new chainsaw blades. More money out of our thousand-dollar payment. Oh wait, that's right! We weren't getting paid . . . we were doing this *for free.*

Sweat ran off me in torrents. My back broke in seven different places. My shorts ripped up the middle and I wasn't wearing any underwear so had to tie a shirt around my waist. Jeff took more than two hours to return. I not only couldn't look at him, I couldn't bear the thought of him.

We worked from 7am until sunset at 6pm. We hadn't thought to bring sunscreen so I was burnt to a crisp.

'Gee, we've got a lot done today,' Jeff said as we drove home.

By my calculations, we'd done barely a third and the worst terrain was yet to come.

We returned the next day. And the next. And we finished the job after four days, two pairs of shorts, one thousand dollars in trunk rental, one hundred and thirty in diesel, forty in takeaway food, two hundred on a chainsaw and sixty for blades and, though we were yet to know it was coming, three hundred dollars in massages for my never-the-same-again back.

'I really can't believe we got all those palings for free!' Jeff said, as if he'd just got all those palings for free. 'Whenever you get the chance would you mind de-nailing them for me?'

There were so many palings dumped at the back of our villa that you could not see over them from the back deck. I reckon the pile was three metres high and ten metres wide. We was hay-chewin' country hicks with a junkyard to call home.

I smiled through gritted teeth.

The next day, the guy massaging me asked, 'Have you damaged your right hand?'

And don't you know, four months after my arm wrestle with the counterweight at the back of the tractor my right hand was fifty per cent bigger than my left. It was puffed up like a pink rubber glove stuck to a schoolkid's head to play Foghorn Leghorn in the Book Week parade. I'd got myself my very first farming battle scar.

As spring 2015 got into full swing to mark the beginning of another grape vintage, reviews for our 2014 wine started coming in. Miraculously, James Halliday in his industry bible *The Wine Companion* gave our Reserve Semillon 96 points and voted it one of the best twenty Semillons in the country! Our Shiraz was awarded 96 points too, and the Estate Semillon 93 points. To boot, our winery was awarded four and a half stars and marked as one to watch. So much for Jenny saying the Shiraz was shit quality! All three of those wines went on to win medals at local wine shows – we never sent the Chardonnay out for assessment because, given its rustic edge, the judges would have been unlikely to appreciate it – but on the back of our reviews I managed to sell the vast majority of the 2014 vintage to a selection of wholesalers and internet clubs that embraced our wine wholeheartedly (though at much lower margins than we would have ideally liked). Still it was income! And it was better than break even (though only slightly, Jeff kept reminding me), and we were beginning to establish a name for ourselves. It tasted like enormous success.

Things at Block Eight stabilised to a degree after I'd left the corporate world and got used to being Jeff's chief labourer. We'd worked out a division of chores and it surprised me just how much there was to do, and that Jeff had been doing it alone for so long while I commuted to work in the city. Massaging results for a weekly report was so damn easy compared to work that left your body feeling ravaged. While it was true we needed whatever money we could get, it was my turn to sit Jeff down and talk about actuals versus inflated profits . . . when we took into account fuel, travelling time, lunch and other ancillary costs, Jeff's Newcastle job simply wasn't worth it. He was much better off staying put on the property as another full-time resource to help get our next villa finished as fast as we could. The longer those villas sat unopened, the longer we went without money and it made no sense at all to me that we should delay a good income in favour of a much paltrier amount in the interim.

'Get excited, Jeffy,' I said, 'we're about to live, work *and* sleep together. It's going to be 24/7, 365-day madness and you're going to love every single second of it! Nobody's spent this much time with me since I was in Mum's womb – and at least she had beer and cigarettes to get her through!'

The Arrival of Rodney and Boulogne

If financial stresses and bloody hard work weren't enough to fill our days, I'd been toying with the idea of expanding our menagerie. You know, just for something extra to do. We had the chooks, of course, but they weren't much of a challenge – though chasing one if it jumped the fence was never a pleasure!

I had long respected farmers who employed a nose-to-tail philosophy when it came to rearing livestock. If an animal was to die for our eating pleasure then the very least we could do to honour that sacrifice was to make use of every conceivable piece of meat the animal provided. The idea was really cemented one night when I took Cheryl to a funky little alleyway restaurant I'd discovered called Berta. Never listen to Cheryl when she tells you she discovered it first; according to her she's been to every single restaurant in the world before you have. At Berta they were hosting a special menu, a pork fest – every dish included some part of their hand-raised pig, including dessert. While accommodation was always going to be our primary income source, I also thought it'd be challenging and rewarding to share our own nose-to-tail approach with the world. This had prompted my initial desire for pigs – to breed them for meat.

Each year, our friend Sheena visited us from the UK and while she was in Australia on business in July 2015, I told her I'd been toying with the idea of getting some pigs.

'I never knew you wanted pigs,' she said, as we sat sharing a bottle of wine. 'I think we should go and get one tomorrow, and I'd like to pay for it.'

Sometimes an actual conversation forced our hands. Over the years we'd shared about a gazillion ideas for Block Eight and few of them had actually stuck. My friend Scott wanted to install a horizontal bungee ride, for example, and we'd toyed with building hidden gardens, a wedding venue, kilometres of raised boardwalks for bushwalking, kangaroo-spotting safaris for foreign tourists, a caper farm (the vegetable, not a circus car full of clowns), a writer's retreat, a writer's festival, a monkey sanctuary (I'd even forego liposuction if I had enough money for that), a water theme-park, a corporate obstacle course, a cactus garden, a pomegranate farm, a small concert venue, an outdoor cinema . . . I could seriously fill this whole book with the ideas we've floated at one time or another. So sure, I'd mentioned I wanted pigs, but did I really want them right now?

'We're not ready for a pig yet, we haven't prepared, we haven't done our research . . .' and the list of reasons (excuses) not to get one went on and on, but Sheena wasn't so easily dissuaded and she insisted on paying for our first real farm animal.

Over more wine, lots of internet research and classifieds browsing (and a new drunken song 'Everybody's talking 'bout my piggy, 'bout my piggy . . .'), a plan was hatched to get a pig the following day from a family raising them in Kurri Kurri, only about thirty minutes from us. A sow. One. Female. Pig. That was the carefully considered plan.

We got to the pig farm full of excitement.

'So you're here for just one sow, are you?' the farmer asked us.

'Yep!' I said confidently.

Her face dropped and she shook her head. 'Oh that's such a shame, that is. You know, it's always much easier to sell the females. It's the males we have problems getting rid of. Nobody ever wants them.'

'What happens to them?' Sheena asked and had she been looking at me she would have seen me waving frantically to *not* ask the question.

'Hmm,' the farmer said grimly. 'Hmm. Well they . . . people just . . . you know, eat them. They get slaughtered at about three months, so in a few more weeks for this lot,' and here she motioned to the adorable little piglets running around the pen and more suckling away at their mother's teat.

'What, no one wants a boy?' I asked incredulously.

'Hmm . . . Hmm . . .' she said again. 'And we've got so many of them too. Just last week we found one had drowned in the water trough so at least he died that way. Anyway, Jimmy,' she called her son over, 'these nice folk are here for a sow so would you jump in and grab them one?'

The boy, about ten, climbed over the fence and into the pigpen. As if they knew exactly what was to come the piglets ran about frantically squealing and the mother grunted out of fear and desperation: *please don't take one of my babies.*

'Which one do you want?' the boy asked.

'That one there,' I said, pointing to a little dark brown one.

The kid picked up the piglet and it squealed harrowingly, its pitch piercing my ears. The mother pig grunted pleadingly. 'It's a boy,' he said with a shrug and threw the piglet back down on the ground.

'What about that one?' I pointed to a tiny caramel and white one.

'That's the runt,' the woman said over my shoulder, 'Don't get that one Jimmy, he's a boy and he's weak and we'll have to send that off next week anyway.'

'I'll take it!' I yelled desperately. 'That one! The runt! Get that one for me Jimmy! Thank you!'

Jimmy reefed the caramel one off its mum's teat and piglet cries again pierced the air. He threw it into Leroy's cat carrier that we'd brought for the purpose and quickly zipped up the flyscreen. The sow grunted and searched about her pen, looking everywhere for her missing baby, hearing its cries.

'Hmm . . . hmm . . .' the woman muttered.

Here we fucking go! I thought.

'You took the runt,' she said, her mouth turned down. 'He's small for his age and he'll struggle so you'll need to keep a close eye on him because he'll get very cold and lonely. They like to snuggle, those runts . . .'

'Jimmy, give me that one too! That brown one you first picked up! Put him in the carrier too, please Jimmy!' I barely even remember saying the words.

The boys, *my* boys, were squealing with so much terror and fear inside the cat carrier that I really needed to get out of there. I could see Jeff and Sheena were distressed too. I just needed to bring those piglets home and show them they would be safe and well-cared-for by us. The squealing of the piglets was shattering and the frets of their mother heartbreaking. This Clarice really wanted the frigging silencing of the lambs, thank you Dr Lecter.

I may as well have been in an abattoir. Maybe I wasn't cut out for the practicalities of animal-rearing when my heart constantly overrules my head. I wanted to rescue all those piglets from their uncertain futures – and take their mother with me as well.

'What the fuck happened there?' Jeff asked as he turned the key in the car's ignition.

'Just drive, Jeff, please. Let's just get out of here.'

In the rush to evacuate, and using Sheena's money, I accidentally paid the higher female price instead of the male, but that didn't really matter. It was only the first mistake of many when it came to those two lovely little piggies.

The bigger, more outgoing piglet I named Rodney just as Uncle Rod wanted, and his little stripy runt of a brother was christened Boulogne, later shortened to 'Billy' by Jeff's mum, Millie, when she returned for another visit. With no time to build them their own pen, Billy and Rodney moved in with the chooks.

They were so small they could squeeze into the tiny space beneath the chookhouse, just twenty centimetres high. They were clearly scared to be away from their mother but at least they had each other and they enjoyed chasing the chooks around. Almost immediately I realised there was no chance I was capable of sending a piglet away for slaughter. Even though we had two boys, I tried to convince myself that the next step would be to get a female and start mating them right away but looking into their inquisitive, intelligent and human-like sensitive eyes, I could no sooner eat their youngsters, I realised, than cut off their heads myself.

Pigs have a very particular scent. The only way I can describe it is like sweet plasticine. It's earthy and kind of rubbery and if you happen to get your nose close to the back of their ears, that's where the real essence lies. The boys' urine also had quite a distinct odour, a sour, yeasty kind of smell. It is the exact smell of a cooked pork bone and from the day I connected the two, I could no longer bring myself to eat any cut of pork on the bone. Raising a fork of that meat towards my mouth would inevitably evoke the trusting eyes of my innocent little pigs.

While it was great they had each other for company, I didn't then realise that getting two male pigs from the same litter would have two significant repercussions in the future: they would never be close to me and inherently lack respect and a sense of hierarchy (kind of like most of the people who ever worked for me, come to think of it), and there would forever be a sibling rivalry between them; the need for one (Rodney) to show continual dominance over the other – just as my eldest brother Grant would always remind me that he was the first in our family to get published – with his poem 'The Hitman', about footballer Brian Battese, being printed in *Rugby League Week* under his pseudonym Jeff Hunt. (I asked him if I could reproduce it here so the world could marvel at his literary prowess, but for some reason he declined.)

When pigs are small they are as playful, malleable and delightful as a pet dog. They play chasings, jump up on you, wrestle with you and give you lots of licks and sniffs. If you take them for walks they will stay by your side, more or less, and never let you out of their sight. When they're small you find yourself (well, I found myself, at least) cutting various fruits and vegetables into bite-sized chunks and their faeces and urine are in such small quantities that you barely have to worry about cleaning up after them.

As a child, one of my favourite books was Helen Palmer's *A Fish Out of Water*. In it, a boy fails to follow advice and overfeeds his fish until it grows to an enormous, comical size. Since bringing Rodney and Billy back to the property, we'd conducted hours of research on how best to raise pigs and one thing was certain across all of the articles – a pig will grow according to the amount of food you feed it. I kept track of the calories being pumped into their little-but-growing bodies and knew I was not overfeeding them, but still the boys were growing so fast I could see them expanding week by week. The way they chased the chickens had become a little rough so within a few weeks we built them a pen of their own next door to the chooks with a waist-high fence so I could easily climb in to be with them or lean over it to scratch them on their bellies.

We encouraged the pigs to climb all over us, jumping up for face-to-face nuzzles, climbing on our backs to play-wrestle on the grass. Charlie and Lucy loved them and enjoyed getting down and dirty with them. Each school holidays when they visited from Brisbane, the kids became fixtures on the daily walk and the pigs gravitated toward them, Charlie in particular. The pigs even became stars of the kids' holiday short films, most notably the one titled *Pignapped*. In the movie there was a scene of the pigs running in slow motion to the song 'Born Free' and to this day it makes me smile. I played an evil pig-napper with a limp who wanted the pigs because of their superpowers, which made them worth two million dollars. We were one big happy human–swine family.

Rodney had learned to sit and I used this less as a demonstration of his intelligence and more to remind him that I was the farmer and therefore the boss. While he could dominate Billy, he should think twice about trying to take top-dog position from me.

We got the local vet to come out and give them their shots and treat them for mites (a common swine affliction and ours probably caught them from their neighbours, the chooks). Hearing Rodney's squeal as the vet held him in place to give him his injections sent adrenaline pumping through my body – I hated every minute of it and was visibly trembling.

'Are you okay?' the vet asked sweetly.

'Yeah, thanks, I'm okay,' I said.

'I was talking to the pig,' she said. Clearly I didn't learn my lesson from the nurse looking after Jeff after his marathon.

I finally let Rodney go, his squeals still ringing in my ears.

'Do you think we should get them neutered?' I asked the vet.

'Hmm, that depends,' she said putting away the needles. 'Do you want to eat them?'

'Definitely not!'

'Because after about three months their testosterone will taint the flavour of the meat and you won't be able to eat it. Are they aggressive at all?'

'Not in the slightest.'

'Then there's no real need to have it done. Besides, you'd need to build a crush cage for them, one that restricts their movement completely and we'd need to make sure everything was just so . . . in order to do the job properly.'

'Okay, sounds fair enough. I think we'll leave it for now.'

And that was the most significant mistake of all.

Just like the fish in the Palmer book, the boys grew and grew and grew. Now they could jump up and rest on the edge of their fence and the sight of the two of them side by side greeting guests and expecting scratches or food was quite adorable. We had the team from the Rivers clothing company come onto the property to shoot a catalogue and Rodney even featured in it, covered in mud and looking right into the lens with a brand-new pair of boots slung over the gate to their pen. We even chose a hand-drawn portrait of Rodney to grace our first ever Rosé, a deliciously dry and fruity wine we made out of our Shiraz grapes in 2015.

They proved to be very popular with the guests, who loved getting up close and scratching the boys' rough hair. Some guests wanted to climb in with them, one even asked if he could bring his wetsuit so he could play with them in the dam (a daily treat they absolutely loved). But as they grew, so too did their independence, and it wasn't uncommon for the boys to trot off on their own, disappear in the vineyard to eat grapes and vine leaves to their heart's content and only when they were good and ready, trot back down the road to their pen and put themselves to bed, bellies stuffed full of goodness – just as Jeff and I had once strolled down the hill from the North Annandale Hotel arm in arm, brimming full of merriment and beer.

Every morning the pigs greeted me with great excitement, their eyes so easy to connect with, their joy in anticipation of food also filled me with happiness. Rodney would be made to sit. (No matter how hard I tried, Billy just wasn't ever close to mastering it. At first I thought it was because he was a bit stupid but in the end I decided that he was the smarter one – *why sit for food like a dumb dog when you know that farmer guy is just going to end up giving it to us anyway?*)

As they grew in size, so did their determination to wrestle with each other. They were adolescent males, after all. It wasn't uncommon to see their long spiralling penises touch the ground and once they were of age, they both worked out how to pleasure themselves. Having a shoe covered in semen was not an uncommon occurrence, commonly known as cumboots.

One day I was busy cleaning the guesthouse and Jeff agreed to take the pigs for a walk with his visiting friends, Cameron and Maggie.

A few minutes later he came running into the kitchen, one eye closed.

'Oh my god! Your bloody pig!' he cried out.

'What? What is it?' I was ready to run out and give one of them mouth to mouth, if required.

'It's so disgusting,' he said, leaning over the sink to wash something from his face. 'Billy got his penis out and was rubbing it on the grass and then when he ran towards me it flicked up and I got cum in my eye.'

'Did you get the money shot?'

I have dined out on that story many, many times and think it will be in my repertoire until the day I die.

With the pigs' adolescence also came the belief that obeying the farmer wasn't a necessity. Increasingly when I took them for walks, the boys would wrestle each other and, in pig language, that meant bashing their necks against each other very hard, using the strength of their muscles to try and push the opponent further and further away. Turning your back on a male pig means you have surrendered and he is the dominant male. You are labelled submissive unless you challenge him in another wrestle and win. On occasion Rodney would wrestle with me, but not in a serious or threatening kind of way, more for fun. I was able to push him away and he knew that I wasn't easy to beat, at least not as easy as his brother. But the wrestles between the two of them were beginning to get more regular, and more aggressive, and I became increasingly conscious of their mood when I took them for walks. Eventually I decided that I would not let them out of their pen if any guests were on the property.

Another school holiday and the kids were down swimming in the dam while the pigs frolicked at its edge. Rodney was getting increasingly excited and swam right out into the middle to be near the kids, grunting animatedly to be a part of their fun. Finally he grew tired and made his way out and then headed straight for me.

It started as a rub against my leg, as the pigs frequently did when they were wet (water without mud makes them itchy so they will usually rub against anything for relief). But the rubbing then turned to wrestling and that soon became something more than just a game. It was the day Rodney decided to send a big fat 'fuck you' to Farmer Todd.

Every time he slammed his neck towards my knees, I pushed him with all the strength I could muster. I never felt in danger of being eaten alive or anything, but I knew if I gave in to him I would never ever be able to control him again. In the least, if he knocked me to the ground and trod on me he could easily have broken a few bones. He must have been over a hundred kilos.

I yelled at the kids, 'Stay in the dam! Do not get out of the dam!' They were both good swimmers and I knew it was the safest place for them.

On and on my struggle with Rodney went, both of us refusing to back down. The kids could see just how panicked I was and my fear sent my legs into melt down, not convenient when you're trying to push off a very determined beast. When Charlie decided to get out of the dam (everyone was disobeying me!) Lucy started crying and all I cared about at that point was making sure the kids were safe.

Mid-gladiatorial battle I managed to work out a strategy. Slowly I would coax Rodney back towards his pen without him realising it but that was about two hundred metres away and I was only gaining about a metre per neck to knee smash. I would have to push his hundred kilos with all my strength over two hundred times and I was already stuffed. I didn't know where Billy was but he was the least of my troubles – he had always been the pig that seemed more or less uninterested in people. Lucy was still crying and also screaming at Charlie for disobeying me, and meanwhile Charlie was confused and coming closer to Rodney. But in the end, Charlie's decision to get out of the dam gave me a better idea than trying to tame old Razorback on my own.

'Charlie run! Run to get Jeff! Be as fast as you can!'

It felt like ten minutes before Jeff arrived when in reality it must have been less than two. Rodney was not backing down and the more I pushed him, the more determined he was to win. Jeff provided enough of a distraction to get Rodney to abandon his struggle for domination. We got him into the pen, locked it securely and went to retrieve Billy, and a cold and shivering Lucy.

I was a complete wreck, emotionally and physically exhausted. I tried my best to laugh it off with the kids.

'Gee, I bet you thought things were serious there for a bit!' *Please excuse daddy while he changes his undies.* 'I had him under control the whole time, I was just worried about you kids.' *Vicky, Jane, it's Todd. I'm sorry, but the kids have been eaten alive by my pet pig. Would you like me to send you their thongs? That's all we have left of them, I'm afraid.*

Sadly, it was the last time I ever took Rodney and Billy for a walk. As loveable as they were, I wasn't a fucking idiot. I had to keep people safe from a Jekyll and Hyde cat, and now from a wild boar high on the scent of human fear.

After that day whenever I got in the pen with them we still bonded – there was more excitement from the boys than anything resembling anger or domination. I still felt close to them but I wasn't about to crawl around on all fours with them as I once had, and those tusks of Rodney's had taken on more sinister undertones.

The following school holidays Lucy came running into the latest villa we were building and yelled, 'Dad! The pigs are fighting and it's serious!'

Sure enough when we approached the pen we could see the pigs were in the middle of a major barney. Billy was bleeding on the side of his head (no doubt caused by one of Rodney's long bottom tusks) and Jeff was brave enough to get in there to separate them. Now he was not only the resident corpse handler, but also the wild beast tamer. The situation seemed to have calmed when Jeff climbed back out but something in Rodney snapped. Suddenly he jumped up onto the fence, reached his front trotters a long way over, and was instantly three quarters of the way out of his pen, all the while barking at me in an *I'm coming to get you, sucker* way I'd never heard from him before. Rodney was angry and he wanted a piece of me! Instinct kicked in and I pushed his snout as hard as I could, forcing him back into the pen, with the fall back onto his trotters taking the wind out of his sails a bit.

I ordered the kids to stay inside while Jeff, Vicky and my friend Scott scrambled around the property for materials to raise the height of the pig's fence. In just over an hour we were done and I breathed a sigh of relief.

But the boys fought more and more over the following weeks and their hormone-laden urine stank up the property. Semen-shined shoes were becoming the norm. When we came up with a solution to move the chickens to a fancy new pen and separate the boys, calm was restored to the property for many months . . . until the day Rodney decided to break through into Billy's pen.

If there is one thing you need to know about pigs, it's that their home is sacred ground. We didn't know how long their standoff lasted but by the time Jeff investigated the banging coming from the pen, there was a lot of blood, and teeth and tusks littered the ground. Can you imagine the force it takes to yank a three-inch tusk out of a pig's jaw? Imagine applying the same force to a wooden fence built to hold in chickens. Again, it was Jeff who went in there with them and somehow managed to coax Rodney back into his own pen, both poor pigs utterly exhausted by their tussle. Rodney's mud bath turned a bloody pink as he slid down into the cool wetness for relief and he breathed heavily in defeat. My heart sank for him.

Jeff boarded up the hole in the fence but we knew this could not go on – it was only a matter of time before they broke through into each other's side again or worse, broke out. Our business was our sole income and if a rampaging pig hurt someone we'd have our arses sued and everything we'd worked so hard for would be lost. As much as I loved my boys, the situation just couldn't continue.

It was too late to chop their balls off. While it might take away some of the pigs' aggression there was no guarantee it would remove it entirely. Besides, by then they were at 150 kilograms so any operation would require major infrastructure and we didn't have the money for that, nor for expensive operations or a fence that could guarantee peoples' safety. No animal sanctuary was going to take intact boars with a history of aggression either. We thought about offering them up for sale but with their strong personalities I feared the boys would be used for only one thing – the object of a hunt by drunken rednecks. The thought of their fear in that situation, in being taken advantage of, filled me with sorrow.

I never told Jeff but at night tears rolled silently down my cheeks. As we also couldn't afford what was required to have them put down by a vet, in order to save our livelihood it looked like the only option I had was to get a guy with a gun to do it for us. If watching *The Yearling* when I was five wasn't bad enough, now thirty-odd years later I was doing the same thing to my own pets. Our builder Pete found someone who was willing to do it – all we had to do was make the call. The gunman wouldn't take their bodies away, we would have to take care of that. And by we, I meant Jeff.

I hesitated for weeks, each morning as I looked into their eyes I sensed them pleading with me. As I scratched their heads and beneath their chins I pictured those same bodies being ripped apart by foxes and goannas, crows and ants. I spoke to them often, went to visit them several times a day. I gave them all the extra food I could find and they feasted on ice cream, chocolate, biscuits and milk. I had failed my boys on every level, I was a failure as a farmer and now they would suffer because of my stupidity and incompetence. Any time I thought of the sound of those gunshots, I cried. But the longer I agonised over making that call, the longer I played Russian roulette with the future of our business.

'Oh Rodney,' I said to him one morning as he grunted excitedly, waiting for his pellets. 'What have I done to you? How stupid am I to have put you through this? I'm sorry. I'm just so, so sorry, my little Rodders.'

But then luck gave the boys and me an incredible lifeline. Pete was working at a property down the road when a pig farmer came to deliver a boar to impregnate the resident sow. He overheard the farmer complain that he didn't have enough boars and how impossible it was to find any that still had their balls.

'You need a few studly pigs, eh? I think I might know of two,' Pete said, and I will never forget how Pete saved my boys.

I couldn't go out on the day they came to take my pigs away. I said my goodbyes that morning, locking eyes with each of them, thanking them for being such a special part of our lives. And I said sorry. Over and over again I apologised to Rodney and Billy and asked them to forgive me.

'Remember that time you knocked Vicky over?' I reminded them. 'How we laughed so much she couldn't get up again? Remember that video we made with the kids? Hey Rodney, you make sure you tell those girls about being on a wine label *and* in a fashion catalogue. And Billy? Sit for your new farmer like I know you can. He'll treat you better if you do, I promise he will. We had some good times, didn't we boys? Enough good times?'

I had to lock myself away in the office on the mezzanine of the shed when the pig farmers came. To begin with, I sat watching through the window until it hurt my heart too much to continue. Billy refused to come out of his pen and was clearly scared and that's all I could take. I put some music on through my headphones and shut my eyes and waited for Jeff to come and tell me that it was all over.

After an hour of trying to coax Billy out of his pen, the farmers gave up and went to Rodney instead. It came as no surprise to me that one sniff of the Tim Tams and fruit laid out to lure him onto the trailer was all Rodney needed, he waltzed onto it like he was a king on a chariot and then he was off on his big adventure. *Gidday, the name's Rodney or Rodders for short if you please*, he'd introduce himself to the ladies. *You might remember me from such wine labels as Block Eight's 2015 Shiraz Rosé? No? How about the Rivers catalogue . . .*

But Billy was another story. He'd always lived in his brother's shadow and after a year confined to his pen he wasn't coming out for anyone. Hadn't he been the pig that'd only ever fought back against the aggressor? He'd never shown me aggression, had he?

'It's not too late to keep him,' Jeff said as he came to find me while waiting for the farmers to return.

'I know, but we have to let him go too,' I said with a sigh. 'We have no choice. There's just no way of knowing how he'll behave. With Rodders not here maybe he'll want to become more dominant. I can't . . . Please go outside, Jeffy. I can't talk about it any more; please stop giving me false hope.'

Two hours later, Billy was finally coaxed onto the trailer and he left our farm for good. I felt empty and avoided their quiet and abandoned pens for several days.

'Do you want me to call the pig farmer and ask how they're doing?' Jeff asked.

'No, I don't want to know,' I said morosely.

If the boys were too aggressive or unable to perform, they would have been killed by now.

I never did hear about Rodney, the once famous Rivers catalogue model, but a few months after they were taken, Pete sent us a photo of Billy's piglets and I knew then we'd done what was best for the boys. I suppose what made it a little bit bearable saying goodbye was knowing that I still had Winston and Wesley.

I Shall Name You Winston

There's a small hobby farm at the end of our road that raises sheep and cows and has a resident emu we named Eddie. One day, as we drove past, we saw a goat – a brown-faced, mischievous-looking goat – poke its head out through the fence.

'Oh look, they've got a goat!' I pointed out to Jeff.

'Cute,' he said, and continued driving us home.

It was December 2016 and Lucy and Charlie were once again staying with us. I got up early the following day, which was already hot, and left them asleep while I went for a run. Jeff was up in the grapevines and the children knew they could call him using my phone if they needed anything.

It's a three-kilometre run to the end of the road and I got there happy to have avoided the swooping magpie (who ignores

165

Jeff every spring and summer but likes to scare the shit out of me, an Aussie kid with a long history of ornithophobia), and on the hobby farm's side of the road I again saw the brown-faced goat. He bleated anxiously at me in an indecipherable way but of course I couldn't help myself and walked over to give him a scratch on his head.

'Hey there, fella,' I said, 'Welcome to the neighbourhood. Aren't you lovely?' It was the first time I'd ever had any interaction with a goat.

Knowing Lucy and Charlie were still alone in the villa, I patted him again then got on with my run, but when my back was turned he'd burst through the barbed wire fence and was now approaching me. All of a sudden those horns of his became a little more threatening and I feared a strike from behind.

'You don't need to butt me, you know Mr Goaty, I'm very friendly,' I urged him against his own nature.

I scratched him to show just how friendly I was and then ran off as fast as my little legs could carry me and I'll be damned if the bloody goat didn't follow, step for step. I thought it best to try to outrun him but after about a kilometre his legs started giving way and I worried that he was going to fall and hurt himself. I stopped running and, seeing how tired he was, turned around to walk him back to his farm.

He bleated at me a few times on the slow walk back, as if to thank me for not making him run any further. Back at the farm I walked up to the fence, spread the wires apart and gave his rump an almighty shove – and then I bolted! And so did the goat, straight back through the fence to chase after me, determined not to let me out of his sight. To the goat, it seemed we were playing one big adventurous game. The kids were still alone and the goat was in danger of hurting himself against the fence if I persisted with these shenanigans.

'Okay, goat,' I surrendered. 'Let's see just how stubborn you are. It's another three kilometres from here . . .'

The goat stayed at my side, fell behind, caught up again, and repeated this pattern several times. He was getting tired so I encouraged him to continue, stopping to let him drink from rain puddles and giving him encouraging pats and scratches.

Almost there, getting closer now, come on you can do it . . . Winston.

'Winston.' I said the name aloud. 'Your name is Winston.' And of course giving him a name meant only one thing: I was instantly, irrevocably attached.

We got to our property's gate and I told Winston we just had to get up the driveway then I would be able to give him some water and food. Jeff had finished spraying the vines and was driving the tractor back to the shed. He looked at me walking down the road towards the house and then detected my four-legged friend. I shrugged, hands held out wide, to show him this wasn't exactly part of my morning's plan.

'Toddy, what have you done?' he asked as we approached.

'Jeff, meet Winston.' I told him the story and he went to wake the kids to meet my new friend.

Winston would not let me out of his sight. Tired after his long walk, he slept on the deck of the villa and let me lie against him like a pillow. When I left him even for a minute, he bleated madly and jumped up against the glass doors, those hooves of his clacking dangerously, making me worried he would smash right through. Having a goat for a pet was not one of the harebrained schemes we'd considered for Block Eight so Jeff called around the neighbours to see who he belonged to . . . but no one knew whose he was, not even the owner of the hobby farm where I first saw the goat at the end of the road. Winston would have to stay with us for the time being, until we could find his true owner. *Yeah right, who was I 'kidding'? I was already head over heels in love.*

Later that morning we locked Winston inside the chicken pen. As we drove off, Winston called out to me not to leave him, climbing up against the wire of the pen to watch us go. It was about a one-hour round trip to the Farmer's Warehouse where we told the girl behind the counter about our new pet. Coincidentally she'd raised goats and told us all about them, what they liked and didn't like, what food to buy, a wormer to give him and that goats preferred human company over all other animals, hence Winston's determination to follow me all the way home. Two hours later, we'd built Winston his new home so at least now I could go about my day without having a goat tap against the windows wherever I was.

He soon was starring in a quirky little movie the kids made called *Careful What You Wish For* where Charlie (who has a habit of eating with his mouth open) turns into Winston, who does the same.

I made sure Winston still got quality time with me: each afternoon we went for long walks around the property. Winston usually stayed by my side or went off to graze on fresh grass nearby. It really pained me to take him for walks but have to leave the pigs behind so I avoided their gazes as best I could and sometimes told Rodney a little white lie: that I was taking Winston to the vet every day, so he shouldn't be jealous.

Winston is a funny little character – very cheeky with a naughty look in his eyes, barrel chested and with a saunter to his gait. He is very vocal, too, and always tells us when he is hungry, or happy to see us, or annoyed by something we do. It's usually Jeff who annoys him, never me. Winston also loves to play, particularly with Jeff, who he often sneaks up on and butts, earning him the surname Buttworth-Jones. He did the same to Cheryl and ever since I've proclaimed him an uncanny judge of character. I worried he was lonely during the day with only the pigs to talk to through the adjoining fence, so early in the New Year Jeff and I drove about an hour to collect him a baby brother.

This little goat was the softest, cutest thing I had ever seen. He was scared to be leaving home so all the way in the car I held onto his hoof and stroked him gently. He was all white, had one ear up and one ear down and tiny little horns protruding from the top of his head.

'What shall we call him?' Jeff asked as he drove.

We went through a lot of names but none of them felt quite right for this all-white little bundle of fur. Eventually we landed on Wesley . . . Wesley Chesney.

The boys liked each other straightaway, though being bigger it was clear at the outset that Winston was the boss and whenever food comes into the equation Wesley is quickly shunted out of the way. Wesley joined Winston and me on our daily walk and quickly bonded, in large part thanks to the bottle of milk Wesley got handfed twice a day.

The simple fact of it was that those times in the pen with the goats were among the happiest of my day. I loved watching their personalities emerge and the way they use their hooves to urge me to continue scratching them. Wesley is always the more vocal goat, bleating out at me from a distance when he wants food or attention (i.e. all the time). His 'voice' is higher pitched than Winston's, whose own bleat is distinctively tainted with attitude. Winston developed a penchant for butting any human other than me, particularly little children, and then one day he took it upon himself to run away from me.

Unusually, the guests in the house had left the front door open. Since all the blinds were drawn, I thought they must have been taking an afternoon nap after a long day of wine tasting. Sure enough, Winston (with Wesley in tow) made a direct line for the house and then bleated with delight when he saw the front door was open. I bolted after them as fast as I could but it was too late, they had disappeared inside. I got to the door to find them both standing on the couch, hoof prints embedding in the leather.

'Winston! Come here!' I whispered harshly. To which he bleated very loudly.

I imagined the guests waking from their rest and asking each other: *Did you hear a bleat coming from the lounge room? No . . . surely you imagined it?* At least it was my hope that no one in their right mind would believe two goats had made themselves at home on the couch. Eventually I coaxed the naughty twosome outside, but ever since that day I have walked Winston in a harness, all the better to grab a hold of him when he gets the notion to cause havoc . . . which happens often enough.

Having learned my lesson with Rodney and Billy, and seeing that Winston had been neutered, we had a band placed around Wesley's testicles to reduce the chances of him showing dominant or aggressive behaviour. It was the least painful way of removing them and after the initial hour of discomfort, Wesley couldn't have cared less.

One morning I made Jeff his favourite breakfast of beans on toast. You can take the boy out of England . . .

'You're being very nice to me today. What did you do wrong?'

'Oh don't be like that, I don't always have something to apologise for, I just thought it would be nice to treat you to something special.'

He sat down happily waiting for me to serve his meal. A plate of steaming hot beans and two overly dark toasted muffins.

I even made him a cup of tea and, after he sat and began eating, I placed down a little side plate with the morning's real treat.

'I got you something extra special for breakfast,' I said.

He looked at it for a moment in confusion and then it dawned on him.

'Is that what I think it is?'

'Sure is! Must have popped off this morning!' Wesley's ball bag was tiny and shrivelled.

'You are truly disgusting,' he said as we got the giggles.

In March 2017, just as Wesley was giving up the bottle, Jeff came inside the guesthouse to interrupt my cleaning.

'You'd better come outside,' he said forlornly. 'And you're not going to like it.'

Winston's original owners had tracked him down. He was raised by a sixteen-year-old boy whose parents had got divorced, and in the separation of lives Winston had been taken to graze on a property five doors down from us, where the boy's aunt cleaned a house rented out to tourists. The boy's dad had run into one of our neighbours and had asked if they'd spotted the missing goat.

'You'll find the goat at the end of the road,' they were told, along with directions to our home.

'He cried for weeks when Stampy went missing,' the father explained before telling the story. 'The plan was to visit him as often as we could and bring him a horse for company but within two days of dropping him off he'd disappeared. We thought someone had stolen him.'

I took them up to the pen and expected a reunion of YouTube-worthy emotion but if Winston (what kind of name is Stampy!) recognised the boy he showed no signs.

'I've become quite attached to your goat,' I tried feebly, 'Are you sure you want to take him back? I could pay you for him.'

'No, I miss him too much,' the boy said shyly. 'I raised him from a baby and I was so sad to lose him. You can come down the road and visit him any time you like . . .'

'I run along that road almost every day,' I explained to the father. 'What do you want me to do if he follows me again?'

'If that happens, we'll have to sort something out.'

Winston was taken from the pen and tied to the back of the truck and, as they drove off, Wesley bleated out great big sobs of anguish. I knew exactly how he was feeling. For all the bullying he'd received he sure did sound sad to see his big brother taken away from him.

I walked into the house dismayed, at a loss. Jeff followed behind.

'I don't think I can do this any more,' I said. 'First the pigs and now Winston, it's breaking my fucking heart. I feel like I've lost my best friend.' Then I burst into tears.

Jeff threw his arms around me. 'It's okay, Toddy. We'll go and visit him as often as you like; we'll get another goat as soon as we can.'

But there was just something about Winston I had grown very fond of. He wasn't just another goat; he'd chosen me to follow home and from that day on we'd been the best of friends. Other people looked at those horns of his and felt threatened, I just saw a loving, lovable young chap who wanted to play and be by my side. I'd never once felt in danger in his company.

'I need to man up! It's a goat for Christ's sake!' I tried to lighten the situation but dammit, I was miserable. 'That kid is just sixteen, it's his goat, he was never really mine . . .'

Wesley was inconsolable so I let him out of the pen and took him into the forbidden area of the vegie patch. Together we weeded the garden beds and he got treats of stolen carrots and spinach. We worked together for two hours or so, keeping each other company, telling each other how much we missed Winston, even his bossiness and the head butts.

'What about the way he ran!' I said to Wesley with a chuckle, like we were reminiscing at a mate's funeral. 'And the way he ate bananas!' I wiped tears from my eyes and knew that Wesley comprehended exactly what I was saying. 'Maybe we will go and get you another brother? Or a girlfriend maybe? Would you like that?' And Wesley stopped chewing spinach for a moment and looked off into the distance, as he always does when he has a mouthful of something delicious, and that day it was as if he was imagining whether life without Winston would ever be the same.

Just as Wesley and I were getting ready to hang up our gardening gloves for the day, my phone rang.

'Hey mate, this is Stampy's dad.' *His name isn't fucking Stampy!* I could have screamed, but did not. 'My boy has got something to say to you.'

My heart sank, my stomach swirled.

'Um . . .' the kid was so nervous it could only mean one thing. 'I . . . I was just thinking . . . he's got such a nice home there with you and . . . you walk him every day and . . . did you say you would be happy to offer me some money for him?'

Bingo! 'Yes,' I said calmly, though internally I was doing cartwheels.

'How . . . how much . . . money were you thinking?'

'Well you tell me what *you* think.'

'I really don't know.'

'On Gumtree you can get a goat for anywhere between eighty and a hundred and twenty dollars.'

'How about one hundred then?'

'Okay. It's a deal.'

'Thanks. We'll bring him back after Dad's finished work down here.'

I sent Jeff off to get the cash, deciding that a hundred and fifty dollars would be my reward to the boy for not being greedy when I was clearly more attached to the goat than he.

'How high would you have gone?' Jeff asked before he left to get the cash.

'Five hundred without blinking,' I said, 'and up to a thousand at a push. Now go get my mate back.'

By late afternoon we still hadn't heard from the boy or his dad so on the way back from the bank I asked Jeff to drop off the cash and see what the situation was. He called from the farm down the road.

'We're coming home!'

I waited excitedly for them to turn up the driveway and then I saw that familiar silhouette of Winston, sitting on the front seat of the Barina no less, his head and horns poking out the passenger side window. When he saw me he bleated excitedly.

'You know, he hasn't made a single sound all the way home and then he saw you and he called out! He knows this is his home, he knows who you are.'

Well of course he did. We are such good friends, in fact, Winston and I were featured in a photographic book, *Outback Mates*.

17

Massaging a Chicken in a Warm Water Bath

Winston and his sidekick Wesley were not the only animals on the property that liked to investigate what the guests were up to. We've had many chickens over the years; lost a lot to foxes, heat stroke and being eggbound, but a few emerged with incredibly strong personalities – and some were complete stickybeaks.

One memorable character was Lizzie Birdsworth, the chicken with a limp. When left in the pen with all the other hens, it was no secret she was the bottom of the pecking order because of her very visible affliction. Most chooks will flee from a pecking attack but Lizzie never could, so when one of the chickens started in on her, she just lay prostrate until it was over. It was truly horrible to see and no amount of shooing away the chickens could deter them from their nastiness. Once the other chickens saw her vulnerability they too would pounce and it wasn't uncommon to see three or four chickens pecking away at her. Things turned nasty one day and the pecking attack had been so savage we found her with a large bloody hole in the top of her head. The only thing to do was to remove her from the pen so Jeff set her up a nice wooden house on the deck of the villa we were building at the time, Water View.

One day as I was building outside (yes *me*, building without Jeff!), a large goanna came to sniff Lizzie the chook out. I think he had his eye on her for lunch. I managed to scare him off by throwing a few pieces of structural pine near him but about an hour later he approached again. This time, Leroy was outside and watching with keen interest as the lizard came towards us and I wondered if he remembered the time he'd watched one eat a rabbit. This day as the goanna got closer, however, Leroy looked determined not to run away.

'Roy?' I called out to him. 'Roy!' I said a little more forcefully.

But Leroy was ignoring me. The goanna was edging closer and closer and I feared the worst but also wanted Leroy to learn a lesson if the goanna got *too* close. By now it was about two metres from Leroy, then one ... and when it took one step further Leroy puffed himself up, arched his back and let out a terrifying growl. The goanna hightailed it out of there faster than I've ever seen one move and Leroy came back to me full of pride, purring around my legs as if to ask for praise for protecting me. He repeated the same feat a few years later when a goanna came hunting after another of our birds. Jeff managed to scare the lizard off in the nick of time and as he turned around to reassure the petrified birds, there was Leroy all puffed up and hissing – Jeff's backup guy for the all-in brawl.

Lizzie loved being the only free-range chook on the property. Each morning we would let her out of her little hut and off she'd go exploring, looking for worms and bugs. She was particularly drawn to the sound of human voices so if Jeff had the radio on while he worked she would limp over to keep him company. One day one of our guests left his villa door open while he took a shower and when he came out of his bathroom Lizzie had made herself comfortable on the couch, thank you very much indeed. She was everybody's favourite animal for some time, limping her way from place to place, but when we finished the fourth villa she had to be moved. A few weeks later I found her hiding and didn't think much of it, but sadly, the next day she was dead.

Lizzie's death reminded me of the time my desk phone at work rang back in early 2013.

'—'s sick,' Jeff said softly.

I didn't catch the name but immediately thought of Leroy. We'd often worried about his tree change and the wide array of wild animals he would be encountering (foxes, snakes, huge goannas, wild dogs, feral cats, to name but a few). All Leroy's urban antics flashed before my eyes when Jeff told me someone was sick because I knew Leroy thought he was tougher than he actually was. Block Eight was no Annandale alley.

'What? What's wrong?'

'I'm at the vet and they can't fix it,' he said, again speaking softly.

'Jeff, tell me what's happened!'

'She can't breathe.'

'*She*? Who?'

'Barry!'

Barry was one of the first chooks we ever purchased, a black bird so named by the kids, for whatever reason. Now that I knew it wasn't Leroy, I calmed down to better understand the situation.

'I went out to feed them this morning and she was rasping heavily, like something was caught in her throat.'

'Has she been smoking?'

'What? Toddy, this is serious!'

'Sorry. What did the vet say?'

'They said they aren't equipped to handle her and that I would need to take her to Sugarloaf because they're good with birds there.'

'What's Sugarloaf?'

'An animal hospital about an hour away.'

'Okay. So what do you want to do?'

'She sounds awful Toddy, really awful.'

'Why don't you take her to the hospital and get their opinion on her and then we'll make a decision from there.'

Sugarloaf admitted her as an emergency.

'What's her name?' the receptionist asked Jeff.

'Barry.'

'Is it a rooster?'

'No, *she's* a hen.'

Dr Alex is an avian specialist. He examined Barry and gave Jeff his diagnosis. She would need to remain in care overnight and be placed in an oxygen tank, just like Michael Jackson but without a chimp for a companion. She might also need an exploratory scope inserted down her throat.

'How much is all that going to cost?' I asked Jeff when he relayed the information.

'Probably around six hundred dollars,' he said.

'Okay,' I sighed. 'I think we need to realise that a chicken is a chicken and she provides us eggs. No chicken in the world is worth that much, we just can't afford that.'

'What are you saying?'

'Is she in any pain?'

'No, I don't think so.'

'So I think you should take her home and see how she goes.'

Almost every day we expected to find Barry gone but she lived on ... and on ... and on. Barry was also immortalised on one of those early wine labels, on our first Shiraz. Barry outlived all but one of her five sisters from our original chook purchase – Brooke (named by Lucy), who'd been the top of the pecking order.

I once asked Lucy where she'd got the name Brooke and she looked at me like I was stupid. 'You know: *brook brook*,' she clucked.

So a few months after Lizzie's death when I saw Brooke lying very still I kept a close eye on her and, noting she hadn't moved the following day, took action. Jeff took her inside and put her on a comfortable bed. He tried to handfeed her and give her water but she pecked at it with very little energy. We thought she might have been suffering from heat stroke or perhaps had been accidently hurt by one of the goats so hoped she would show signs of recovery after a few days' respite. On the third morning, however, she still looked as though she was paralysed and when I went to tend to her, she was sitting in a stinking pool of her own faeces. Her eyes were more or less lifeless.

'What are we going to do?' Jeff asked. He is the true birdman on the property; my affections are more with the mammals.

'I don't think she's going to recover, I think she's paralysed and we need to put her out of her misery.'

'Put her down at the vet, you mean?'

'No. I mean, man up and put her out of her misery.'

'Toddy, what are you saying?'

'I think we need to kill her quickly and humanely, and take care of it ourselves like normal farmers do.'

To be honest, I'm not sure where the bravado had suddenly come from. It just didn't feel right to run off to the vet asking for a lethal injection every time one of our chickens showed a sign of irreparable illness. I had seen Paul West chop off a chook's head on *River Cottage Australia* and the imagery had been utterly disturbing (admittedly even for him) now here I was suggesting that we (Jeff) should do the same. Part of the justification was financial – we certainly didn't have a few hundred dollars for a needle every time a chook was close to death, and part of it was taking ownership of the lives we'd brought onto the property and their accompanying deaths, when it was within our control and the most humane thing to do.

'How would you do it?' Jeff asked.

'I think you should chop her head off with an axe,' I suggested. 'She won't even know what's hit her and then you'll have relieved her suffering.'

'Oh Toddy, I couldn't . . . I can't . . . Can't you do it?'

'No way!' I said determinedly. 'Not a chance in hell.' But then I looked at poor Brooke, who'd once been the very top of the pecking order, a big fat healthy hen full of her own sense of importance, and that was a far cry from the pathetic lifeless bird that I saw lying at my feet. 'Go get the axe,' I commanded. 'But I can't remove the body, you'll have to take care of that.'

Feel free to skip over the next paragraph because I can tell you – without question – that it is the hardest thing I have ever had to do.

We got a thick wooden board to lay Brooke down upon, and made sure the axe was sharp and rust-free. We carried Brooke outside, stroking her gently on the back. Jeff gave her a spoonful of strawberry yoghurt and she licked at it without much gusto, but even that small amount was a symbolic last meal of a richness she had never had before. We lay her down on the board ensuring she was as comfortable as possible, coaxing her neck out straight. I had told Jeff that I would do it with my eyes closed but I now saw that would be foolish and unfair to Brooke – if I missed the results could have been catastrophic. I raised the axe over my shoulder and brought it down with all of the strength I could muster, careful to aim it precisely on her neck. The blade went through with ease and the blood ran quickly from the top of her shoulders and out of her mouth came some of the strawberry yoghurt. I was at once disgusted with myself, and proud in a bizarre kind of way, that I could force aside my own squeamishness to bring a swift and hopefully painless end to Brooke's suffering. I can categorically say that I will never, ever kill a bird ever again.

Brooke's death haunted me for many days. In my dreams I saw her head separated from her body, the blood, the yoghurt, and just how ridiculously easy it was to take her life. Jeff had disposed of her body (it was always our philosophy to place dead chickens in the bush far away from their pens so that they could be eaten by hungry animals) but the blood pool had remained behind.

I had spent most of my twenties as a pescetarian and my philosophy was simple. If I wasn't prepared to kill an animal for myself then I wouldn't eat it – so, as I found catching and preparing fish easy, it felt acceptable to me to continue eating them. But killing Brooke had blurred the line . . . I had killed her to end her suffering, I knew now I could never, ever kill a bird to eat it, so why was I eating supermarket-packaged chicken several nights a week? Killing Brooke brought with it, in many ways, that dilemma of whether it was acceptable having industry do your dirty work for you so you could push it far back into the recesses of your mind. I could no longer eat pork on the bone; would never consider eating goat but now I had to decide: was it still okay to eat other meats?

Over the years you get to know chickens and their illnesses better. There are products you can buy to place in their water on particularly hot days and this medication helps them stay cool during heatwaves. Five years after Barry's trip to the vet, another of our chickens, Nicks, came down with a mystery illness similar to the one I'd seen in Lizzie and Brooke, only she could at least still walk.

It was 31 December 2017 and we were due at the neighbours' house to celebrate New Year's Eve. But it was getting later and later in the afternoon and Nicks wasn't getting any better and the water we'd been force-feeding her didn't seem to be making a difference.

'Do you think she might be eggbound?' I asked Jeff. We looked it up on the internet and sure enough, Nicks was displaying nearly all the symptoms.

'Sorry we're late,' I said to Natalie and Andrew about an hour later. 'We've been massaging our chicken's abdomen in a warm water bath.'

'You've what?' Natalie asked with a laugh.

I explained further. As we were still without running water inside the villa we were now building for ourselves, Jeff had sponged himself down while standing in a large crate of warm water from the kettle so we'd placed Nicks in it to help ease her straining. 'Apparently it's what you need to do if you think they're eggbound.'

'You guys ... honestly ...' she said and introduced me to one of her friends.

As odd as it may sound, it worked. When we came home later that night Nicks had laid an egg on the bathroom floor where she'd been placed on a plush cushion for comfort. I picked her up and placed her on my chest and stroked her for half an hour or so before we went to bed, the chicken gradually falling asleep in my arms. The next day she was completely back to normal and while we'd lost many other chickens to heat stroke (and fox attack), I wondered, had I been smart enough to think of them being eggbound as the cause, whether I might have been able to save Lizzie and Brooke from their horrible deaths.

Nicks and her sister Stevie are the most tactile birds we've ever owned. I named them for Stevie Nicks because the night we saw her in concert at a local vineyard with Chris and Verity was also the night a fox had taken five of our six chickens. Stevie and Nicks love to be picked up and stroked and rarely struggle to be set back down. At dusk all Jeff has to do is call 'Chook, chook!' and they will come running to him, ready to be carried back to their roost and locked away for the night in the Taj Mahal of chook pens that Jeff built, safe from foxes and other nasties. If they hear voices, they gravitate towards humans, always wanting in on the action, just as Lizzie had.

Naturally, when any of the chickens died it was Jeff's job to come and retrieve the body. He was so proficient at handling carcasses it just didn't make sense to train me in the same skill.

The chooks weren't the only fowls on the property.

We'd taken Mel, Jesus, and their young daughters, Sophia and Amelie, to the Hunter Valley Zoo in the spring of 2016. Watching the girls interact with the animals was a genuine pleasure. I also looked at the various creatures speculatively. Over the years we'd featured different animals on each of our wine labels but after perch, yabbies, ducks, chickens, pigs and kangaroos we were running out of logical options.

Mel pointed to a peacock trailing its magnificent tail: 'That's what you need next, one of those. Aren't they lovely?'

I laughed but didn't seriously consider it and for the rest of the zoo visit we played 'spot the possible wine-label animal' but nothing was an actual contender.

Strangely enough, two weeks later I walked into the local pet shop to buy some supplies and the owner, Trevor, showed me a peacock in a small cage and a peahen housed in with the chooks. I'd never really entertained the notion of owning exotic birds but I knew we could give them a good home and . . . hmm, maybe a peacock strolling around the grounds would be just a little bit fabulous.

Spencer and Katharine (Kate for short), as I named them, were soon ours. The next few hours were spent researching online how to keep peafowl. They moved in with the chickens at first because we needed to keep them confined until they learned where home was, otherwise they would roam away. After three months it was time to let them out, and take our chances on Spencer's instinct to flee, but they seemed happy to stay with us and in the evenings made their (separate) homes high up in the gum trees, safe from predators.

The first time we ever saw Spencer display, in early October, was a monumental occasion, though thanks to his cramped cage at the pet shop a lot of his lovely feathers were broken and tatty. He's a bird of breathtaking beauty and the dance he does to woo Kate is spectacular in itself. In autumn he loses all his tail feathers, only to have longer ones emerge the following spring. By nature, peafowl are very skittish so we've never really had the chance to get close to them or bond, but Spencer loves displaying for people so often shows off in front of our impressed guests.

Our first summer with the birds, Kate sat on six eggs. Peafowl sit patiently for up to five weeks, only leaving the eggs for something to eat and to ward off potential enemies in a very vocal and impressive run about the property. Kate hatched four of her eggs on our friend Lachlan's birthday in March and we assumed she would not need any help from us, but then the beautiful little chicks began to die. By day three we knew it was time to intervene and decided to remove the chicks from Kate so we could look after them in a cage inside our villa. Separating a mother bird from her chicks is something you will only try once. Kate was beside herself, running around calling out for the chicks and the whole scene was so distressing we decided to bring them back together. I was pretty adept at the tractor and other equipment, but I just couldn't master the art of being an unfeeling farmer when it came to animal welfare.

Jeff built Kate a separate little home inside the chicken pen. But when another chick died we re-thought the situation and brought Kate inside the shed with her two remaining chicks, and went and bought a heat lamp to keep them warm through the chilly autumn nights. The following day yet another chick died which left Kate with just one, the strongest we supposed, named Freddie by Sophia. It wasn't long until Freddie grew to be as large as her mother and it became a lovely sight watching them patrol the property together, or coming up to our window begging for some of Leroy's cat biscuits.

Jump forward a year and Kate was again sitting on six eggs. This time she had chosen to roost under the house and we assumed the eggs would be vulnerable to goannas but decided to let nature take its course. I was watering the orchard on the day of our twelfth anniversary in February when she emerged with six chicks. We immediately swung into action and cornered Kate into the cat carrier, each chick quickly followed. They spent two nights under a lamp inside the house then were moved to a large covered lean-to next to the shed and we watched them anxiously. This time none of them died. Finally we'd mastered how to help Kate see them through.

185

There was a small gap in the top of the wall of the lean-to and one of the chicks escaped one day and flew straight down to the bush in front of one of the villas. I couldn't find it and assumed the little chick would perish pretty quickly without its heat lamp or Kate to keep it warm. Two days later it returned, but refused to be caught. Freddie heard the chick's squawks and flew down to tend to it. We watched her fly up into the tree and down again, over and over, trying to show her little sibling how it was done, but eventually the chick gave up and flew away. Surely this would spell its end? But two days later, it had not only returned but had found its way back inside to be with Kate.

This adventuresome chick was white, one of two. At the end of their first three months, when we'd originally planned to sell all of them, we decided instead to keep the two white chicks. Jeff named them Tom and Shelley for the actors in his favourite film/ lifestyle inspiration, *The Money Pit*. I suppose it was better than naming them Mary and J. Blige but I'd secretly been hoping to name them Meryl and Jack from *my* favourite film, *Heartburn*.

By her third season, we were confident that Kate would allow us to help her through to hatching but close to the date we noticed she was limping. Poor Kate had broken her toe, which made sitting on those eggs all day very uncomfortable. I called Dr Alex at Sugarloaf and between us we agreed the best course of action was to leave Kate until the eggs hatched. Whether it was because of her gimpy foot, or thanks to Tom and Shelley, on hatching day, three of her eight eggs had been broken and contained dead chicks, and Kate abandoned two more eggs so she was left with only three chicks, one white and two coloured.

When we did get Kate to the vet, the prognosis was not great. The toe had become infected and would need to be amputated. Jeff called me and delivered the news and without any hesitation I said for him to go ahead. It was going to be a very expensive little procedure, but after five years of raising all these animals, I suppose I had become dedicated to their wellbeing and unlike poor old Barry when we first began, and Brooke's disturbing fate, leaving Kate's toe untreated was not an option. We went through the stress of administering her painkillers and antibiotics twice a day by forcefully shoving them down her throat and switched on the heat lamp every night to keep the chicks warm. Wearing our new grey Block Eight uniforms, I'd never felt more like a zookeeper but given half the chance I would have spent all day every day tending to the animals.

'She's only got three chicks . . . should we keep them all?'

I'd sworn Tom and Shelley would be the last peafowl we added to our family, but separating Kate from her three just seemed a little cruel and senseless.

Tom and Shelley, as is a peafowl's nature, got hold of one of the chicks and traumatised it. Kate knew its fate and ignored it so we brought it inside and I stroked the little warm body until it died in my hands. Though we knew nothing of this bird or its personality, it was still a very sad moment; senseless that one of the birds should attack its brother or sister, just because.

'She only has two babies now . . .' Jeff said.

'Okay, we'll keep them,' I said.

The next day we discovered that Freddie was sitting on six eggs of her own. Again on hatching day some of the eggs looked to have been cracked and, being a new mother, Freddie abandoned the others and raised only one. It was such a lovely sight watching Freddie and Freddie Junior roam the property, just as Kate and Freddie had done before, and have them come to eat the morning porridge Jeff so dedicatedly provided them.

18

When a Father Calls

In July 2015, Dad called from Gosford Hospital: Mum had been admitted to Emergency. Mum's lifelong fear of hospitals and the fact that Dad was calling (Dad rarely called) told me the situation was serious. Mum had been experiencing abdominal pain for a few weeks but tests failed to detect the cause. She'd woken that morning in extreme pain, went to her GP and was finally referred for a scan, which had shown a large black mass somewhere near her appendix. I was in the middle of feeding the animals when I took the call and became completely distracted. I knew Mum would loathe being cooped up in a hospital bed and would be petrified of an uncertain diagnosis, filling her mind with horrific worst-case scenarios. I hoped Dad would be able to keep his cool and guide her through this.

Mum never gets sick. In fact, the only story she ever tells of being ill was back when she was a young mother in the seventies. She'd got my two older brothers ready for school while dealing with a particularly nasty head cold and once they'd left she had zero energy so was forced to climb into bed. Usually an active and demanding toddler, I'd crawled right into bed beside her and quietly lay there against her spine for hours as she slept. We emerged from bed together late in the afternoon, Mum feeling refreshed and able to face the after-school onslaught of my brothers. She tells the story often and I love that she remembers it so fondly.

More tests in the hospital proved inconclusive. In short, no one was able to tell her why she was in pain, or what the black mass was. It was such a large and obtrusive growth the doctors and specialists couldn't get a clear view of what was going on. Mum was administered pain relief and it was decided that rather than cut her open for investigative surgery, the safer course of action was to put her on an antibiotic drip. Hopefully this would clear up the mass a little, perhaps even diminish it, and then they'd be able to identify the root cause of her pain. Thankfully the treatment worked and it, coupled with a heavy dose of more medication at home, showed a clearing up of what they now assumed was a significant infection, though not of the appendix. Outwardly, Mum slowly returned to normal but she would later confess that inside she knew things were not quite right.

It was a few months later that the bleeding began. Mum was referred to her surgeon, the doctor who'd come close to opening her up that July night in Gosford Hospital. He sent her for more tests, an MRI and another scan and I drove down to his surgery to meet Mum and Dad and get the results. Mum was quiet and pale. I overcompensated for her fear by talking too much, making stupid jokes about the world's ugliest tissue box cover in the waiting room and generally trying to take her mind off things. Finally it was our turn to be seen and once we were seated, the doctor cut to the chase.

'We have identified a small number of malignant cells in your bowel.'

Tears welled in my father's eyes, Mum tried her best to be stoic. I focused intensely on what the doctor was saying so I could relay it to my brothers, and remind Mum and Dad of what he'd said once the shock had worn off.

'Our first course of action is to remove that part of your bowel. Whenever these types of cells are present this is our best treatment, a preventative course.'

'Will I need a bag?' Mum asked barely above a whisper. Thankfully she was told no. A colostomy bag represented ill health, sickness . . . states of being my mother resists at all costs.

Mum was booked in for her major operation for late October. About one third of her bowel would be removed and though it would result in a long period of considerable digestive problems, it should also mean that malignant cells would never return. The operation was a success and after five days in hospital Mum returned home to continue her recuperation.

Every year for the past twenty-one years, my mother and I treat ourselves to a fancy meal on Melbourne Cup night. It began in response to my father's decision to take my eldest brother, Grant, out to the races one year and while their tradition soon fizzled, ours only grew in strength. Our rule is simple: no one else is ever invited except my middle brother, Glen, when he is home from Canada, and we can never visit the same restaurant twice. This night has provided the three of us with a lifetime of funny tales and fond memories.

One year we decided to take Mum to a drag show at the Albury Hotel, affectionately known around the scene as The All Blurry.

'Well, well, well, what do we have here?' One of the drag queens asked my mother, mid-act. Not usually one for public attention, my mother stood up fearlessly.

'My name's Judy!' she said boldly.

'And what the fuck brings you to a place like this, Judy?'

'I'm here with my two gay sons,' Mum said proudly. It was the first time I'd ever heard her say those words.

'You lucky fucking mole,' the drag queen said. 'They're never going to love another woman as much as they love you.'

'I know,' Mum said as she sat down, 'I know.'

I'd never seen my mother so bright eyed and in her element but then she had been somewhat of a disco queen in her thirties. Complete strangers came up to her and asked what she was doing there and when she told them her story, many of them cried on her shoulder that their own parents had rejected them, kicked them out of home or never spoken to them again. It was as if Mum had become a celebrity for the night and though she was new to the role; she took to it like a second skin.

Mum was sworn to secrecy; that evening was never to be mentioned to Dad, it just wasn't something he'd be all that fond of, to imagine his wife in that sort of environment playing den mother to Sydney's gay children. Months later, my parents were driving Glen and James to the airport and Mum piped up: 'Isn't that the All Blurries?'

'What's that?' Dad asked.

'Have we been there?' Glen asked.

And the car fell silent. We could only imagine the thoughts running through Dad's mind.

At another Melbourne Cup dinner, Glen told us of his fear that his death would be at the hand of an axe-wielding madman.

It was little wonder he worried about it given that during his adolescence Grant hid scary photos of Rasputin beneath Glen's pillow and left Glen's Western Suburbs Magpies clown hung from his wardrobe pole, knowing full well that Glen checked the wardrobe every single night before sleep (thanks to watching *When a Stranger Calls* as a young kid). One night he spent the best part of an hour crouched in said wardrobe so when Glen checked it just before turning out the lights Grant burst out with a yell. To this day Grant likes to give his daughters frights and I've no idea how his long-suffering wife, Bec, deals with living with a boy-man who loves playing these little games. But then, nothing quite fills me with the same joy as hiding around corners to frighten Jeff.

With Mum just out of hospital, still in pain and with barely any appetite, she and I decided to delay the dinner until she was better. I teed it up with Dad to surprise her with a home-cooked meal instead on Melbourne Cup night. Dad was out calling bingo so it gave Mum and me a chance to have a proper catch up.

Over the ensuing weeks Mum got better and aside from gastro problems everything else seemed to return to normal. That she'd sailed through the trauma with hardly any painkillers, zero complaint and no talk of doom was no surprise to any of us. My mother is the backbone of our family and she wasn't about to let a little thing like the removal of a third of her bowel get her down.

'You're looking thinner,' I said to her. 'Has half your poo shoot been removed or something? I know Cher had a rib taken out to look thinner, wouldn't that have been easier?'

'Don't make me laugh, Toddy; it hurts too much to laugh.'

'I'd be avoiding mirrors in that case . . .'

'Stop it!' she said, clutching her stomach.

We finally celebrated our actual Melbourne Cup dinner at a local Hunter Valley restaurant shortly before my birthday in December.

'Were you scared of dying?' I asked over the second bottle of wine.

'Yes,' she said simply. 'But I'm not the type to dramatise things. I had to face the operation, what other choice did I have? Get on with it.'

But then in May 2016 the bleeding returned. Mum was sent for yet more tests, just like the ones before and we were once more summoned to her surgeon to receive the results.

'Bleeding after an operation like that is completely normal, Mum,' I'd said to her repeatedly. 'You'll see, it's going to be nothing at all.'

'You have bowel cancer,' her surgeon said frankly.

Mum and Dad were both crying. I felt like I'd been smashed into by a road train. It was the worst possible news and a scenario I'd never entertained – not even for a millisecond.

Just a few months since her operation to remove part of her bowel where cancerous cells had been found, a cancerous growth in the remaining bowel was now visible. Mum would require intensive radiation – every weekday for six weeks.

Outside the surgery I gave my mother a long hard squeeze.

'We'll face this together, Mum, you have my full support. This bastard is not going to beat you!'

I drove them both home and made us all cups of tea.

'You heard the doctor, Mum,' I said to her concerned face, 'You're not going to lose your hair and they have such good medication for nausea now it's likely you won't even get sick. It'll be a walk in the park for someone as strong as you.'

Dad, who always wore his heart on his sleeve, was not quite so firm in his positive resolve and was already on the phone to my mother's family sharing the news and crying. I raised my eyebrows at Mum.

'It's important *you* stay positive, Mum. And I will be with you every step of the way.'

I went with Mum to most of her initial appointments and we were both shocked to learn that she would also be undergoing chemotherapy when her surgeon had said it would just be radiation. But the meeting with the oncologist was the worst. While most of Mum's appointments and treatment had taken place at the new, light, airy and rather lovely Central Coast Cancer Centre (which coincidentally had a painting in the waiting area by our friend Cheryl's painter ex-husband, making me feel Cheryl's positivity was with Mum and me every step of the way), that first meeting with the chemo guy was at Wyong Hospital and it was the drabbest, most soul-destroying environment you would never want to see.

The gravity of the situation slapped my mum hard and on the way out she stopped in reception to pick out two cheap and nasty headscarves. She was crying as we walked to the car.

'What have you got there?' Jeff asked her. (He also came to most of the initial meetings.)

'Just some scarves, just in case . . .' Mum tried her best to hide the tears.

'Oh Jude, if you go bald you won't be wearing some two-dollar op shop scarf, give those to me.' He took them off my mother and ran to put them back in the basket. I threw my arms around Mum as we waited for Jeff to come back.

'It's okay to be scared, Mum,' I whispered in her ear, 'but you don't need to be, because you have me.'

'If you go bald, after I slap your head like Benny Hill used to do to his sidekicks, I will be going out to buy you the fanciest scarf I can find. You don't need to look sick *and* cheap, Jude,' Jeff said when he came back.

We all got the giggles.

'Shame my old boss threw away his toupees,' he went on, 'I could have saved them for you.'

'Oh, what about hair in a can, Mum? I hear these days it comes in more colours than just baby shit green and mission brown.'

'Leroy loses a lot of fur too . . . I'll brush him every night and pop it all in a freezer bag for you.'

'I think you'd look even better than Liz Taylor with a shaved head,' I offered. 'But you won't be gettin' no diamonds so don't even think about it.'

'Thanks, you two,' Mum said wiping away tears that were thankfully now happy ones, 'I really don't think I could do this without you.'

'Rubbish,' I said. 'You're the strongest person I know.'

For six weeks I took Mum to some of her radiation and chemotherapy sessions and Jeff came whenever he could. Those hours with my mother were among the most beautiful we have ever shared, or are ever likely to share again.

At one of her first treatment sessions, the nurse couldn't find a vein to insert the chemo needle. She poked and poked, and having never been a fan of needles (or doctors or hospitals or medicine) Mum turned green but never once lost her cool.

'You should be used to that sensation,' I told her after the nurse had left, 'Dad's been sticking pins into a doll resembling you for years.'

When Nurse Andy came to Mum's bedside Jeff got all giddy. Andy was tall and muscular with a kind and handsome face. I swear Jeff blushed.

'Are you kidding me?' I said, after Nurse Andy had left.

195

'What?' he played dumb.

'My mother is about to get her first bout of chemo and you're flirting with her nurse?'

'I wonder if he offers sponge baths?'

'Mum! Don't be crude!'

And this is how most of our time played out. Waiting hour after hour, answering the same questions about cigarettes and alcohol and family history, surrounded by some very sick people and some very loving and dedicated hospital staff members. And crosswords, lots and lots of crosswords – though clearly the poison in Mum's system was also taking a few brain cells.

'Thirty-seven down? You can't get that? It's obviously "make" and the "d" you had is wrong. It can't be "made", you silly old bag because now "kilt" fits in perfectly.'

I feel honoured and privileged that Mum allowed me to share those moments of intimacy and fear. Yet in our determination to defeat cancer, we also shared some of the biggest belly laughs of our lives. I remained a bastion of positivity and hope while in the presence of my mother but would come home to Jeff and burst into tears, overwhelmed by the sickness surrounding her every day; amazed at her strength.

Each Monday morning I drove the ninety minutes to Mum's house to collect her for treatment ('Morning, my lady! Ready for another dose of lethal poisons?') then drove her back to Block Eight for a brief respite of a decent meal, a glass or two of wine, a visit with the animals and a night of talking and laughing before turning around the next day and taking her back to face the music all over again. On one hand the six weeks flew by, on the other it dragged like time had stood still and Mum and I were the only two trying to move forward. Mum's hair thinned but that public sign of sickness, a bold bald scalp, never came – much to her relief. I would sit looking at her jumper covered in long grey strands and wonder how close she was coming to losing it, a physical sign so innocent yet so menacing and pitiful. Mum pushed through the few days of nausea she experienced and never gave even one split second of complaint. Not even on the days the staff failed to explain things properly, or made her wait for unnecessary hours with me by her side shifting in my seat, got the dates slightly wrong and told her she needed even more radiation than the exact number she'd been counting down with a highlighter pen on her calendar on front of the fridge; not even when thick heavy bruises appeared on her arm from more failed attempts to find her veins, when countless professionals prodded her up the bum, and she nearly shit her pants more times than any person would ever wish on their worst enemy, when she was forced to drive herself to treatment on some days because none of us could get to her in time . . . As I write this now I wipe away heavy tears of pride, pain and unquantifiable love.

'How have you stayed so calm and positive, Mum?' I asked toward the end of the treatment.

'There are a lot of people a lot worse off than me.'

Jeff and I took Mum and Dad to their favourite Central Coast restaurant overlooking Terrigal Beach to celebrate the end of her treatment. Then we simply had to wait. Weeks of anxious not-knowing.

Cancer had changed my mother, a little. Any ailment made her fear the worst. Her severe back pain especially, she feared, was the disease coming back to ravage her; and test after negative test failed to convince her otherwise. Then the professionals thought to fucking X-ray her and noticed her *fractured pelvis* – which turns out to be a fairly common side-effect of intense radiation in that area. *Oh yeah, the fractured pelvis! Sorry, we forgot to check for that.*

A few months after her final radiation treatment my mother was given the all clear. We'd been surrounded by so many sick people throughout her treatments that we couldn't believe how lucky she was to make it through without a graver prognosis. Nothing quite solidifies the love you have for your mother than seeing her go through something as terrifying as a cancer treatment. And similarly, nothing like witnessing it first hand makes you reflect on your own health more intensely.

Tales of the Unexpected: A Farmer's Life

For the first five years at Block Eight (and let's face it, for many before that), Jeff and I were renovation junkies, living in the shell of each villa as it was built. Who needed creature comforts, warmth or a clean plate to eat off when we could just rough it and live like street bums? As each was completed, we moved into the next. Thus we lived and built our way around the various construction sites, stepping over tools and materials, making do without a flushing toilet or electricity, and braving bitter winters first in Orchard View, then Barrington View, followed by Tree Tops and finally Water View, until all four of the villas plus the house had been completed. If ever there had been a princess inside me, she was long dead. Daddy's Gold Amex had been destroyed many years before. I eventually stopped pining for luxurious items like a clean glass to drink from, a warm shower, water from a tap and a fridge tall enough to hold a bottle of wine.

By the final villa we had honed the interior designs and the online listings and photographs. Our guests love them: the compliments and thank you notes are constant, the five-star reviews almost universal. It's so rewarding to realise that our dream has been worth pursuing and we love sharing our beautiful corner of the world with those who come to stay. The income from the villas is steady and provides enough to keep the property going and keep the wine in production.

Of course growing grapes for wine was never as straight-forward again as it had been in 2014. To say Bacchus blessed us for our very first season would be putting it mildly. The Semillon is the most hardy and resilient crop and we've managed to get a harvest out of it every year – some years the quality of the grapes is better than others but that's all down to the weather. The Chardonnay is not quite so robust – its thick leaf growth and tight little grape bunches make it particularly susceptible to mould and mildew, which can decimate the crop.

After the paltry five hundred kilos of fruit in 2014, 2015 was a bounteous year with over eight tonnes but then just when we thought we were on easy street, in 2016 mould attacked the fruit and we made the decision not to harvest a single grape because of the cost of labour involved in manually sorting the good bunches from the bad. In 2017 we were back, this time with ten tonnes of fruit, a brand new label designed by Chris that can only be described as a striking Eden-like floral image and then, in 2018, thanks to the drought, the kangaroos took care of most of the leaves at the beginning of the season and whatever grapes did make it through to harvest time, the starving birds made an absolute feast of, so again we picked not a single grape.

The income from the villas also helped us make our own olive oil.

The olive groves have always been at the bottom of our list of priorities. Grapes and accommodation have consumed so much of our time and resources that the olives, those robust and carefree trees, more or less look after themselves. The most we ever do is spray them if they become infested with lace bugs, we de-sucker them and keep the grass around them low. But we never prune them, never fertilise them and rarely water them, which (we'd been told) were imperative in order to harvest any crop.

In March 2017, as I went through the grove mowing the grass, I was amazed to see for the first time in five years that the trees had produced fruit, and a lot of it. I called Peter from the Olive Association who also owned the olive processing plant in Lovedale – the same guy we'd called for advice just after we moved in – and asked him to come and take a look.

'There's definitely enough here to harvest,' he said, as we walked around the groves. 'The fruit looks good. You boys have done an amazing job on the grove, it looks one hundred per cent compared to how it looked five years ago.'

'Ever eaten a raw olive?' he asked. 'That's a mistake you'll only make once!'

After he'd left, I couldn't help myself and took a bite out of one. It was part earwax, part Drano with a healthy dose of rotten avocado thrown in.

'Ever eaten a raw olive?' I asked Lucy during her next visit. 'They're delicious!'

She put a green one in her mouth and immediately spat it out. 'Oh Dad, that is absolutely disgusting!'

'Which colour did you try?'

'Green.'

'Sorry sweetheart, I thought you knew. They're the unripe ones, you need to try a black one instead.'

And she did!

It can be so much fun being a dad.

A few weeks later, we harvested our first crop of Frantoio olives for oil. A machine with claws at the front came to shake the trunk of each tree and catch the fruit in a skirt extended around its base (see, skirts do have a place on a farm, Phil!). By the end of the day we'd collected six tonnes of fruit – to us, it felt almost like a free crop. But of course there were costs, from harvest to processing, bottling and labelling. Olive oil, it turns out, is quite an expensive game.

Much like the first time we ever tasted our own wine, my eyes filled with proud tears the first time we tasted our own oil. You can't compare it to the rubbish sold in supermarkets. It has a fruity full flavour at the front of your palate and a wonderful peppery kick at the back. Block Eight had another feather in its cap.

20

Helga Hagatha Van Hoggett

'I'm thinking of getting another pig,' I said to Vicky on the phone in July of 2017. We often call each other for updates – me on the kids, and she about the latest news at the property – and she is never surprised by one of my whims.

Jeff overheard the conversation and when I'd hung up the phone said, 'I didn't know you wanted another pig.'

'I just miss having the boys around,' I said with a shrug. 'I can't explain it. Obviously I wouldn't get a boar this time . . . I was thinking I'd get a sow and name her Helga.'

'Why "Helga"?'

'I don't know, it just seems right. "Helga Hagatha Van Hoggett" rolled off my tongue with very little thought.' It was as if she already existed.

I didn't really want to go into detail but Rodney and Billy's absence had left a hole in my heart that went all the way to China and, much as I loved Winston and Wesley, only another piggy could come close to filling it.

As is his way, the next day Jeff was on the internet looking for a pig to buy me as a surprise, but sows were hard to come by and none were available within an easy drive of our property. Then he had a brainwave and called Trevor at the local pet shop where sometimes pigs were for sale. Over the years we'd got to know Trevor at the Branxton Pet Shop and his love for animals shines through in everything he does, like converting his shop's yard into a petting zoo for kids to come and feed and pat the farm animals. We know he sources healthy animals from reputable local farms where they are given good lives and not taken from their mothers too soon, so aside from Spencer and Kate the pea fowl, he's also sold us quails and chooks. It also helps that he is rather easy on the eyes. I'm sure quite a few local mothers visit that shop often, 'just to show the kids the bunnies'.

'Yep, I've got one,' Trev told Jeff over the phone.

Not knowing any of this, I walked into our villa carrying cleaning equipment.

'Are you ready?' Jeff asked.

'I'm not up for another trip to Bunning's today,' I said, 'you can go on your own this time.'

Jeff does all of the building and fixing on the property and for him it isn't unheard of to go to the hardware store three times in one day, choosing different locations so the staff members don't comment on his frequency. *Third time today! You must be busy . . . or forgetful!* His cushion fetish had been replaced by a love of tools . . . but then I still bought cookbooks so there were no grounds for complaint. Though it must also be said that guests at Block Eight love poring over the cookbook collection as they sip our wines on their private decks so my little obsession has not gone to waste after all. And in his defence, Jeff's newfound love of building has saved us tens of thousands of dollars in labour – maybe even more than a hundred thousand but then, it's hard to put a value on my contribution of cookbooks that capture the hearts of our guests, isn't it?

I did try to help Jeff build whenever I could. He'd worked with Pete at loads of off-site jobs and Pete had taught him a hell of a lot about many facets of building, ever the patient mentor who wanted his grasshopper to produce work of sheer perfection. I would have loved being a fly on the wall at those building sites – ocker Pete with his footballer's build and gay Jeff with his eye for precision and desire to rid the world of prejudice. Pete's wife, Ange, and I wanted to sign them up for *The Block*, knowing they made for an unlikely but very engaging team. Pete and Ange were another pair of locals who embraced Jeff and me. They invited us along to many family get-togethers and insisted we go to their house for Christmas and Easter meals. Pete was a never-ending source of advice for Jeff, who frequently called him up just to ask if 'this way or that' was the best way of doing things, often to be given a completely different method. Ange and I bonded as the builders' wives and made jokes about the boys whenever we could. We felt genuinely loved and accepted by them.

'You know,' he told Jeff one day, 'I'm really glad you two are here at my family table, mate.'

Jeff took all the knowledge Pete shared with him, along with hours of YouTube viewing, and invested in the tools that would allow him to do most of the building work that remained to be done on Block Eight. He's turned his hand to carpentry, plastering, tiling, plumbing, roofing, stone masonry, concreting ... you name it.

'Can you just cut this down to one-forty for me?' Jeff asked one day when I was employed as his labourer – and I was butch enough to know that meant millimetres.

I was once scared of power tools (never a good thing to close your eyes when dealing with them but perhaps I should have learned that on the cricket pitch my one and only season, when I shut my eyes at a speeding cricket ball heading straight for my face), but gradually I've come to know my way around the saw, nail gun and others fairly competently. I handed Jeff the piece of wood, proud that I'd got the measurement just right.

Jeff put the wood in place, looked at it strangely.

'Are you kidding me?' he asked. 'You've cut it at an angle!'

'No I haven't!' I objected.

'What's this then?' He held the piece of wood up to the light and the angle was difficult to ignore.

'I'm sorry . . .'

'Why don't you go and weed the vegie patch? I may as well do this myself.'

'I'm sorry!' I said again.

'I just thought you could cut me a piece of wood, that's all, but it's okay, don't worry about it . . .'

I skulked off to the vegie patch, defeated. But then I turned on my heel and marched straight back into the shed to confront Jeff.

'You don't understand,' I pleaded. 'I cannot cut in a straight line like you! I have an affliction, Jeff; it's beyond my control!'

'You have a . . . condition . . . that prevents you from cutting in a straight line?' he asked, deadpan.

'No, an *affliction*. You've seen me with scissors and I can't cut straight. Now you've seen I can't saw straight either.'

'Okay . . .'

'Well . . .' clearly losing this one, I looked about the shed for ammunition. 'Well . . . you try writing a bestselling guide on how to use eBay! So what if I can't cut straight? I'm so sorry I'm such a burden to have around. We each have our weaknesses – now you know mine.'

'Oh, I've known yours for quite some time,' he said snarkily.

Back at the villa, talking about a second trip to Bunnings I said to him, 'I don't get it. When I bake a cake I read the recipe thoroughly, write down the list of ingredients then go to the shop and buy all those ingredients at once. I don't make things up and keep going back to the shop for all the stuff I've forgotten.'

'Building doesn't work that way,' he said with a shrug. 'You wouldn't understand. Sometimes I don't know what I need until I need it.'

'Doesn't make any sense to me at all . . .' I said.

'Doesn't have to! But we're not going to Bunnings again, anyway. We're going to Branxton.'

There's also a hardware store in Branxton that Jeff often goes to for last-minute building emergencies. 'Nah, you go. I've got more cleaning to do.'

'But Helga's waiting for you!' Jeff said excitedly.

Needless to say the mop and bucket were promptly dropped and my Crocs were replaced with less comical shoes for Trevor, though I had been known on occasion to wear them out in the real world.

'I reckon this one's a real corker,' Trevor welcomed us in his Steve Irwin-lookalike uniform. 'I get a lot of pigs through but she's gonna be a ripper.'

There she was! Helga was incredibly small for her age. She had fine black stripes down her back and the rest of her was dark brown. The pink patterns on her belly and inside her hind legs reminded me of giraffe markings. Helga was living in a small wooden crate with hay for a floor and a male piglet for a playmate. She was about the size of a chihuahua.

I picked her up and held her in one hand, pressing her snout to my cheek. She squealed a little bit, but nowhere near as much as other piglets I'd handled.

'She'll soon settle if you hold her every day,' Trevor said, but she'd already quietened in my arms and I think I did detect just the slightest hint of him being impressed with me. Lucky I hadn't worn the Crocs on this occasion.

The male pig in the pen began to fret so I took Helga away, trying to block out his cries. Trevor placed her in a comfortably sized box with hay on the bottom but as soon as we got her in the car I picked her up and held her against my chest. She settled almost straightaway, a good sign that she was going to be a good companion, comfortable with humans.

After the ten-minute drive, I decided it would be good to get Helga to appreciate her new home right away.

'She's been in that wooden crate for a while,' I said to Jeff, 'Maybe we should let her down on the grass, get her used to some land beneath her feet again?'

'Do you think that's a good idea?' Clearly he didn't!

'She'll be all right, I'll look after her.'

I put Helga down on the grass and watched her get used to the soft sensation. Her trotters were so tender, pink and smooth to the touch. I was marvelling at how her nails were different colours, some black and some pink, when without warning, she bolted. A piglet, even one as small as a chihuahua, can move *very* fast. Helga was sprinting and we set off after her from our standing start. There wasn't a chance in hell we were going to catch her but we chased her anyway. Jeff and I were running flat out and she was still tens of metres in front of us, squealing with fear and disorientation.

Then I realised: Helga was running directly for the dam.

This is it, I thought, *she's going straight into the water and she's going to sink to the bottom.* I mentally prepared myself to follow her in fully clothed – it was all very *Baywatch* only without the muscly bodies, big boobs and red budgie smugglers. *No pig was going to drown on my watch!*

Helga hit the water and thankfully stopped in her tracks – it was still winter and the dam's temperature was a little chilly. She took an immediate left and started heading for the bush where the creek runs through – it is densely treed and has very long grass so she would be lost to us within seconds. Another horrible thought flashed before my eyes – *Helga will perish out there, scared and alone.*

'Come on, Todd!' Jeff yelled. 'Keep up!'

I started to worry that we were chasing her away. Maybe if we stopped running after her she might miraculously decide to stop too but, whenever I slowed, she showed no signs of fatigue. Just as I feared the worst, she turned ninety degrees and ran straight toward the house again. Fortunately for us she headed to a little gate, which meant she was coming to a dead end and I lunged for her and took a firm hold, careful not to panic her any more than she already was. Helga was out of breath, cold and wet, great big heaving lungsful of air came from her tiny frame.

I put her inside my jacket, wrapped my arms across my chest and held onto her tightly. Within seconds she began to relax. Helga was safe and warm, enclosed.

'Yep, great idea,' Jeff said and we took her inside to get her used to her new home.

It was clearly inevitable I would be making some mistakes with Helga but hopefully nowhere near as many as I had made with Rodney and Billy.

So there we were in the middle of winter 2017 with a new pet pig and living in the basic shell of a fifth villa – this one, for the time being at least, was to be ours to live in permanently (though probably not 'forever'). Electricity came in via long extension leads from the shed, the toilet was a very basic outdoor portaloo and the only running water was a cold tap over a laundry tub. Man, this was living! Our internal walls were cobbled together and the floor was bare wooden sub-flooring. It didn't seem that having a pig indoors would create all that much extra havoc.

At first we tried confining Helga in a spare bathtub, but its walls were too slippery and she was desperate to jump out. Inside the shed Jeff had built us a small laundry (needless to say it was unfinished and had no appliances) so with hay for a floor and a newly purchased dog bed, Helga was pretty happy in there, but it had no daylight and not a lot of room for her to move around. We quickly developed a routine. She would messily eat her meals on the 'living room' floor and at the end of the day I'd let her in for playtime and to chase Leroy around a bit. Given his temperament, we were surprised this never ended in a fight. Helga loved the taste of freedom and being returned to the laundry was soon met with grunts of disappointment and protest that were loud enough to disturb our guests in the villa next door, so we moved her into our unfinished bathroom, where Jeff had recently installed a real, actual flushing toilet!

It wasn't uncommon to have a pig between your legs while you went about your business, as Helga soon made the space her own. Mealtimes resulted in smears of bread and peanut butter, cheese and a wide array of other sloppy mess all over the floors and walls.

Because I was working so hard, one day I treated myself to a massage at the local shopping centre. They're very professional but part of the treatment involves pulling down my underwear to expose my buttocks, which are so intimately connected to the muscles in my lower back. This particular day, however, when the guy lifted the towel to tuck beneath the top of my lowered undies, I heard him make this weird sort of coughing nose and rather than pulling my pants down, he did something very strange – he placed the towel over the top of them and never once massaged my glutes. It was the most disappointing treatment I've had there and on leaving I decided to find another provider.

Later that night as I got ready for bed, I looked down and noticed right at the back of my underwear was a familiar snout print of Helga's, brown and distinct.

'Oh my god, Jeff, look at this!' I said holding it out for him to see. 'My massage guy thought I shat myself!'

Our neighbours Natalie and Andrew (with daughters Chelsea and Amber in tow), Jenny, Nat and Dan, Pete and Ange (with their daughters Tejay and Jorja) and family would drop by our place, take one look at 'Helga's room' and give us a disapproving stare. But giving Helga space inside our own meant that we could bond more deeply than any other Block Eight animal and I had done before. Her behaviour was so similar to a dog's as she excitedly ate her meal then ran about looking for things to play with. She discovered Leroy's cat flap into the shed and then that was it, game on! Helga disappeared for a few minutes then returned with a piece of cardboard in her mouth, shaking it from side to side just like a dog. She grew bored easily, disappeared again, for longer this time, then brought a medium-sized piece of irrigation pipe into the living room. As she shook her head the pipe smacked her so she soon grew tired of that sensation and disappeared again.

'Are you worried about her?' Jeff asked after about five minutes.

'A bit,' I lied, fearing she was ripping the shed to shreds.

But sure enough, we again heard the cat flap push open and there Helga was, bursting into the room with an enormous plastic bag in her mouth, easily thirty times the size of her and she thought she was the cleverest thing on the planet, proudly shaking it about the room with glee. We paused Netflix and waited for her to tire of this latest, very noisy, game.

It didn't take very long for her to come and lie on my lap, nuzzling into my hand where she eventually fell to exhausted sleep beneath a blanket we'd purchased to keep her warm (we still had no heating for ourselves). Her soft snores were mesmerising. Had she not lived with us, I would never have had the chance to get to know her on such a level. And anyway, as usual, I think I was slowly beginning to fall in love.

When you live with a pig, the most pressing issue is ensuring she's toilet trained. It's one thing to live in a permanent state of renovation; it's quite another to have it reeking of pig urine, which is particularly pungent. Thankfully Helga was very small and the volume of her business was to scale, for the time being. While Google often has the answer to any single question you can fathom (except dead kangaroos in dams), when it comes to learning about raising and training animals, you quickly discover that most of the information on the internet is based on personal experience. But everyone's experience with animals is different. There's no such thing as a parental bible, just as there is no such thing as a foolproof way to toilet train a pig, though I was convinced Helga was smarter than most.

I first tried shredded newspaper. Some forums suggested it was the perfect material, soft and absorbent, and recycled to boot. Each morning I would meticulously hand-cut paper into shreds (though never in straight lines), trying to get it to a consistency I thought would appeal to Helga. During the newspaper trial, however, it wasn't uncommon for a television show to be interrupted by Jeff running through the living room carrying a squealing piglet in his hands. A pig doesn't like to be interrupted from the task at hand and a piglet's squeals can be ear-piercing.

Helga had this funny little way of grunting three times quickly to let you know she was unimpressed, a sort of warning alarm, before launching into her full volume squeal, surely loud enough to be heard in all four corners of the property. Despite our best intentions to get her onto that shredded paper every time, it soon became clear that Helga didn't find that material a suitable enough match. Hidden puddles were often discovered, stray pellets stumbled across at inopportune moments or while friends were visiting. Her excursions into the shed, it also became apparent, weren't just about finding a toy to play with but also about adding to her considerable stockpile of weapons of mass destruction.

I next tried mulch, figuring the earthy smell and texture would be just what the piglet ordered. It was a marked improvement, certainly there were still a lot of misses but once every six or so attempts Helga would get it right and remember where she was supposed to be doing her business. I had read that leaving a reminder in the box was also helpful and at times she went straight to the same corner of it, but one in six was clearly not good enough odds. More grunts and squeals, more moments of Jeff running through the room carrying an interrupted piglet, followed by more encouragement from him to try another option. I'd seen pigs on television walk to the door and wait patiently to be let out to complete their business, but we had Leroy to consider and his alley-criminal past meant he wasn't allowed outside at night, particularly when we had guests on the property. Helga would just have to get used to the concept that either she was going to be constantly interrupted by Jeff, or she'd have to work out a more practical solution.

'Why don't you try dirt in the tray?' Jeff suggested one evening.

Now I am not one to easily admit that someone else has come up with a good suggestion for training *my* pig but as the bark still wasn't hitting the mark, after a few days I secretly replaced it with lots of lovely earth. And if I'm not one to embrace someone else's suggestion, it goes without saying that I'm also not the kind of guy to admit that Jeff was right. I'm sure trying dirt was my next logical step after mulch and no doubt I would've tried it without his prompt.

Almost immediately, it clicked with Helga. The dirt beneath her trotters, the scent of the ground, the texture of the stuff, everything clearly just felt right to her and within two days of my placing it there, Helga was miraculously toilet trained. She never once missed making it to the tray, though on occasion she overshot its edge and spilt a little mess onto the floor, but as our bathroom was still concrete she was easily forgiven.

Like the proudest of parents, our television watching was no longer interrupted by the squeals of a determined little piglet, but now by cries of 'Good girl! Good girl, Helgy!' and the like – and dammit if that pig hadn't been playing me all along and was just waiting in her own good time to get the toilet training right. Of course she wanted to do her business in dirt! That's what nature intended and how dare I try to mess with a millennia-old formula. The next test would be to see if she could come to me on demand.

It made practical and logical sense to have Helga spayed. In the very least, as much as I love animals, I believe it's irresponsible to breed animals without having a very clear solution for the lives you help bring into the world. It's not good enough to just hope you'll find a suitable home (or purpose) for them some time after they're born. Poor preparation led to the horrible situation with Rodney and Billy and I just couldn't let that happen again – it wasn't fair to them, and let's face it, I would've had an emotional breakdown going through that again.

Research also told me that sows could develop many internal issues such as cancers, uterine infections and other problems associated with hormones and of course there was also the practicality of Helga potentially bleeding around the house, on guests and around the property. Plus, unspayed pigs can be quite moody and temperamental and there simply wasn't enough room on the property for two of us behaving the same. The urine scent of a pig on cycle is also strong and I feared this might attract wild boars from neighbouring bushland. I have read countless articles that insisted a spayed sow would make for a more reliable pet and reduce the risk of Helga roaming or wandering in search of a potential mate.

I called our local vet to book Helga in for the operation but was told they didn't have the necessary equipment and I would have to speak to the staff at Sugarloaf Animal Hospital.

From the moment I first spoke to the woman who answered the phone at Sugarloaf, I knew my little pig was going to be in safe and loving hands. I was asked her age and temperament and told that one of the vets would call me back personally to discuss when the best time would be to have her spayed. Less than one hour later, Dr Alex telephoned me and advised that it was best to wait until Helga was between twelve and fourteen weeks, so we'd have another four or so to wait before she was big enough to cope with the operation.

When the day of her procedure came, I was a complete mess.

'Maybe we shouldn't do it,' I suggested to Jeff. 'I'm sure she'll be a good pet without having her vagina carved out of her.'

'You know they're not really touching her vagina don't you?'

'Hmm, you know that's not really my area of expertise, don't you?'

'Anyway, Toddy, we've been through the pros and cons,' he reminded me. 'She'll be a happier animal if you go through with it now. Come on, I'll do the driving.'

After Mum's cancer, we reached the conclusion that she should be closer to Jeff and me so we could help take care of her if she ever needed us. After lots of searching Mum and Dad finally settled on a house in a town about fifteen minutes' drive from Block Eight. I'd taken Helga over to my parents' house a few times so she was used to the car and didn't seem to mind taking a trip. She sat contentedly on my lap, watching the world whizz by her window, often she would simply fall asleep and start snoring sometimes while nuzzling on my finger and those soft wet sucking sounds would tell me she was happy. Even the forty-minute drive to Sugarloaf proved a breeze for her – she rarely stirred.

The Sugarloaf staff were excited to welcome Helga as it wasn't often they saw more exotic pets, let alone had the chance to operate on one. Dr Alex came out to greet her personally.

'Thank you for giving us the opportunity to show the staff a different kind of animal,' he said as he ushered us into his treatment room. 'She looks like a very healthy little pig, small for her age.'

Helga was still in my hands; she hadn't shown any need for us to put her in the cat carrier we'd brought along just in case.

'I had pigs growing up in Russia,' Dr Alex continued, 'so I know firsthand what amazing animals they are and how easy it is to form a special bond with them.'

The chitchat was doing its job, putting me at ease.

'You need to know the risks of the operation before we proceed,' he continued. 'Particularly with pigs because they can react differently to the anaesthetic and it is very difficult to predict how any one animal will perform under it, or how she will come out of it.'

I looked at Jeff and furrowed my brow. He knew my doubts were again creeping in.

'Of course we'll do everything we can to make sure she is comfortable and the operation is a success.' Dr Alex must have sensed my paranoia. 'Helga looks very fit and alert and you told me how playful and responsive she is at home and all of this points to her coming out of the anaesthesia without a problem but it's my job to inform you of the potential complications.'

'I understand,' I said and handed over my baby pig.

'We'll call you as soon as the operation is complete and again a few hours later when she is fully awake.'

'Will you need to keep her in overnight?' I asked, trying desperately to keep my voice from wavering.

'That will depend on how she recovers,' Dr Alex said, 'but I see no reason for her not to be home with you this afternoon.'

With some doctors, nurses and veterinarians, you can just see in their eyes that they love what they do and have no intention of letting you down, or harming your loved one. We signed the necessary paperwork and walked out of the surgery.

'We don't have to put her through it if you really don't want to,' Jeff said, reading the anguish on my face.

'No, no, it's the right thing to do,' I said, trying to sound brave. 'This is about giving her a better life and . . . well . . . if the worst happens then that is what's meant to be . . .'

For the next several hours we filled in time as best we could, trying not to think about what Helga was going through or how she was coping. During lunch my phone rang: it was the team at Sugarloaf. Helga's operation was a complete success and she had woken from the anaesthetic. She was alert and they would monitor her progress over the next few hours but all was pointing to the likelihood she could be picked up around 5pm.

A wave of relief swept through my body and I could have cried with happiness. I never expected the worst to happen to my baby pig – that just wasn't an option – but having the best possible outcome was utter perfection.

By the time we went to collect Helga, the staff at Sugarloaf had fallen madly in love with her. She had bonded best with the two male veterinarians, frolicked in the surgery's yard with the other staff and generally won them all over with complete conviction. Helga's interactions with people beyond me, Jeff and my parents were few. True, our local baker's driver had fallen in love with her and requested to see her every time she dropped off bread, but that was about Helga's only interaction with the outside world. I already thought she was magnetic in every way but to have that confirmed by people with no obligation to say such wonderful things about a little pig made me realise that Helga held appeal for a broad range of people.

I began posting more photos of her on Instagram and they were viewed and liked by more people than other subjects I posted about. People I'd never met asked me to keep posting regularly, commented with real affection about this little pig they'd never met. And one of my friends in publishing, Lou, even suggested I write a book about her. I wasn't becoming a Hollywood 'stage mum' was I?

As we drove home that afternoon with Helga seemingly back to her normal self, sitting on my lap and reaching up to look out the window at the passing scenery, suckling on my hand for comfort and falling asleep to the slow rhythms of my scratches and back rubs, I felt she was ready for more interaction with the world – but first we had to keep her confined within our villa for fourteen days to allow her stitches to heal.

Before her operation, I'd given Helga a few hours outside each day. We'd cordoned off a corner of the goats' pen and furnished it with straw and a 'swimming pool' and a few toys for her to play with. She seemed to enjoy being out there, particularly in sunlight, and even tolerated Winston's frequent head butts against her fence. The fourteen days of recuperation therefore were a struggle for a pig who was just beginning to get a taste of independence, but selfishly for me they were a memorable and lovely last two weeks of indoor bonding.

The plain and simple fact is that Helga loves cuddles. Any time we spent inside the villa without allowing her to run around our feet and sit on our laps was met with disapproving grunts. By now she had taught herself how to jump up onto the couch and while Leroy found this completely annoying and inappropriate, it meant she could bond with us wherever we sat, not just if we lay on the floor. Her routine was always the same – she liked her food served a particular way, loved milk in the mornings, wanted cuddles during lunch breaks and demanded playtime and falling asleep in between my legs of an evening. The four of us watched our favourite shows on Netflix, Leroy with one eye constantly on Helga, ready to bolt if she decided it was time to play with her furry black friend. Despite his tendency to attack humans without warning, Leroy has been nothing short of the perfect gentleman when it comes to our pets.

Because Leroy's fearlessness knows no bounds and he can be unpredictable, it was a pleasant surprise to watch him persevere with baby Helga, who was more robust in her demands than any other animal we'd introduced him to.

In the mornings I used rice crackers, one of Helga's favourite foods, to teach her to come to me on demand – a task she managed to master within three or four days. She was a cunning little animal because I could clearly see in her eyes that she knew what I wanted her to do and that she knew how to do it but this game of 'Here, Helga!' was boring for her and if it didn't end with treats . . . well she'd rather be off exploring or playing in the shed, thanks all the same. Eventually though, she came more and more frequently. It didn't work every time, but often enough to appreciate that she knew what 'Helga! Here!' meant and if she wasn't coming it was purely because she was being stubborn, or had engaged herself in a new game of 'see what's in the shed' or eating Leroy's cat biscuits.

'I don't think I'm ready for her to go outside,' I said to Jeff as the day marking Helga's full recovery drew near.

'We can still let her sleep inside if you like but don't you think she'd prefer to be outside during the day?'

We talked through the pros and cons. And really, the only pro was for me: I'd miss having so much time with my pig. Helga was growing at an astronomical rate, even in the two weeks since leaving Sugarloaf it looked like she'd doubled in size. She needed more exercise than an occasional explore of the shed and all that aside, she needed to do what a pig does best and a pig can't forage or root on concrete or wood.

Any time outside meant freedom, mud and dirt. Inside meant constriction and, in time, broken furniture and fixtures. What would happen when we'd finished our renovation and had all that new stuff and of an evening Helga barrelled in and ran about, just like a pig should? Rainy days would result in trotter prints and body smears all over the house (and more gasps of horror from the masseur). There was only one scenario worth entertaining – it was time for Helga to leave the nest – and though I longed for her company often, during the day she bounded with happiness, playfulness and independence. Helga was always going to grow from piglet to pig and it would have been grossly unfair to force her to stay in my semi-ordered human world.

Outside, I made sure I spent quality time with her every morning and brought her treats throughout the day. Some of those first mornings she spent outside I'd lie with her or just sit and watch her for anywhere from ten minutes upwards to an hour, then every afternoon I took her and the goats for walks around the property. I missed her most in the evening, when I'd stroked and scratched her as she snored lightly in my lap, and I had to be strong during her first rains and storm, forcing myself not to go outside and check on her or (and yes it was considered) climb into her wooden house and comfort her if she was scared. But rain also turned her pen into her favourite thing: mud. Within days she'd turned over the entire floor of her pen, churned up all the hay and forest debris we'd lined it with, and found herself a discreet corner to do her business in.

My longing to spend evenings with her eventually subsided but I was convinced it was more than mere coincidence that on those first few nights without Helga in the villa Leroy became more needy and was regularly smothered with cuddles and affection.

*

Two goats, a pig and a farmer walk into a bar . . . it's a line that occurs to me almost every time I take the goats and Helga for a walk. I try to do it every day, whether that's a quick trip for some grazing or a longer walk exploring corners of the property. I realise how ridiculous my life might look to those outside looking in – a middle-aged man taking his pet goats and pig for a daily walk – and it's true that more often than not when guests see me on the walk they point and laugh. I guess it is truly a spectacle for the mostly city-dwelling visitors we get at the farm. But I enjoy being the punchline because not only does it bring joy to others; it never fails to make me laugh too.

One stubborn and strong-willed goat, barrel-gutted with a stumpy gait and mischievous eyes, Winston is so independent I always have to put that dog's harness around his chest just in case I need to pull him away from a guest's private deck, or pot plants or some other no-go zone he gets the notion for. The bright orange straps of the harness only add to the humorous nature of the scene, I am sure. ('You really need to get his permission if you're going to post photos of him in that bra,' Vicky wrote once.)

Wesley, by contrast, is so determined to do the right thing he rarely gets much further than a metre or two from my side and often insists on walking right against my legs so I can tickle the hairs on his back. But on some days Winston leads him astray and he then thoroughly enjoys leading me on a wild goat chase into some forbidden corner of the property. Helga remains every inch my baby, and while she will run up to about twenty metres from me, she will then come straight back to be by my side, and if I rest on the ground she insists on lying on my lap for belly rubs and scratches, even though she is way too big and much too heavy for it nowadays.

Barely a day passes that I don't find myself chuckling at their antics on these walks. The bouncy way Helga runs (particularly that view from behind), her excited barks as she laps up the open space, Wesley's Nadia Comăneci impressions off the bench we'd placed to admire the view in front the olives and yes, even Winston's naughtiness; it all fills me with such glee that I don't care how funny I appear to others.

Helga is like those kids who can't stand to have different foods on her plate touch each other – only for her it isn't the touching that's a bother, it's eating in a haphazard order. For her evening meal I deliver a carefully divided tray of different food groups, which Jeff christened her 'bento box', claiming Helga got better meals than he did. She immediately sets to it with her snout and in mere seconds has systematically rated the food items from most to least interesting. Poor farmer choices get shoved over to the side of the tray to perhaps be considered for afters. The most appealing morsel is greedily devoured, with Helga (who quickly mixes up all my careful division) rooting through the whole tray in search of any hidden gems. Only when she's confident the best choice is all gone will she consider moving on to ingredient number two, her second favourite, and so on.

Cheese is almost exclusively the first choice, particularly her favourite: herb and garlic fromage frais, which I buy just for Helga from our local dairy when I'm placing orders for our guests' cheese platters. A close second is cookies leftover from my baking for the guests, or rice crackers (also loved by Winston but never ever by Wesley). Bread generally follows next, especially if I hide chunks of peanut butter within, or if it's been soaked in milk, or if it is sugary bread like brioche, which our guests sometimes leave behind. One day, felafels were her second choice. Unlike Rodney and Billy before her, who would eat practically anything (except onion and capsicum), Helga has a more refined palate and doesn't enjoy herby crackers, cereal, eggplant or cucumber and, like the boys, onion and capsicum are a definite no-go.

The goats are also fussy eaters. Anything that has touched dirt is met with utter disdain. Wesley scoffs at any food he does not like, sneezes over it and shakes his head violently from side to side. *I will not be eating that, thank you very much!* (Just like Charlie with tomatoes.) Over-ripe bananas are the most disgusting things on the planet, apparently, and the goats also deign only to sup at water freshly supplied from the tap.

Sometimes I checked on Helga before the sun went down and the two or three items in the tray she had chosen not to devour straightaway had found their way into her gut, as though, on realising she was getting no more of her first choices, she had shrugged and figured *might as well.*

It took me a few more days, but in time I also taught Helga to sit. When she achieved it, she seemed to open her mouth in an enormous, proud-of-herself smile. She so enjoyed walk time with the goats that I worried she was getting lonely through the day, so Jeff did some research.

'It does say here that pigs are really prone to loneliness . . .'

'Do you think we should get her a friend?'

The thought of going through more months of training, the anguish of having another pig spayed . . . as much as I loved my Helga, repeating all of that held little appeal. But if your baby piggy needs a friend, well then you just do what you have to do, so within a few days we were on our way to purchase her a friend. On the way to the pig farm I decided to do a bit more last-minute research.

'I found this article listing all the animals pigs get along best with. Guess what's number one?'

'Goats?'

'Yep!'

We turned the car around, called the pig farmer to apologise, then cut a hole in the fence between Helga's pen and the goats'. Now in case you hadn't guessed I'm probably the world's guiltiest person when it comes to anthropomorphism but I swear when she burst in to be with the goats, Helga's whole face lit up. It melts my heart to watch them sleeping together, or Helga chasing Winston around the pen, proving she indeed has become the boss of them all.

21

A Reality Self-check

While I'd taken care of all of the animals over the years, I'd neglected to look after myself. By the middle of 2016, just after Mum had beaten her cancer, I was teetering on morbidly obese on any BMI scale. Let's not mince words here – I was fucking *fat*. It felt like my blood had solidified and my organs were struggling. I had never been less happy with my body. I felt as if I was walking around in a fat suit made of jelly. Everything was heavy and clumsy. I've struggled with eating and weight my whole life but never knew I was fat until some kid called me 'Ten-tonne Toddy' when I was about ten.

Around the same time, my family went on our first-ever beach holiday. The first morning we suburbanites trudged up to the local beach and it was jam-packed – I'd never seen so many lovely semi-naked bodies in all my life. I suppose I was on the cusp of puberty but didn't know it at the time.

As we settled onto an impossibly small area of sand, wedged between other families that all looked tanned and taut, I suddenly began to feel uncomfortable. Ten-tonne Toddy had no place being here. My family members stripped off but I sat quietly drinking it all in, psyching myself up to show the world what I'd only recently become so conscious of.

'Why don't you take your shirt off, Toddy?'

'I will soon, Dad . . .'

'Why don't you take your shirt off, Toddy?'

'I said, I will soon!'

'No, why don't you take it off now?'

Then in one fell swoop, my father jumped to his feet, marched over to my side of the blanket and literally ripped the t-shirt from my back.

'There. Now it's done,' he said, rather pleased with himself, and plonked back down onto the sand to puff away on his cigarette and help himself to another joint of Kentucky Fried Chicken.

Though I wasn't conscious of it at the time, that afternoon I'd joined a new club.

'Hello? Body Dysmorphia Association.'

'Hello, yes? I'd like to take out lifetime membership.'

'Oh you're in luck. We have an easy payment plan on offer at the moment! Each month, all you need to do is alternate between binge eating and crash dieting.'

'Where do I sign up?'

'In the fine print you just need to promise never to like what you see when you look in the mirror.'

'It's a deal!'

'One last thing?'

'Yes?'

'When you grow up to realise you're gay, you will never ever feel comfortable on the gay scene so you'll only get intimate with anyone when you're drunk enough to forget what you look like and you'll find yourself being alone until well into your thirties as a result.'

'Great! Where do I sign?'

Thirty-odd years later, to realise at the age of forty-two I was heavier than ever, and having seen what Mum went through, gave me the kick up the arse I needed.

Mel and Jesus were visiting and I expressed how unhappy I was.

'Let's do it!' Jesus said.

We got out the scales and weighed ourselves and agreed to check in with each other every week – we called it Weigh-in Wednesday. Like Vicky, I love a competition, so it was a great motivator.

In essence, I stripped fat, alcohol, dairy, gluten and sugar out of my diet and I exercised for between forty and eighty minutes every single day. I was running more than the equivalent of a marathon every week and as my body began to change, I became addicted to seeing those kilograms fall away. Over the years I've learned the only way for me to lose weight is to religiously keep track of calories in and calories burned, because seeing the numbers in print is the only way I can hold myself accountable. My body becomes a spreadsheet, a scientific experiment in weight loss.

As the diet progressed, we ate less and less meat. Meat just represented one big fat chunk of calories to avoid. Portions went from five hundred grams pre-diet to a hundred grams. White fish dishes became a much more sensible spending of calories. Jeff would often leave his meat until the last thing on his plate and then only eat it because he didn't want it to go to waste.

'Can we have vegetarian tonight?' he would ask. But I resisted because all meals aside from breakfast were just *better* with a slab of meat, even if it was only a hundred grams.

I lost more weight than Jesus almost every week and in just over three months I lost a total of twenty-six kilograms. I had never felt better, never looked better. One day I caught my naked reflection in the mirror at the local swimming pool and did a double take. I truly could not believe that the body I was looking at was mine, the eternal fat kid. Parts of my body now revealed themselves for the first time and I no longer had one iota of self-consciousness. Would my BDA life membership be revoked?

When we were spending cosy evenings watching Netflix with Helga on my lap, some of the films we watched were *Cowspiracy*, *What the Health?* and *Forks Over Knives*. It was eight months after my initial weight loss and shamefully I'd put twelve kilos back on thanks in large part to too much wine and a reduced exercise regime. Watching those films (which I admit are propaganda for their own causes), I could not believe how closely diet was linked to significant diseases such as cancer and diabetes, and when I looked at my immediate family I found a *Who's Who* of dietary and genetic problems: many cancers (though Mum's was perhaps the most severe), type 2 diabetes, Crohn's disease, diverticulitis, gout, high blood pressure, high cholesterol, kidney stones, gall bladder stones, arthritis, obesity . . . add my grandparents and the list grows to include heart disease, stroke and yet more cancers. I was still within a healthy weight range but I could not deny that with my family's history I felt like a ticking time bomb. And we had one thing in common aside from genetics: we were all raised on a diet high in animal protein from meat and dairy. In their later years my parents' food pyramid has dramatically shifted to be laden with meat, dairy, white bread and fried foods, and is breathtakingly light in grains, legumes, leafy green vegetables and fruit. Why had not one of Mum's health practitioners bothered to ask her what she ate, and talk to her of the dangers of certain foods, and their link to cancer? And as I looked into my sleeping piglet's tiny face, could I seriously, with clear conscience, hoe into strips of greasy bacon or munch on a pork fillet ever again?

I preached to my parents about their diet and lack of exercise but deep down knew they considered themselves too old and set in their ways to make any significant changes. I would tell anyone who'd lend me five seconds of their time just how much I loved animals and I couldn't stand to watch the singer Morrissey's film about animal cruelty, and yet every night I was still feasting on flesh. When our neighbours Natalie and Andrew had us over to dinner I insisted I could not eat goat or pork on the bone, yet it was hard to deny just how delicious Andrew's slow-cooked pork belly was and I'd invariably help myself to seconds. I may have been a walking goat and pig joke, but I'd also become a walking contradiction on animal welfare. I'd killed one chicken and swore never to do it again, and I'd go to the ends of the earth (and the pits of our bank account) to make sure all our animals were healthy, but in Coles I'd stack half a trolley full of nicely packaged body parts. Could I love my animals as intensely as I did and still happily munch on their distant relatives?

Caring for Winston, Wesley and Helga also gave me a sense that I was honouring them more profoundly. They aren't just pets, but a reminder each and every day of the horrors that animals face in the meat industry. Road kill now seems even more senseless; a greater loss. And any suffering I see in animals (like when Wesley's hooves grew too long and he found it hard to walk – who knew you had to trim their nails?) affects me more deeply.

On top of all of this, Jeff and I live on a property at the mercy of drought and rainfall. We see firsthand the effects of global warming: even within the six years we've been here our grape-growing season grows shorter and shorter and we find ourselves harvesting weeks earlier every year. By mid-2017 we'd had so little rain that our main dam almost dried up completely and even the water we'd had pumped in via the PID did little to help us. In drought, the kangaroos had desperately turned to grape leaves and their hunger robbed us of our entire Shiraz crop, whose leaves had hung at the perfect angle for roo grazing. We harvested eight tonnes in February 2017 but just six hundred kilograms in 2018.

We know the statistics: it takes over nine thousand litres of water to produce four hundred and fifty grams of meat – one meal! – and over eighty million hectares of rainforest have been destroyed to raise livestock or grow plants for their consumption. While we might not have been showering very often, because we simply didn't own a shower, the grim reality is that even stopping showering altogether would have practically zero impact on the environment, whereas foregoing one Quarter Pounder is the equivalent of skipping about one hundred showers. We are farmers and water is our precious fuel for production and therefore our livelihood. Checking the weather app is not about assessing the need for an umbrella, it's about checking to see if we'll survive.

All these were contributing factors but I can say with absolute certainty that the bond I share with Helga was what prompted me most to turn to veganism. (That word 'veganism' sounds like

I started a daily ritual of smoking crystal meth. I will be a social outcast forever!)

My decision can be illustrated by two very distinct scenarios: if Australian supermarkets packaged dog meat for sale, would we consume it? No, because many of us have bonded with dogs (and cats, exotic birds – the list goes on). Our culture regards these animals as domestic companions so the thought of eating them revolts us. But as I've developed equally strong bonds with goats and pigs, the thought of eating neat little polystyrene and cling-wrapped packs of their bodies was unconscionable. Secondly, if I asked any omnivore to go out and slaughter their own animal then slice it up for consumption, no one I know has the stomach for it. Because an animal's death, terror, pain and suffering in the meat trade are not visible to us, most of us manage to compartmentalise its existence.

In January 2017 I was driving to meet my brother Glen and his husband, James, for a brief two-day holiday in Forster, the first little break I'd taken in recent memory. Our poor Barina had been so battered over the years the air conditioning no longer worked so I was driving with the windows down. Suddenly I smelled shit. I figured I must have stepped in some on the farm, so while driving I bent down to try to sniff my shoes – nothing. Confident it was not a personal hygiene issue, I assumed some farmer had just fertilised their roadside fields with mountains of dung. But the longer I drove, the more intense the smell became.

This game of 'where the hell is this shit smell coming from?' continued for several minutes. At last I turned a bend in the freeway and finally saw its source. Ahead of me was a truck full of animals headed for slaughter. The smell of their fear had been trailing behind them for several kilometres and now that I was close, it was unmistakable. I caught the eye of one of the sheep and its look was one of pure terror. I could not help it. I promptly burst into tears.

So taken altogether it simply became unacceptable for me to continue eating meat (not to mention asking for trouble, given my genetics).

I know 'vegan' is a word that often causes meat-eaters great stress, conjuring up images of barefoot, smelly hippies and hemp-clothed, placard-waving types, so I've come to a simple philosophy: if veganism is a scary word, just tell yourself Jeff and I have transitioned to a plant-based lifestyle.

One of the very unfortunate side effects of turning vegan was that I had to learn a whole new way of cooking. I'd amassed a vast repertoire of dishes over the years but none were vegan. The only solution was to reignite my cookbook collection, filling it afresh with vegan titles – and as if the gods of my previous Annandale life were still smiling down upon me, more vegan books seem to be released each week. Using these books as my guide, I had to reinvent the entire way I cooked. Meat was no longer used as the main flavour and texture, so at first I experimented with replacing my meaty staples with a vegan alternative. Cauliflower became the butterflied chicken in my one-pot signature dish, tofu replaced chicken breast in Asian dishes, marinated garlic mushrooms replaced pepperoni on pizza. It was a challenge to continually inspire myself to add to my repertoire but each week I'd master another dish, so in time I had thirty or forty stored in my memory bank and each I've tweaked to suit our palates.

I also experimented with meat substitutes. The worst thing in the world, believe me, is fishless tinned tuna and I didn't go much on fishless fish cakes either, though I did make my own 'chorizo' out of strong gluten flour and while it wasn't disgusting, it wasn't exactly something I'd be rushing to create again. There's a basic rule in our house: if you crave the texture and density of meat, use tofu instead. Some vegan cheeses are plastic and bland but others are barely distinguishable from the real thing and I often make my own cashew cheese, boosted by nutritional yeast, one of those 'secret' ingredients vegans use to trick the mind into thinking the tongue can taste dairy.

Eating at friends' and family's houses is a hassle we choose not to put them through so more often than not we take our own dishes, though Mum has grown quite adventurous and often goes out of her way to make us vegan meals. She and Dad even enjoy going vegan when they eat at ours (at least, Grant never passes on any second-hand complaints so I can only assume there haven't been any). Most of the time if I add enough flavour (which I'd always been a huge fan of doing) no one I cook for ever thinks twice about what's being served. Meat has just gone on a little holiday – it will be back in their lives soon enough. Even Charlie, his whole life one of the world's fussiest eaters, has ventured so far out his comfort zone that I've got him eating tofu and mushrooms and he enjoys them so much he goes back for seconds, while Lucy was inspired by us (and reading about the chicken farming industry) to go vegetarian a few months after we went vegan.

After giving up animal protein, I also started exercising with more intensity. One of the beautiful things about living where we do is observing the animals when you go for a run. I can't recall a single occasion when I haven't seen a kangaroo – usually they graze by the side of the road. Most often they jump skittishly out of the way, afraid that's a rifle I'm packing in my gym shorts. Sometimes they'll let me run past within a metre or so of them and it never ceases to amaze me how beautiful, inquisitive and mesmerising they are.

'Are they ever aggressive?' guests sometimes ask and in the past I'd dismiss the suggestion as outrageous.

However in February 2018, I'd completed a six-kilometre run and was about one hundred metres from our driveway when I heard something skid on the gravel. In my own little running world, it scared the bejesus out of me. I spun around so fast it pulled a muscle in my neck and my heart was beating even faster than usual.

About thirty metres behind me stood a large male kangaroo eyeing me suspiciously.

'You scared the fuck out of me,' I said aloud to him, then turned on my heel and kept on with my run.

Now it may have been because I was wearing a bright orange t-shirt, or perhaps the kangaroo felt confronted by my turning around to look directly at him and me being such a fine masculine, aggressive-looking specimen, but within seconds I heard the distinct hopping sound of a large kangaroo. Then he produced a deep guttural grunt, the kind I have often heard when male roos challenge each other around the property.

Still running, I turned my head to look behind me (hurting my neck again) and saw the kangaroo making a beeline for me. *Holy shit I'm a goner!* was the only thought to fill my head. I knew I wouldn't be able to outrun him and if he got close enough he could rear up on his hind legs and push me from behind. In another split second I made the snap decision to head for Natalie and Andrew's fence to place anything between my marauding mate and me.

Like the most adept stuntperson, I slid beneath that fence seamlessly because I genuinely thought my life depended on it. With two planks of wood as my safety cage, I stood and faced my attacker, waving my hands in the air and screaming at him like one of those desperate victims in the horror films we watch with Pet. *Gew* became *Shoo!*

The kangaroo stopped, stood high up on his hind legs and puffed up his chest. *I'm ready to fight*, I thought. *I'm going to have to fight for my life.* I could hear the thumping of my heart. I raised my hands again and screamed out some more and this impressive display of strength and scariness was enough to make the roo think otherwise. He skipped on a few lengths.

Oh my god, that was close, I said to myself, *wait till I tell Jeff!* I was ready to come out from behind my hidey-hole when the kangaroo stopped and turned to face me again. He gave me what I was sure was a menacing glare. *All in good time*, I swear I heard him mutter to himself before laughing wickedly.

I still go for runs, but I remain a little edgy whenever I come across a male kangaroo, and often cross the road to put a few more metres between my nemeses and me.

With a plant-based diet combined with a return to exercise, I lost ten kilograms in a little over a month and I felt as though my veins and arteries had been flushed clean. I cannot stress that point enough: I felt renewed on the inside. It's almost beyond words the overall feeling of healthiness I felt. I have experienced no side effects, no deficiencies of any kind, and my energy levels are higher than they were with pieces of meat rotting inside my gut.

I believe so many things have led me to the realisation that I no longer want to support industries that shamelessly take advantage of animals with little regard for their welfare. Moving out of apartment life made it possible for Flo (our little break-and-enter feline) to remind me how much I loved animals and missed having them in my life, which opened the door for Leroy's adoption. Dissatisfaction with the corporate world led to our desire for a tree change. Having a property large enough to accommodate animals led first to the chickens, then the pigs, goats, ducks and peafowl, and their accompanying lessons led me to a little piglet who has grown up with me and with whom I have formed an incredible bond. Helga has become the embodiment of my belief that animals deserve compassion and respect and it makes me sick to the stomach to think how much meat gets thrown away across the world – unfinished portions, meat past its use-by date, parts of the animals we choose not to eat . . .

I look into Helga's eyes and I feel at one with nature, knowing that a life of overcrowding, stress, smog, traffic, meat consumption, wealth creation and, frankly, never being satisfied with your lot in life, is worlds away from the existence Jeff and I have forged for ourselves and our menagerie of strong-willed and incredibly beautiful individuals. And if I listen closely, I'm sure I can hear Enya playing somewhere in the distance.

22

Our Little Army

There is never a day that Jeff and I wake up with nothing to do. The list of jobs is eternal; for every one completed another three are added. Emergency repairs frequently pop up. A lot of days I find myself bent over a toilet scrubbing away other peoples' excrement. This is one of the realities of our new life. I worked my guts out to get a great HSC mark, went to university for five years to study law then gradually worked my way up the corporate ladder for fifteen years to become a respected leader and yet here I am, basically a cleaner. For some, this realisation might prove depressing and it's true there are occasions when I do not enjoy the more mundane chores of running a hotel. Woe is me, I have to remind myself; billions of people around the world clean bathrooms and make beds for their spouses and kids, and they do it all for free, often with little or no thanks.

But whenever I think there might be something else I would rather be doing, I remind myself of all those city dogs chasing their own tails – a life I never want to participate in again. I would rather scrub other peoples' shit than lick more corporate arse. And besides, there will come a day that Jeff and I hire a cleaner to do the dirtier work. But for the time being it is about maximising profit margins and maintaining our high level of quality. The more people we get involved in the running of our business, we reason, the less control we have over our guests' experience.

In truth I have grown to prefer physical work to office politics. From day to day I am 'employed' at any number of trades – cleaner most regularly, but also gardener, landscaper, shopper, chef, wine-taster, barman, vine pruner, painter, handyman, animal handler, builder, fencer, concierge, water checker . . . our time is free to fill as we please with only a few pressing deadlines like the arrival of guests, the spraying of crops or harvesting.

I am always dirty. Dust and grime are everyday realities. My clothes are always getting stained or torn; my sweat is continually drying then running again. My fingernails are naturally filthy and it's rare I'm not sporting some smear from Helga's snout or the rubbing of her freshly muddied body. No job on a property the size of Block Eight is simple or small – repairing a fence can take all day, your muscles so sore by the end of it, your neck so stiff, that the dull ache permeates your entire body.

But we still love to help out friends and family where we can. We drove to Sydney and helped Jesus work on his pergola and once again I was chief labourer, carting over a hundred and thirty kilograms of pavers from one side of the yard to another. Even when Jesus left a metal clamp fastened at (my) head height and it wedged into my forehead to carve a deep Harry Potter scar, you would not have heard me complain. It's a far cry from corporate life, where I spent my time worrying whether someone in another team was telling my boss lies about me.

When Mum and Dad decided to sell their property on the Central Coast to be closer to us, we drove down to them several times to present their house for sale. I painted the entire outside from top to bottom, Jeff built them a stunning outside deck to take in the water views and we hacked down the neighbour's three-metre-thick hedge (with permission) to reveal more of that lovely enough-money-can-buy scenery. Then when they moved, we spent hour after hour landscaping their barren backyard. I pulled my back so badly I could not get up off the ground.

'Which one of you is giving me some of your Endone?' I asked politely. Both my parents' GPs handed out the drug like it was candy at a school fete and dammit, I knew they were packing.

'Endone?' Dad said vaguely. 'I don't even think we have any on the premises at the moment.'

Got ya! I thought. Dad would never use a word like 'premises'!

'One of you go and get your son a god-damn Endone!' I yelled. 'I've thrown my back out for you, now it's the least you can do.'

And of course Mum was the one to part with her precious bedmate. But that was as nasty as I got.

With debts piling and more work than we could ever complete, Jeff and I thought it would be a good idea to self-manage our super fund and buy an investment property in the town of Branxton. Mid-2017, we bought the biggest hovel; I mean the ugliest, shittiest pile of dump you have ever seen, knowing we'll have to do all of the labour in restoring it to its former lovely cottage self.

'Now remember, Jeff,' I said to him, 'this property is not worth taking risks for. No daredevils; safety must always come first.'

During demolition he said: 'Just be careful of those planks of wood you're pulling off the walls,' and I gave him that look – it was I who'd reminded him to be safe in the first place, after all.

Two minutes later a rusty nail went into my elbow but I continued demolition after the blood stopped flowing. It was going to take more than a bout of tetanus to stop this labourer from working! That night as we sat watching television, my arm went numb at the elbow and it hurt every time I moved it. Waves of pain spiralled up and down the length of my arm.

'I know you think I'm a hypochondriac,' I started defensively, 'but I think I might have done some serious damage to my elbow.'

So off we went to the hospital. Again.

After I'd been seen by the doctor I texted Jeff in the waiting room.

It's amputation, as feared, I wrote. *This is the last text I will ever send with my right hand.*

Ask if you can keep it, he texted back. *What's the 'arm in h-asking?*

In no uncertain terms, it takes a particular kind of couple to thrive when you both live and work together. You're each other's boss but also self-employed; you're each other's harshest critic but also most ardent supporter. You want everything to be perfect but have to realise that your perception of perfection is not the same as anybody else's – some days you grossly under-bake it; others you over-deliver with ease. Money is at the core of every problem you face – where it's coming from, where it's going. Financial stress is the one that can cripple any couple, no matter the depth of your love. Somehow Jeff and I scrimp from day to day and just assume that the next 'cheque' will come in before the next bill is due.

One day we played a game where we listed all the local companies we support in the running of our little business: two dairies, bakery, butcher, egg co-operative, a water company, bottling company, winery, electrician, plumber, builder, grape consultant, grape-pickers, transport companies, laundry . . . the list went on. It was only when we made a conscious effort to go local that Jeff and I truly got a sense of the local community.

Unlike the city, everyone is up for a chat; it's just part of your day. Gai-Lee at the laundry taught me how to make beds using the three-sheet method and every time we drop off or pick up the linen there's a chat and a laugh to be had. I cannot recall a single occasion of picking up the mail at the local post office, that didn't end up with the licensees, John and Margaret, and us in hysterics. Janell who organises local grape contractors is always up for a chat and a giggle, and whenever I need a single thing it seems she drops everything for her 'boys on the hill'. Her main tractor driver Beryl never visits without a hug and asking after the kids, and telling us how beautiful we are. Drivers who deliver the milk and bread each day stay for a chat, and over time we got to know more of the neighbours on our street – there are now dinners and wine aplenty. As we got talking to more of the winemakers and cellar door staff, I got to know most by name, and I'm always met with a genuine welcome and a *How are you?*, which has extended to include the staff at local restaurants and the wonderful team at the cheese factory. Even local supermarket staff know us by name and ask us how Block Eight is going, a familiarity I doubt many people enjoy in the city. All of us locals shared our fears and concerns throughout the heatwave of January and February 2018 that kept tourists away. Block Eight's income plummeted to depths we'd never seen in the six years of our tree change. It was comforting to know we were not alone, and rewarding to discuss potential strategies for plugging the gap. When you drive a vehicle emblazoned with your logo and branding, it's a daily occurrence that someone toots their horn and waves and you find yourself waving back, whether you know who it is or not.

A whole host of other companies provide assistance from further afield: designers, printers, coffee supplier, toiletries manufacturers, accountants, lawyers, insurance agencies, furniture suppliers, hardware stores, nurseries, online travel agents, payments processors, channel managers, Google . . . For every dollar we make (for the time being at least), the same dollar is being spent on all these businesses and one day in the not-too-distant future we hope some of those dollars might even find their way into our own pockets.

But over the years of our tree change, the number of people who have volunteered their time is nothing less than extra-ordinary. Mel and Jesus, of course, are always helping out but then other friends like Meredith and Lachlan came to every single working bee, as did Merv. Pet brought her parents, Rod and Anne, to work and they did so without complaint, in their late sixties performing tasks at twice the speed of people half their age. Our kids know that holidays spent at our house aren't in actual fact holidays – there is always work to be done, chores to be completed. Vicky throws herself into them with gusto.

One time we tried to instil a work ethic in the kids by making them face that pile of fence palings Jeff had scored 'for free'. Usually it's Charlie who baulks at such a massive task whereas Lucy dives right in, eager to please and get the job done right. This time, however, Charlie (in a display of earthy manliness he clearly didn't get from his father) pulled off his shirt (at least I didn't have to tear it off his back myself) and started piling those palings in the neat stack requested of him. The enormity of the task was too much for Lucy, however, and within minutes she was in hysterics, crying that she was getting splinters (no, sorry children, no gloves supplied) and that Charlie was getting in her way. But with Vicky and me dismissing the dramas and embracing Charlie's enthusiasm (that admittedly didn't last for much longer than fifty or sixty palings) we managed to get all six thousand four hundred and fifty two of Jeff's 'free' palings stacked neatly on a pallet, as per his instructions. (Disclaimer – the exact number may have been significantly less than this.)

We did try our hand at hiring help. One day a fifteen-year-old neighbour rode up our driveway on his bicycle. He introduced himself and said he was looking for work. We'd heard from our neighbour Andrew that Matthew charged himself out at twelve dollars an hour and particularly loved doing anything that utilised machinery but there was no way Jeff was going to risk hearing 'please don't hate me' from a teenager so I told him we had nothing at the moment but that he should call me in a month or two.

Two days later my phone rang. 'Hi, it's Matthew, I was just thinking maybe you had work for me now instead of in a few months.'

You had to love the kid for his mettle and industrious nature.

'Actually, I do have a job for you.'

I introduced Matthew to the paling mountain. 'You can come any day you like, work any hours you want, and all you have to do is bill me for the hours you work,' I explained. 'We need every nail removed from these palings.' (Another cost to subtract from Jeff's 'free' score.)

After an hour or so, my phone rang. 'Do you have another job for me to do? This is really boring and it's really hard.'

I showed Matthew the pigpen and instructed him how to distract Rodney and Billy in order to retrieve their not insignificant piles of poo.

'Are you over it?' Jeff asked him at the end of the day.

'I'll see you over the school holidays,' I said, miming a hammer de-nailing planks of wood.

Eerily, he never returned.

For other working bees, friends roped in friends, about half of eBay came at one point or another to pitch in, even overseas visitors like our pig-buying friend Sheena and my mate Andy who I'd met in Africa and have remained penfriends with for twenty-five years, spent hours and hours in the vines doing what needed to be done. And my lovely friend Belinda is always on hand to help, roping her mum, Virginia, in whenever we need an extra pair of hands. When she's here on holidays from Melbourne our friend Nic transforms into not-so-Lazy Susan, our work experience cleaner. The list of people who have helped is long.

But when all those people go back home to their city lives, it is just Jeff and me, two sets of hands (though one with a right hand slightly bigger than his left), shaping Block Eight from a one-house, sometimes-harvested, no-animal farm into a thriving, busy, never-dull and never-resting business and farm – and the closest-to-perfect home we could ever hope to share.

Missing in Action:
One Pig

Ten years ago de-stressing after work meant fighting through city crowds to find a bar with enough seats for the group, waiting an eternity for the bartender to catch our eye and take our order, then struggling to be heard over the noise of office workers debriefing. We'd have a few twelve-dollar glasses of wine then laziness would lead us to a fifty-dollar taxi ride and a greasy meat-laden pizza, and the whole night would set us back about two hundred dollars. Our ears would be ringing from the bar noise, our voices hoarse from yelling above it. And it might have ended with my face in a bucket thanks to my friend Belinda's bright idea to challenge me to a Rosé-drinking competition.

Our home was in Annandale on an alleyway littered with garbage bins on a plot of land tightly sandwiched between others, where the only outlook was the neighbours' roofs and walls.

But Jeff and I were content with that . . . until we got a taste of an altogether different life.

This morning we were woken by the unmistakable sound of a gas cylinder shooting flames. When we went outside in our pyjamas, a hot air balloon was directly above our villa, about thirty metres off the ground. There's something majestic, otherworldly and completely mesmerising about watching those enormous balloons float on the breeze. We waved at the passengers high up in their basket then got ourselves cups of tea to watch the balloon eventually land on the property next to ours, skimming tree tops as it came down.

Around 5pm, while Jeff was finishing tiling the bathroom, I walked up to the animal pen. I let Helga out first because she never wanders and Winston is embarrassed when she sees him stepping into his harness and won't do it if she is present. Once Helga was outside, I placed Winston's harness around his front legs – lately he had taken to licking me as I completed the task. I tapped each foot I needed him to lift and he complied with a minimum of fuss. Wesley had already gone to the lead and bit it playfully – he loves walks and knows as soon as he sees his brother in his bra he'll soon be galloping freely and munching on delicious grass.

I took the animals to the dam in the dip between our two olive groves. The water was lower than it's ever been since we moved here but there was still enough for my pig. It had been a hot day and Helga made a beeline for the mud, rolling in it awkwardly to cover herself in wet stinky sludge. Wesley found a patch of long grass to eat and Winston used his front foot to bring a branch of a gum tree closer to the ground so he could feast on its young leaves. He's a bit of a Gumby at these kinds of things but eventually he got some leaves between his teeth.

Jeff brought two glasses of our own Rosé (Belinda and I have shared many happy nights over it) and we sat on the deckchairs we'd been told we'd never get to use and talked about our day: jobs we'd finished, jobs we were yet to begin. We watched the animals frolic and feast and their antics made us chuckle as we glanced past our vineyard to the commanding view of the national park, and the silhouette of the Great Dividing Range beyond. For as far as our eyes could see there was not a single man-made object. We never tire of this beauty.

Two of our guests walked over to join us. Patrick and Veronica are a young Italian couple living in Sydney and this was their second visit to us in a matter of weeks: they had fallen in love with Helga and returned with the specific purpose of seeing her again.

Helga lived up to her reputation and showed them great affection. She crawled over Patrick and leaned up to place her snout against his lips as he kissed and cuddled her with genuine fondness.

'This is his real girlfriend,' Veronica said teasingly but Patrick was oblivious. His attention was solely on my pig and she was feeding off it; lapping it up.

Helga sat for him like a good girl and that strange look of pride came across her face. She opened her mouth in what initially looked like a smile but soon developed into a yawn – her bottom teeth are small and comical and the yawn made us all laugh.

I try to be objective but cannot ignore Helga's magnetism. There is something about this pig that is hard to define – her joie de vivre is infectious but more than that, this sow seems to touch people in a profound way. They flock to her, feel a need to touch her and bond with her. Later Veronica would post photos of their Helga encounter on Instagram and the caption read: *Be kind to all kinds.*

It feels as though life with Helga is the end of the first chapter of what has proven to be one of the greatest experiences of our lives and every step along the way has got us to this point, to wine by the dam late in the afternoon with people we would never have met in the bustle of a crowded city. Unlike the boardroom, there are no lies or deception here; there is no self-serving ulterior motive. It just is.

Later that night I told our neighbour Natalie about Helga's biggest fans.

'You should write down all your Block Eight stories,' she said.

'As if I have time for that,' I scoffed, and poured her another glass of our latest Chardonnay.

The following morning, I had reached the last part of my routine and the bit I savoured the most. I delivered Helga her bowl of milk and she vacuumed it up in a few hungry seconds like it was the last she'd ever receive. Drunk on its goodness and brimming with excitement, she trotted around her pen then came to me for cuddles.

Once she was comfortable she started to nuzzle gently into the meaty part of my thumb, making quiet sucking noises. Her breathing steadied and as I scratched her lightly on the belly in regular circular motions, her eyes slowly began to close and I could imagine that she thought she was back with her mother, safe against the warmth of mum's gut with siblings by her side.

A sneeze from the goats startled her and she opened her eyes, but only for a moment, and when she saw me above her she knew she was safe. She closed her eyes again to continue her suckling.

This moment never lasts long because Helga is very busy and has much to do, but for those few minutes each morning we are closer than I've been with any other animal. Together we are quiet and calm.

While Helga suckled I made a mental list of all the jobs I had to complete and I took deep, contented breaths.

In an instant she was off, bursting back into the goats' pen to chase Winston and hunt for their spilled food. I got up and brushed myself down.

As I began my work day, I thought, *How lucky are we?* And then, *But dammit we deserve this after everything we've done to get here.*

The following night, Jeff and I celebrated our fifth anniversary at Block Eight by going to our favourite local restaurant. We had fifty-six dollars in our bank account and were in debt to the tune of a million dollars but to us, it was worth toasting our 'magnificent success'.

Two urban yuppies who could barely grow a pot of herbs had thrown in ludicrously lucrative careers to try their hand at farming, building, hotel-running, animal husbandry and everything in between. Our business still wasn't profitable but it was bringing in more gross income than we received as employees in the big smoke. We now knew how to grow high-quality wine grapes, turn them into award-winning wine and sell out of it each and every year. We had an accommodation business with a weekend occupancy rate in the ninetieth percentile. We knew how to care for animals we'd never encountered before, and even how to massage an eggbound chook. Sure, I still had sleepless nights over finances, but what small business owner doesn't?

We'd suffered the heartbreak of losing entire crops and animals we loved but these were balanced by the insurmountable highs of sharing Block Eight with our kids, and Mel and

Jesus's daughters. We'd endured floods and severe droughts, prepared for the worst as thick clouds of bushfire smoke darkened our property, and ran out to see hot air balloons land on our open fields. My in-remission mum was also helping out at Block Eight, getting the villas ready with stock for the guests' arrival, and the sight of her in her little Block Eight uniform was as cute as a button. Try as I might, I'd also let those stupid bloody tanks run out of water again and again and to this day I have lost count of the emergency phone calls I've placed to Phil.

We'd never worked so hard but we were happier than we had ever been sitting around boardroom tables, and with all of that behind us, the business was edging closer to being in the black – so what if our own villa lacked a shower or kitchen because quite honestly I'd forgotten what those things actually were.

'To five years,' Jeff raised his glass.

'To us,' I chinked mine with his. 'You know, I think it's time we expanded the business.'

'Yeah, right,' he said with a chuckle.

'No, I mean it. I've been thinking . . .'

And two months later we purchased a tour bus and were in the midst of building a wine bar that levered out over our main dam. It's a structure we built ourselves, with no help from anyone. I even proved myself a better than competent labourer to Jeff's builder, pre-empting his needs by fetching this tool or that, keeping a spotless work site just like Pete demanded of Jeff when he taught him all he knew. Me, a builder's labourer and chief saw operator! Yes folks, I had finally overcome my affliction – well, nearly . . . just don't ask me to cut along a line with a pair of scissors. We had plans to build our animals a beautiful large enclosure so I was in search of the next addition – undecided between a deer, llamas, a cow or a donkey.

If boredom in Annandale was our nemesis, at Block Eight the only thing we ever had to worry about was exhaustion (and angry kangaroos).

Just when you think you're on top of things, Block Eight sometimes finds a way to knock you back a peg or two, keep you honest and remind you that you're at its mercy.

It began with a broken whipper snipper, but that was fine; we were in drought so the grass wasn't long. The following week, an air conditioner in one of the villas broke during a forty-degree heatwave. Then, in the same villa, an electrical fault caused the spa bath to stop working. We had to wait on spare parts so apologised to our guests but received our first complaints since opening. It was depressing to have things out of our control impact our guests' experience. The heatwave had been keeping guests away – for two months our business had been down forty per cent on the previous year – but at least the new tours were helping plug some of that gap.

Taking advantage of some of the guest-free days, Jeff and I continued to work on the wine room, taking four long, hot, exhausting days to build and install the roof, forcing me to face my fear of heights and just concentrate on getting the job done. It was such a happy milestone for us when we had it all in place. Not long after, the rains finally came and our fields turned from dead brown grass to thick lush green. Then the ride-on mower broke and it took weeks to get the replacement parts and the grass went crazy.

Our friend Richard was staying with us and, being a builder, he reminded Jeff to strap down the fancy new roof we'd built or one strong wind would blow the whole thing off. But it was a job Jeff was dreading so he put it off.

Then the front door lock broke in the same villa where we'd just repaired the air conditioner and spa and, after replacing the blades in the mower, I was two hours into my eighteen-hour mow-a-thon when it got a flat tyre. I moved on to whipper snipping with the new machine we'd bought because repairing the old one would have been too expensive.

But at least the wine room was coming on in leaps and bounds. We'd even started talking about dates for a launch party.

I took the animals for their afternoon walk and, as it began to drizzle, we took shelter in the wine room with Jeff, who was just putting away all his tools. The rain got heavier, then it began to hail, then the wind whipped up and began to blow the rain horizontally into the unsealed room. The animals panicked and, though the storm was ferocious, we concentrated on keeping them calm. Then in the roar of the wind and rain the entire roof of the wine room peeled off and disappeared. Jeff and I just looked at each other in complete *What the fuck?*

But there wasn't time to think. Helga was terrified and wasn't having a bar of that shit – she ran off into the rain, heading for the bush. I knew my pig and I worried she would keep running until exhaustion took over and then she would be lost to me forever, disoriented in the bushland adjoining our property and never able to find her way home. My heart sank; I had to go after her. The rain bucketed down and I bolted in the direction she had run but the goats wouldn't let me out of their sight and, even though they hate rain more than anything in the world, they chased after me.

I called out Helga's name as loudly as I could, but I could barely hear it myself so there was no way she was going to know I was looking for her. Lightning lit up the sky, thunder crashed overhead and that wind – the one capable of ripping an entire roof structure off a building – was bending trees about us at incredible angles. It wasn't safe for the goats outside, so I ran all the way back to their pen to lock them away. By now Jeff had joined me so we could look for Helga together. The thought of losing her was pure agony.

As I got to the pen with my confused, drenched and frightened goats I knew my search for Helga might take hours but I would do anything to make sure she was safe. I walked through the open gate . . . and there she was. She was terrified and moaning with exhaustion. I doubt I had ever been happier to see a pig. My lovely little pig.

Animals corralled, it was time to face the situation at the wine room. Hours and hours of work, thousands and thousands of dollars wasted. But how incredibly close that roof had come to the overhead power lines, which could have severed and shot sparks around wildly, just metres from where the animals and Jeff and I had stood.

'We have to concentrate on how fortunate we were that things weren't much worse for us,' I said to Jeff.

'But sometimes you just feel like throwing in the towel and walking away,' he said. I had never heard him sound so dejected since moving to the property. 'I had the strapping of the roof down on my list of things to do tomorrow.'

'Don't worry, Jeffy,' I said. 'I'll help you build it again. I'll be with you every step of the way. Now come on, let's go shopping to buy some lovely cushions for our soon-to-be-finished wine room.'

And just like magic, his face lit up.

Easy Recipes

Smaller Meals

Crumbed Mushrooms with Roasted Vegetables

Serves 4

Once after a long day driving the tour bus, I came home to this delicious meal Jeff had invented. The mushrooms were so soft and creamy, the coating so crunchy, it was amazing! Naturally I had to tweak the recipe a little, but full credit to Jeff for coming up with the hummus-and-breadcrumb coating.

Ingredients

For the roasted vegetables

4 potatoes

2 onions

1 fennel bulb

2 apples

4 cloves garlic

Olive oil spray (make your own spray with a high-quality olive oil and put in a mist gun you can buy at department stores)

2 sprigs rosemary

Sea salt

For the mushrooms

1 cup vegan breadcrumbs or corn flake crumbs

2 tsp garlic salt

1 tsp onion powder

½ tsp freshly cracked pepper

1 tsp dried thyme

4 tbsp hummus

2 tbsp non-dairy milk

500g medium-sized flat field or brown mushrooms

Olive oil spray

Method

- Preheat oven to 180 degrees Celsius.

- Cut the potatoes, onions, fennel and apples into equal-sized cubes of around 2cm.

- Place vegetables in a roasting tray with four peeled whole garlic cloves (or more to taste).

- Spray with olive oil, sprinkle with rosemary and sea salt and toss to combine.

- Bake in the oven until the potatoes are soft, around 45 minutes.

- While the vegetables are roasting, in a bowl mix together breadcrumbs, garlic salt, onion powder, pepper and thyme.

- In another bowl mix together the hummus and milk.

- Roll the whole mushrooms in the hummus mixture then roll in the breadcrumb mixture until each mushroom is completely coated.

- Once the potatoes have been baking for 25 minutes, place the mushrooms on a baking tray and spray generously with olive oil. Bake for around 20 minutes or until the breadcrumbs are nicely toasted.

- To serve, divide the roasted vegetables between each plate and top with the crumbed mushrooms.

The Raw and the Cooked

Serves 4

I'm still stuck in the 1980s so the name of this recipe gives a nod to the Fine Young Cannibals album (ironic, being vegan!). Sometimes salads can be boring. I wanted to create one with a great variety of textures, flavours and a little chilli hit but which is still fast and easy to make. I like the contrast of the hot potatoes with those crunchy raw salad vegetables.

Ingredients
For the salad

4 medium white potatoes, washed but unpeeled

1 red onion

1 large raw beetroot (yellow if you can find it)

6 button mushrooms

1 red capsicum

1 Lebanese cucumber

4 radishes

½ cup fresh parsley

For the dressing

1 punnet cherry tomatoes

½ cup pitted olives

2 tbsp capers

2 tsp sea salt

1 tbsp balsamic vinegar

1 tsp seeded mustard

1 chilli, chopped (red with seeds for maximum heat, green without seeds for a slight hit)

Method

- Prick the potatoes thoroughly with a fork, then space evenly on a microwave-safe plate. Microwave on high until the potatoes are completely tender, around 12–15 minutes.

- While the potatoes are cooking, slice all the other salad ingredients as thinly as you can – a mandolin gives good results.

- In a mortar, place all the dressing ingredients and carefully smash with the pestle. (Cherry tomatoes will squirt so be careful, or you could use a food processor.)

- Assemble the salad by placing hot potato slices on each plate first, then the onion. Sprinkle with a little sea salt.

- Top with the rest of the salad ingredients, ensuring all the colours are visible.

- Spoon the dressing on top of each salad.

Oregano and Chilli Charred Tofu on an Orange, Fennel, Rocket and Cashew Salad

Serves 4

I used to make a version of this salad using pork fillets. It's fast, easy and delicious and tofu makes it even simpler and tastier. The contrast between the softness of the tofu and the crunch of the salad makes it very more-ish. Barbecuing the tofu lessens the heat of the chilli but you can also cook it in the oven or grill for spicier results.

Ingredients
For the tofu
1 tbsp dried chilli flakes
1 tbsp dried oregano
1 tsp sea salt
375g firm tofu
Olive oil spray

For the salad
1 bulb fennel
4 stalks celery
1 red onion
2 oranges, peeled and segmented
1 handful rocket
½ cup salted cashews, crushed

For the dressing
½ cup vegan mayonnaise
1 tbsp Dijon mustard
2 tsp apple cider vinegar
1 tsp sea salt

Method
- Preheat a barbecue hot plate.

- Combine the chilli, oregano and sea salt in a shallow bowl.

- Slice the tofu into eight even-sized lengths (about 1cm wide).

- Spray each slice of tofu with olive oil then roll in the chilli mixture. Set aside.

- Slice the salad vegetables thinly and toss in a bowl with the orange segments and rocket to combine.

- Stir together the dressing ingredients then mix through the salad and leave the flavours to intensify.

- Spray the chilli tofu slices with a little extra olive oil.

- Cook the tofu on the barbecue for 1–2 minutes each side, until the chilli starts to blacken.

- To serve, pile salad on serving plates, top with two slices of chilli tofu then sprinkle with the crushed salted cashews.

Stuffed Sweet Potatoes with Chilli, Garlic & Shallots

Serves 4

This is another great lunchtime meal or a flavour-packed entrée. The secret to these stuffed spuds is to keep the flavours raw and cooking the sweet potatoes in the microwave first makes it fast and fuss-free.

Ingredients
2 orange sweet potatoes, washed but unpeeled
2 green spring onions/shallots, sliced
2 cloves garlic, crushed
2 green chillis, sliced (with seeds for extra spice)
2 tbsp chopped parsley
1 tbsp chopped dill
80g vegan cheese (fetta- or mozzarella-style)
1 tsp sea salt
2 cups mixed salad greens
1 tbsp olive oil
2 tsp balsamic vinegar
Salt and pepper

Method
- Preheat oven to 180 degrees Celsius.

- Prick the sweet potatoes all over with a fork, then space evenly on a microwave-safe plate. Microwave on high until tender, around 12–15 minutes.

- While the sweet potatoes are cooking, combine the spring onions, garlic, chillis, parsley, dill, cheese and sea salt in a large bowl.

- When the sweet potatoes are cooked, cut each in half lengthways then scoop out the soft flesh, leaving about 1cm against the skin. Place the flesh in the bowl with the onions and other ingredients and mix well.

- Spoon the sweet potato mixture back into the skins.

- Place the stuffed sweet potatoes on a lined baking tray and bake in the oven until piping hot.

- Serve with salad greens that have been tossed with olive oil, balsamic, salt and pepper.

Roasted Cauliflower Wraps

Serves 4

Charred cauliflower brings whole new meaning to that humble vegetable. Topped with hummus and some crunchy pickled vegetables, it's hard to find a tastier, healthier lunch.

Ingredients
1 head cauliflower
2 tbsp olive oil
1 tbsp sea salt
4 tbsp hummus
4 vegan wraps
¼ jar of pickled vegetables, sliced
½ red onion, finely sliced
1 cup rocket
Sea salt
Chinese chilli sauce (optional)

Method
- Preheat the oven to 180 degrees Celsius.
- Break the cauliflower into evenly sized florets, about the size of golf balls – they will shrink a little when cooked.
- Toss the cauliflower florets with the olive oil and sea salt.
- Place on a lined baking tray and bake for around 25 minutes, or until the cauliflower has developed a toasty brown colour.
- Spread 1 tbsp of hummus on each wrap.
- Top with cauliflower, pickled vegetables, onion and rocket and sprinkle over a little sea salt and chilli sauce (if using).
- Roll up the wrap and eat immediately.

Midnight Friday Special

Serves 2

I'm the first to admit this isn't really a recipe that requires a lot of cooking but Jeff and I stumbled across this one night in the middle of a drinking session. Non-vegans would fortify their stomachs with salty melted cheese but we have found this to be a delicious alternative.

Ingredients
4 thick slices vegan white sourdough bread
4 tsp vegan butter (I use Nuttelex Buttery)
4 tbsp no-sugar crunchy peanut butter
Sea salt

Method
- Pop your bread in the toaster and toast to your taste (I think it's better just blonde, Jeff prefers it dark).

- Spread 1 tsp of butter on each slice of hot toast.

- Spread 1 tbsp of peanut butter.

- Sprinkle with sea salt to taste.

- Eat while binging on your favourite Netflix show and drinking a glass of dry Rosé.

Todd Alexander

Tahini Creamed Spinach with Cherry Tomatoes and Toasted Pine Nuts

Serves 2 (or 4 as a side dish)

This is based on a dish Cheryl used to make us for dinner in Petersham. I've upped the flavours of this one a bit and added some wine to create richness, while the nuts add a lovely crunch. She'll insist I've tampered with an original but sometimes you *can* improve on perfection.

Ingredients
3 tbsp pine nuts
2 tbsp olive oil
2 cloves garlic, crushed
1 punnet cherry tomatoes, halved
1 bunch spinach, chopped
2 tbsp tahini
1 cup Semillon

Method
- Place pine nuts on a baking tray in a 180-degree-Celsius oven and roast until toasty brown, about 8–10 minutes.

- Heat oil in a saucepan then add the garlic, stirring constantly to ensure it doesn't burn, and cook for 1 minute.

- Add the cherry tomatoes and cook for a further minute.

- Add the spinach and stir until the leaves have all wilted, about 2–3 minutes.

- Stir in the tahini until all of the spinach is nicely coated.

- Pour in the Semillon and cook until most of the liquid has evaporated, stirring occasionally.

- Serve immediately topped with the toasted pine nuts.

Larger Meals

Easy Silverbeet Filo Tart

Serves 12 (makes 2 tarts)

This is vegan fast food at its best. I usually keep a few of these pre-cut in the freezer so whenever we want something quickly we can just pop one in the oven until hot.

Ingredients

1 packet frozen vegan filo pastry (18 sheets), defrosted
    overnight in the fridge (most are made with oil, not butter
    but double check)

3 large bunches of silverbeet

4 cloves garlic, peeled

1 tbsp sea salt

Olive oil spray

200g vegan mozzarella cheese, grated

1 tsp nutmeg

Method

- Preheat oven to 180 degrees Celsius.

- Wash the silverbeet in cold water then strip the silverbeet from its stalks by ripping the leaves into smaller pieces.

Do not dry the leaves as the water will help them cook. You will now have a massive pile of torn leaves, but don't worry – they wilt down a lot.

- Place the garlic cloves and sea salt in the bottom of a large saucepan then place the silverbeet on top. Cook until the leaves are all tender (they will turn a dark green colour), ensuring you keep stirring them around so the heat disperses evenly and they cook at the same rate.

- Once cooked, pour the leaves into a colander, and remove the garlic cloves.

- Once cooled, squeeze as much moisture out of the leaves as you can – you should end up with about two cups of densely packed leaves.

- Roughly chop the silverbeet.

- To assemble the tart, unroll the filo pastry then carefully remove the first sheet.

- Spray the bottom of a tart tin with olive oil spray, then put the sheet of filo on the bottom. The sheet will come up over the edge of the tray. Spray lightly with oil.

- Keep adding layers of filo pastry one on top of the other, spraying with oil each time, allowing the excess pastry to overhang opposite sides of the tray.

- Once you have used half the packet of filo (9 sheets), repeat this layering process for the second tart.

- Spread half of the grated cheese on the bottom of each tart, then sprinkle over the chopped silverbeet.

- Fold over the pastry overhangs so they become the top of the tart, then spray the top lightly with olive oil and sprinkle over the nutmeg.

- Bake for 20 minutes or until the top is golden brown.

- You can slice each tart into six pieces and place in the freezer until you're ready to eat it.

- To re-heat, place frozen portion in a 160-degree-Celsius oven for 15 minutes or until a knife inserted into the middle of the tart comes out hot.

Roasted Cauliflower with Semillon Vegetables

Here is my vegan version of the one-pot chicken dish I created when we moved to the Hunter. It's loosely based on Maggie Beer's Chicken & Grape Pie.

Ingredients

4 white potatoes, thinly sliced

300g brown mushrooms, sliced

2 brown onions, thinly sliced

1 cup large green olives (with pips tastes better but makes it more difficult to eat)

10 sprigs thyme

Sea salt

2 heads garlic, cut in half horizontally

1 whole cauliflower, sliced into 3cm 'steaks'

1 cup vegan vegetable stock

1 cup Semillon

Olive oil spray

Salt and pepper, extra

2 tbsp flour

Method

- Preheat oven to 180 degrees Celsius.

- In a deep (about 10cm) roasting dish, layer the potatoes, then mushrooms, then onions, then olives, then thyme, sprinkling each vegetable layer with a little sea salt.

- Place the garlic heads skin side down and then place the cauliflower steaks on top.

- Pour over the vegetable stock, then the Semillon.

- Spray the cauliflower with the olive oil then season well with salt and pepper.

- Cover dish with foil and place in the oven.

- After one hour, remove dish from the oven and carefully turn over the cauliflower steaks. Cover with the foil and return to the oven.

- After another hour the cauliflower should be tender, and so should the potatoes at the bottom of the dish.

- Remove the foil and place dish back in the oven for a further thirty minutes until the cauliflower is nicely browned.

- Remove from the oven and, using a ladle, remove two cups of the liquid from the bottom of the dish.

- Place liquid in a saucepan and bring to the boil, then sprinkle flour over it using a sieve.

- Stir the gravy constantly to ensure there are no lumps, and cook for 2–3 minutes until thick. Check for seasoning and add a little more salt and pepper if required. Transfer to a pouring jug.

- Serve the roasting dish and jug in the middle of the table so people can help themselves.

Kale, Quinoa and Mushroom Bowl

Serves 2

We have a little local wholefoods café in East Maitland that specialises in organic and vegan foods – it's always a treat to discover a restaurant that caters to vegans and it's becoming more common even in rural areas. This is my version of their quinoa bowl – packed full of flavour and freshness. I use micro-wavable quinoa to make this dish super-fast and easy.

Ingredients

3 tbsp sesame seeds

1 tbsp sesame oil

2 cloves garlic, crushed

2 inches fresh ginger, grated

1 red chilli, sliced, seeds removed

500g mushrooms, sliced

3 tbsp salt-reduced soy sauce

1 bunch kale, sliced

1 packet microwavable (semi-cooked) quinoa

4 tbsp sauerkraut

4 tbsp hummus

1 avocado, sliced (optional)

Method

- Gently toast the sesame seeds in a frying pan until golden brown, then remove from the heat and set aside.

- Heat the sesame oil in the frying pan then add the garlic, ginger and chilli, stirring frequently to ensure they do not burn. Stir-fry for 1 minute.

- Add the sliced mushrooms and stir well, ensuring the mushrooms are coated nicely with the garlic mixture. Stir-fry for 2 minutes.

- Add 2 tbsp of the soy sauce and stir-fry for a further two minutes until the mushrooms are tender.

- Add the kale and quinoa and stir-fry 2–3 minutes until the kale is tender.

- Add the remaining 1 tbsp soy sauce and stir well.

- To serve, place the quinoa mixture on a plate, top with 2 tbsp each of the sauerkraut and hummus and half a sliced avocado (if using). Sprinkle over with toasted sesame seeds.

Tofu with Green Thai Sauce

Serves 4

Here is my vegan version of a steamed chicken dish I was addicted to when I worked in the city. I use microwavable rice so I can make this dish in a hurry, usually in less than fifteen minutes. Jeff can't stand Szechuan pepper so I'm not allowed to use it but I can't get enough of its lemony numbing taste, so if you're more like me than he, replace the chilli powder with ground Szechuan.

Ingredients
2 cloves garlic
2 inch piece fresh ginger
4 spring onions/shallots, dark green ends only
½ stick lemongrass
½ bunch coriander leaves (don't use the stalks)
1 tsp vegan stock powder
3 tbsp sesame oil
3 tbsp coarse breadcrumbs or corn flake crumbs
2 tsp chilli powder or Szechuan pepper
375g firm tofu
Olive oil spray
Mixed Asian greens
1 pack microwaveable (semi-cooked) jasmine rice
4 tbsp salt-reduced soy sauce
2 tbsp Chinese chilli sauce

Method

- Preheat oven to 180 degrees Celsius.

- Place the garlic, ginger, shallots, lemongrass, coriander and stock powder in a mortar and bash with the pestle until you end up with a thick green paste. It should take about 3–4 minutes.

- Stir in 2 tbsp of the sesame oil and set aside.

- Mix together the breadcrumbs (or corn flake crumbs) and chilli powder (or Szechuan pepper) in a shallow bowl.

- Cut the tofu into 12 even lengths (a little less than 1cm wide).

- Spray each piece of tofu with a little olive oil, then dip into the breadcrumb mixture and roll until each piece is well coated.

- Place the tofu on a lined baking tray and spray each with a little more oil.

- Bake for 10–15 minutes or until the breadcrumbs are lightly toasted.

- While the tofu is cooking, heat the remaining 1 tbsp sesame oil in a frying pan then add in your chosen Asian greens. Stir-fry until tender.

- Cook the rice according to the packet directions.

- To serve, place a mound of rice on one half of each plate and top with the tofu. Place the vegetables on the other half of the plate. Drizzle each piece of tofu with some of the soy sauce then top with dollops of the green sauce.

- Top with Chinese chilli sauce, to taste.

Pumpkin 'Burrito' with Beans and Rice

Serves 6

Every once in a while, I don't mind cheating by using store-bought spice mixes. Most of the packs available in the Mexican section of the supermarket are vegan and, in an effort to avoid bread for the day, I played around with this idea to create a really tasty bread-free Mexican meal.

Ingredients
2 butternut pumpkins
2 tbsp olive oil
2 red onions, sliced
2 red capsicums, sliced
250g mushrooms, sliced
½ red cabbage, shredded
2 packets burrito seasoning
1 cup water
240g vegan mozzarella cheese
1 tin red kidney beans
1 family bag microwaveable (semi-cooked) rice
½ bunch coriander, chopped
4 tbsp jalapenos, sliced
4 tbsp pitted kalamata olives, sliced

Method
- Preheat oven to 180 degrees Celsius.

- Cut each pumpkin into thirds so that you're left with six roughly evenly sized pieces – each with at least one flat end. Carefully scoop out the flesh from each of the pumpkin lengths using a spoon, leaving behind about 2cm of flesh against the skin. Discard the scooped out flesh – use in a soup or another recipe.

- Heat the olive oil in a large frying pan, then add the onions, capsicums, mushrooms and cabbage, and cook until all the vegetables are almost tender (about 5 minutes).

- Stir in the burrito seasoning with 1 cup of water and continue cooking, stirring occasionally until nearly all the liquid has evaporated (about 5 minutes).

- Place 40g of cheese in the bottom of each pumpkin piece, then top with the burrito vegetable mixture.

- Place pumpkin on a lined baking tray, wrap in foil and bake for 45 minutes or until the pumpkin is squishy and tender.

- Drain the beans in a colander and mix together in a micro-wave-safe bowl with the rice.

- Cover with plastic film and microwave on high for 2–3 minutes, until the rice is fluffy and tender. Stir through the coriander.

- To serve, place the pumpkin on the rice mixture and sprinkle over the chopped jalapenos and olives.

Vegan Pizzas – Even Better than the Real Thing

Serves 4

I was vegetarian for seven years in my twenties but the thing that brought me back to meat was pepperoni pizza. It's the one dish I could eat every day of my life and never grow tired of. I'll be honest and admit I miss it (a bit) but veganism has forced a whole new way of thinking about pizza. The secret to these pizzas is to cook the toppings first so the flavours and textures are more intense.

Ingredients

For the bases
2 vegan pizza bases
6 tbsp tomato or barbecue pizza sauce
200g vegan mozzarella cheese
Vegan parmesan cheese (optional)

For the toppings
NUTTY CAULIFLOWER PIZZA
½ cauliflower
Olive oil spray
1 tbsp vegan butter
150g almonds, roughly chopped

GARLIC MUSHROOM PIZZA
200g brown mushrooms, sliced
2 cloves garlic, halved
6 sprigs thyme, leaves only (removed from stalks)
2 tbsp vegan butter
2 tsp sea salt

POTATO & ROSEMARY PIZZA
2 large white potatoes
2 sprigs rosemary
2 tsp chilli flakes
2 tsp sea salt
2 tbsp olive oil

MEXICAN PIZZA
2 tbsp olive oil
Kernels from 1 corn cob
1 zucchini, sliced
200g red kidney beans
1 red onion, sliced
1 red chilli, sliced
1 avocado, sliced

Method
- Preheat oven to 180 degrees Celsius.

NUTTY CAULIFLOWER PIZZA
- Break the cauliflower into evenly sized florets, spray with olive oil and bake until browned and tender (about 20 minutes).

- Place butter in a microwave-safe bowl and heat on high until butter is melted. Add the chopped almonds and heat on high for a further 2 minutes.

GARLIC MUSHROOM PIZZA

- In a microwave-safe bowl, mix the mushrooms, garlic cloves, thyme, butter and sea salt in a bowl. Microwave for 8 minutes until the mushrooms have absorbed most of the liquid. Remove and discard the garlic cloves.

POTATO & ROSEMARY PIZZA

- In a bowl, mix the potato slices, rosemary leaves, chilli flakes and sea salt with the olive oil. Place in one even layer on a lined baking tray and bake in a 180-degree-Celsius oven for 15 minutes, or until the potatoes are evenly browned and tender.

MEXICAN PIZZA

- In a frying pan, heat olive oil, then add the corn, zucchini, beans, onion and chilli. Stir-fry for 5 minutes until all vegetables are tender.

- Set aside avocado for assembly.

TO ASSEMBLE THE PIZZAS

- Spread each pizza base with half of the pizza sauce and cut each base in half.

- Top each half with 1 of the 4 toppings.

- Sprinkle each pizza half with 50g cheese, and bake on oiled baking trays for 10–15 minutes or until the cheese is melted and the bases are firm.

- To serve the Mexican pizza, top with sliced avocado.

Smoky Roasted Pumpkin with Chardonnay Lentils

Serves 4

Pumpkin is a vegan's best friend and I find slow roasting it with smoky spices turns it into something out of this world. Here it's served with vinegary Chardonnay lentils – one of our go-to meals at least once a week.

Ingredients

For the pumpkin

1 butternut pumpkin, cut into 8 thick wedges

3 tbsp extra-virgin olive oil

1 tbsp smoked paprika

1 tbsp cumin seeds

1 tbsp sea salt

For the lentils

1 tbsp olive oil

2 red onions, sliced

2 cloves garlic, crushed

2 carrots, finely diced

3 celery sticks, finely diced

2 red apples, unpeeled, cored, finely diced

1 tbsp dried oregano

12 Brussels sprouts, sliced

400g tin brown lentils, drained

2 vegan vegetable stock cubes

250ml Chardonnay

3 tbsp fresh dill, chopped

For the dressing
150ml extra-virgin olive oil
50ml sherry vinegar
Ground black pepper

Method

- Preheat oven to 180 degrees Celsius.

- Place the pumpkin wedges in a bowl with the 3 tbsp olive oil, paprika, cumin and sea salt. Mix well to ensure each wedge is coated nicely.

- Place wedges on a lined baking tray and bake for 40 minutes, or until tender.

- In the meantime, prepare the lentils. Heat 1 tbsp olive oil in a frying pan then add onions and garlic and cook for 2 minutes, stirring constantly so they do not burn.

- Lower the heat and add carrots, celery and dried oregano, and cook for a further 5 minutes or until the vegetables are tender.

- Add the sliced Brussels sprouts, apples, drained lentils, 2 stock cubes and Chardonnay and stir well. Cook for 3 minutes then stir through with the chopped dill.

- For the dressing, combine the olive oil, sherry vinegar and black pepper and whisk well.

- To serve, divide the Chardonnay lentils between each plate and top with 2 pumpkin wedges. Pour over with the dressing.

Best Ever Felafel Rolls

Makes 8–10

When I used to do the Thursday night shift at Dymocks we'd go out for beers afterwards and, without fail, I'd stop off at the kebab shop in Glebe and grab myself a felafel roll. Unlike most fast food, nothing beats a homemade felafel – shop-bought are always dry and tasteless. The added crunch of pomegranate seeds in these wraps makes them completely irresistible. Inspired by a recipe in the Hippie Lane cookbook.

Ingredients
For the felafel
400g tin brown lentils or four-bean mix
½ bag microwaveable (semi-cooked) quinoa
2 cloves garlic, crushed
2 tbsp lemon juice
1 small red onion, finely diced
1 bunch of parsley, chopped
1 tbsp chilli sauce
2 tbsp chick pea flour (or any gluten-free flour)
2 tsp vegan stock powder
Olive oil spray

For the hummus
400g tin chick peas
2 cloves garlic
3 tbsp lemon juice
3 tbsp tahini
6 tbsp iced water

For the salad
1 bunch parsley, chopped
½ bunch mint, chopped
2 tomatoes, diced
1 red onion, finely diced
½ bag microwaveable (semi-cooked) quinoa
2 tbsp lemon juice
1 tsp sea salt
Seeds of 1 pomegranate

To serve
Vegan Lebanese bread

Method
- Preheat oven to 180 degrees Celsius.

- In a food processor, blend all the felafel ingredients except the olive oil spray until it comes together in a wet dough-like consistency. (I've also tried cutting everything by hand and mashing the lentils/beans – this gives a meatier, chunkier texture, which I prefer.)

- Shape the felafel into small balls, about the size of a golf ball (you may need to wet your hands a little as the mixture can be sticky).

- Place on a lined baking tray, flatten slightly with the palm of your hand and spray with olive oil.

- Bake for 10 minutes, flip the felafel and bake for a further 10 minutes.

- In a food processor, blend all the hummus ingredients except the ice water until you get a chunky, paste-like consistency.

- Add 2 tbsp of iced water at a time while the food processor is running. Once you've added all the water, keep the processor running until the hummus is ultra-smooth and creamy (up to 5 minutes).

- Mix all the salad ingredients together and let sit for 15 minutes to allow the flavours to develop. (The best way of getting the pomegranate seeds out is to cut the fruit in half, hold a half seed-side down over a bowl and hit the top of the fruit – the skin side – with a wooden spoon. Most of the seeds will fall out without the white membrane, but if any membrane does fall into the bowl, just pick it out.)

- Spread the Lebanese bread generously with the hummus. Crumble two or three felafel on top and spoon over the salad. Wrap up tightly and eat.

Something Sweet

Oreo Choc-orange Mousse Cups

Serves 4

When I found out that traditional (plain) Oreos were vegan, I knew it was a very dangerous discovery! Here is a simple and delicious dessert that will impress guests who will never know it's vegan.

Ingredients
For the base
1 packet plain Oreos
4 tbsp orange marmalade

For the mousse
¼ cup coconut milk
1 cup vegan chocolate buttons
2 ripe avocados, peeled and de-seeded
¼ tsp sea salt
2 tsp vanilla extract
3 tbsp maple syrup
4 tbsp toasted hazelnuts

Method

- Place the Oreos inside a tough freezer bag and crush carefully with a rolling pin.

- Divide the crushed biscuits evenly between 4 serving glasses or dishes.

- Place 1 tbsp orange marmalade on top of each biscuit base by dropping small amounts evenly over it.

- Place coconut milk in a microwave-safe dish and heat on high for 2 minutes.

- Pour the vegan chocolate buttons into the hot milk and stir until completely melted, then transfer to a blender bowl.

- Add the avocado flesh, sea salt, vanilla and maple syrup, and blend until completely smooth.

- Spoon the chocolate mixture evenly over the orange marmalade.

- Place in the fridge to set at least 30 minutes, or until serving.

- Before serving, sprinkle over toasted hazelnuts.

Chocolate Olive Oil Cake

Most recipes for olive oil cake call for mild (read: bland) olive oils but I love using our extra-virgin olive oil in desserts because the fruitiness of it really complements the chocolate and the peppery kick it gives adds a mellow spiciness.

Ingredients
For the wet ingredients
150ml extra-virgin olive oil
150ml water
1 tbsp vanilla extract
1 tbsp balsamic vinegar

For the dry ingredients
250g self-raising flour
125g caster sugar
100g brown sugar
½ cup almond meal
4 tbsp cocoa powder
1 tsp instant coffee powder
½ tsp sea salt

To serve
Coconut vanilla yoghurt

Method
- Preheat oven to 180 degrees Celsius.

- Grease and line a 20cm round springform cake tin.

- In a small bowl, mix together all the wet ingredients until well combined.

- In a larger bowl, sift together all the dry ingredients.

- Pour the wet ingredients into the dry and stir until completely combined.

- Pour into the prepared cake tin and bake for 30 minutes – the centre will still be a little squidgy.

- Once cold, remove the spring outer of the tin.

- Serve with coconut vanilla yoghurt.

Cinnamon Scrolls
Inspired by Ina Garten

I love watching cooking TV shows and when it is done in a setting as stunning as Ina Garten's Hamptons home I could sit and watch it all day. One day she introduced me to her fast and easy cinnamon scrolls using nothing more than ingredients most of us have on hand – here is my vegan version. Warning: these are seriously addictive.

Ingredients
100g vegan butter
8 tbsp brown sugar
8 sheets vegan filo pastry
Olive oil spray
130g pecans, chopped finely
250g raisins
½ tsp cinnamon
Coconut ice cream, to serve

Method
- Preheat oven to 180 degrees Celsius.

- Place the butter in a microwave-safe dish and heat on high for 1 minute.

- Pour the melted butter into a lined square slice tin (about 15cm × 15cm).

- Evenly sprinkle half of the brown sugar over the melted butter.

- Place the filo sheets one on top of the other, spraying generously with olive oil between each sheet.

- On top of the eighth sheet, evenly sprinkle over the remaining brown sugar, along with the pecans and raisins, avoiding the edges of the pastry (about 1 cm).

- Carefully roll the pastry lengthways so that you end up with a log of about 26cm.

- Trim 1cm (without filling) off each end.

- Carefully cut the log into 2cm slices – use a sharp knife in a scissor action with your hand so you don't push down on the log. You should end up with 12 slices.

- Carefully pick up each slice by lightly squeezing the sides so the filling does not fall out and place facing upwards in the tin.

- Push the slices down lightly with the palm of your hand so they soak up some of the butter and spread together slightly.

- Sprinkle over any of the spilled filling and then the cinnamon, then spray generously with olive oil.

- Bake for 15–20 minutes until the pastry is golden and let cool for 3 minutes before inverting onto a serving tray.

- Serve warm with coconut ice cream.

Lime and Frizzante Granita

Sometimes after a meal you just want something light and sweet to cleanse your palate, not a rich, heavy dessert. You can serve this sorbet between courses or as a light, fresh, boozy dessert at the end of a heavy meal. The wine is not cooked off so you will still be able to taste it but it is perfectly balanced by the lime's iciness. Best made the day before.

Ingredients
1 cup water
¾ cup sugar
750ml Frizzante (sparkling Semillon)
⅓ cup lime juice

Method
- Place the water and sugar in a saucepan and boil for around 5 minutes until all the sugar has dissolved and it has thickened slightly.

- Into a large, shallow container that has a lid, pour the sugar syrup, the Frizzante and the lime juice (you can strain the juice if you prefer a smoother mixture but I keep mine rustic) – stir well.

- Place the container into the freezer.

- After three hours, stir the mixture with a fork.

- The following morning, stir the mixture with a fork again.

- One hour before serving, stir the mixture with a fork one final time – the end result should be sweet, boozy, citrusy ice crystals that melt in your mouth.

- Serve straight from the freezer in cocktail glasses.

Oat and Vanilla Cookies

I have lost count of the number of people who have asked me for this recipe. These are the cookies we leave all our guests when they check in with us at Block Eight. Inspired by a recipe from Rachel Allen, over the years I have tweaked her recipe to create a saltier, moister cookie that our guests just can't get enough of. Here is a vegan version that is just as good.

Ingredients
225g vegan butter
200g caster sugar
2 tbsp vanilla extract
250g plain spelt flour
½ tsp sea salt
100g rolled oats
50g desiccated coconut

Method
- Preheat oven to 180 degrees Celsius.

- Beat the butter, sugar and vanilla in an electric mixer until pale and creamy.

- Sift in the flour and sea salt.

- Add the oats and coconut, and stir to combine, ensuring the oats are evenly dispersed.

- Work to form a firm dough.

- Roll the dough into a sausage shape, about 5cm diameter.

- Wrap tightly in cling film and place in the fridge to chill, at least 30 minutes.

- Slice the dough into 1cm rounds and place on a lined baking tray.

- Sprinkle each slice with extra sugar and bake in the oven for 15–20 minutes or until the edge of each cookie is slightly golden.

- Remove from the oven and allow to cool before handling.